evangelical
awakenings
in LATIN AMERICA

evangelical awakenings
in LATIN AMERICA
J. EDWIN ORR

Bethany Fellowship INC.
MINNEAPOLIS, MINNESOTA 55438

J. EDWIN ORR completed his theological education at Northern Baptist Theological Seminary, but he studied at six other graduate schools as well. He earned a D.Phil. at Oxford, and an Ed.D. from UCLA. In all, he has eight earned degrees.

Recognized as a careful scholar and authority on spiritual awakenings, he has been a professor at Fuller School of World Mission for ten years. He has been guest lecturer in numerous colleges and universities around the world.

He is the author of over thirty books.

Copyright © 1978
Bethany Fellowship, Inc.
All rights reserved

Published by Bethany Fellowship, Inc.
6820 Auto Club Road, Minneapolis, Minnesota 55438

Printed in the United States of America

Library of Congress Cataloging in Publication Data

Orr, James Edwin, 1912-
    Evangelical awakenings in Latin America.

    Bibliography: p.
    Includes index.
    1. Revivals—Latin America—History.   I. Title.
BV3777.L3077   269'.2'098   77-16148
ISBN 0-87123-130-1

Introduction

EVANGELICAL AWAKENINGS

An Evangelical Awakening is a movement of the Holy Spirit bringing about a revival of New Testament Christianity in the Church of Christ and in its related community. Such an awakening may change in a significant way an individual only; or it may affect a larger group of believers; or it may move a congregation, or the churches of a city or district, or the whole body of believers throughout a country or a continent; or indeed the larger body of believers throughout the world. The outpouring of the Spirit effects the reviving of the Church, the awakening of the masses, and the movement of uninstructed peoples towards the Christian faith; the revived Church, by many or by few, is moved to engage in evangelism, in teaching, and in social action.

Such an awakening may run its course briefly, or it may last a lifetime. It may come about in various ways, though there seems to be a pattern common to all such movements throughout history.

The major marks of an Evangelical Awakening are always some repetition of the phenomena of the Acts of the Apostles, followed by the revitalizing of nominal Christians, and by bringing outsiders into vital touch with the Divine Dynamic causing all such Awakenings—the Spirit of God. The surest evidence of the Divine origin of any such quickening is its presentation of the evangelical message declared in the New Testament and its re-enactment of the phenomena therein, in the empowering of saints and conversion of sinners.

It is more than interesting to compare the characteristics of the Awakenings of various decades with the prototype of evangelical revivals in the Acts of the Apostles, a perennial textbook for such movements.

Our Lord told His disciples: 'It is not for you to know the times or seasons which the Father has fixed by His own authority. But you shall receive power when the Holy Spirit has come upon you; and you shall be My witnesses . . . to the end of the earth.' Thus was an outpouring of the Spirit predicted, and soon fulfilled.

Then began extraordinary praying among the disciples in the upper room. Who knows what self-judgment and confession and reconciliation went on? There were occasions for such. But, when they were all together in one place, there suddenly came from heaven a sound like the rush of a mighty wind and it filled all the house. The filling of the Holy Spirit was followed by xenolalic evangelism, not repeated in the times of the Apostles nor authenticated satisfactorily since.

The Apostle Peter averred that the outpouring fulfilled the prophecy of Joel, which predicted the prophesying of young men and maidens, the seeing of visions and dreams by young and old. He preached the death and resurrection of Jesus Christ. What was the response? The hearers were pierced, stabbed, stung, stunned, smitten—these are the synonyms of a rare verb which Homer used to signify being drummed to earth. It was no ordinary feeling; nor was the response a mild request for advice. It was more likely an uproar of entreaty, the agonizing cry of a multitude.

Those who responded to the Apostle's call for repentance confessed their faith publicly in the apostolic way. About three thousand were added to the church. Then followed apostolic teaching, fellowship, communion and prayers.

What kind of fellowship? Doubtless the words of Scripture were often used liturgically, but it is certain that the koinonia was open. What kind of prayers? There are instances of individual petitions of power and beauty, but there are also suggestions of simultaneous, audible prayer in which the main thrust of petition is recorded, as in the prophet's day.

The Apostles continued to urge their hearers to change and turn to God, which they did by the thousands. And no hostile power seemed for the moment able to hinder them. Persecution followed, but the work of God advanced.

The events recorded in the Acts have been repeated in full or lesser degree in the Awakenings of past centuries. From the study of Evangelical Revivals or Awakenings in cities and districts, countries and continents, generations and centuries, it is possible to trace a pattern of action and discover a progression of achievement that establish in the minds of those who accept the New Testament as recorded history an undoubted conclusion that the same Spirit of God Who moved the apostles has wrought His mighty works in the centuries preceding our own with the same results but with wider effects than those of which the apostles dreamed in their days of power.

Although the records are scarce, there were Evangelical Awakenings in the centuries before the rise of John Wycliffe, the Oxford reformer. But such movements in medieval times seemed very limited in their scope or abortive in their effect. What was achieved in the days of John Wycliffe—the dissemination of the Scriptures in the language of the people —has never been lost, nor has the doctrine of Scriptural authority. Thus the Lollard Revival led to the Reformation, which would have been unlikely without it; and the principle of appeal to the Word of God in the matter of reform has not been lost either. The Reformation thus led to the Puritan movement in which the essentials of evangelical theology were refined; and the Puritan movement prepared the way for the eighteenth, nineteenth and twentieth century Awakenings occurring in more rapid succession.

A student of church history in general and of the Great Awakenings in particular must surely be impressed by the remarkable continuity of doctrine as well as the continuity of action. Anyone could begin reading the story of the Gospels, continue on into the narrative of the Acts of the Apostles, then without any sense of interruption begin reading the story of the poor preachers of John Wycliffe, the itinerants of the Scottish Covenant, the circuit riders of John Wesley, the readers of Hans Nielsen Hauge in Norway, or the Disciples of the Lord in Madagascar.

Not only so, but the student of such movements would find in the preaching of the Awakenings and Revivals the same message preached and the same doctrines taught in the days of the Apostles. But non-evangelical Christianity, with its accretions of dogma and use of worldly power, would seem a system utterly alien to that of the Church of the Apostles, resembling much more the forces both ecclesiastical and secular that had opposed New Testament Christianity.

The reader of the Acts of the Apostles must surely notice that the Church began to spread by extraordinary praying and preaching. So too the 'upper room' type of praying and the pentecostal sort of preaching together with the irrepressible kind of personal witness find their place in Great Awakenings rather than in the less evangelical ecclesiastical patterns.

The first three centuries of progress were followed by a millenium of changed direction when the Church was united with the State and political force compelled the consciences of men. These centuries are rightly called the Dark Ages, though they were not entirely without light.

Before the fifteenth century, a change began, commencing a progression of awakenings that moved the Church by degrees back to the apostolic pattern and extended it all over the world. Not only was theological dogma affected and missionary passion created, but society itself was changed.

From the times of the Lollards onward, the impact of the Evangelical Revivals or Awakenings was felt in the realm of personal liberty— knowing the truth made men free, and made them covet freedom for all. Thus the Social Rising of 1381 championed a charter of freedom based on evangelical conviction. Its daughter movement in Bohemia defended its freedom against the forces of tyranny for a century.

The consequent Reformation that soon began in Germany caused such a ferment in men's minds that a rising became inevitable— but it was crushed, only because some of those responsible for the hunger for freedom betrayed it. The hunger for righteousness of the early Puritans brought about another attempt to establish freedom under the law, but, like various ventures before it, the Commonwealth failed because it relied more upon secular force than persuasion.

In the eighteenth, nineteenth and twentieth centuries, the revived Evangelicals re-learned an earlier method. New Testament counsel began to prevail, helping persuade free-thinkers and Christians, traditionalists and Evangelicals, that freedom was God's intent for every man, everywhere. Thus the nineteenth century became in itself the century of Christian action, taking Good News to every quarter of the earth, to every phase of life. Those whose hearts the Spirit had touched became the great initiators of reform and welfare and tuned even the conscience of unregenerate men to a sense of Divine harmony in society.

Yet Christians believed that the horizontal relationship of man to men was dependent upon the vertical relationship of man to God, that social reform was not meant to take the place of evangelism, 'so to present Christ in the power of the Spirit that men may come to put their trust in Him as Saviour and to serve Him as Lord in the fellowship of His Church and in the vocations of the common life.'

What are known as the Great Awakenings began in the second quarter of the eighteenth century, among settlers in New Jersey and refugees from Moravia about the same time. The First Awakening ran its course in fifty years, and was followed by the Second Awakening in 1792, the Third in 1830, the Fourth in 1858-59, the Fifth in 1905.

TABLE OF CONTENTS

Introduction

1

THE NEW WORLD AND THE OLD GOSPEL

What an opportunity it was for Christendom when, in 1492, Columbus landed on an island in the Bahamas, and opened a door to the civilization, colonization and settlement of the Americas! A vast New World was brought into the circle of a nominally Christian society.

That same year, Alexander Borgia—whose personal life it is a kindness to ignore—ascended the papal throne. That same year, the last Muslim kingdom in Spain was reduced, releasing a burst of energy in the Iberian peninsula which helped create an empire in the West.

The same Alexander Borgia arbitrarily drew a line from the north pole to the south, designating the lands to the east of the Azores the proper domain of the King of Portugal, to the west, that of the King of Spain. By agreement, the line was shifted more than a thousand miles farther west, thus permitting the Portuguese to retain the land discovered by Cabral, the sub-continent of Brazil.

Within a couple of generations, the far-ranging Spaniards had explored Atlantic and Pacific coasts of the Americas, from Nova Scotia to the Horn to Oregon; the Aztec empire in Mexico had been annexed by Cortés, and the Inca empire in Peru by Pizarro. Lasting settlements were made in the Antilles, in Central and South America, forever fastening a Hispanic language and culture upon a score of countries.

The Portuguese, meanwhile, began to occupy the shores of the vast territory of Brazil, and sent explorers inland— all the while extending their conquests in Africa and Asia. As with the Spaniards, the Portuguese 'agreed to bring to the Christian faith the peoples who inhabited the islands and the mainland.'[1] Hundreds of missionaries followed military conquerors and commercial exploiters, and won thereby an 'outward acquiescence to the Christian faith'[2] of a large majority of the indigenous inhabitants. It would be far from correct to say that they had been evangelized, even in the best sense of the Roman Catholic understanding of the term. In many instances, 'it was superficial in the extreme.'[3]

It should not be forgotten that the Spaniards began to colonize the Americas a full century before the English first settled in the West. The settlements differed much in kind, a majority in the English colonies coming to make a living and to worship God in peace, a majority in the Spanish colonies to win a fortune through mining and planting.[4] The English settlers invariably brought their wives and families; the Spanish often took wives of the native inhabitants; the English colonists performed their own menial work at first; the Spanish used force to compel the Indians to work for them.[5] Most of the English colonists were nonconformists; all of the Spanish were as intolerantly conformist as their home society. Even the evangelization of the Indians was achieved by force, rather than persuasion, Bartolomeo las Casas being one of a number of heroic exceptions.[6]

The important differences between Spanish colonization and its later English counterpart lay deeply in the history of the peninsular and island kingdoms. From the Moorish conquest till the military triumph of Christian forces over Islam, Spain was a battleground out of which emerged a dominant military and religious totalitarianism; and once the internal struggle ceased, the Spaniards overflowed the bounds of the Old World as soldiers and priests. England, on the other hand, remained isolated from the Continent, and became a land of traders and independents, submitting to neither Roman authority nor Anglican uniformity.

Portuguese expansion resembled much the extension of Spanish power, yet it never seemed as harsh in enforced conformity. Also, the Portuguese failed to find in the vast outreaches of Brazil an indigenous civilization, such as the Aztec or Inca empires, where submissive lower classes accepted the transfer of power and acquiesced in religious changes.[7] The Brazilian Indians were less civilized and more inaccessible, hence Brazil was less 'evangelized.'[8]

The dictum of the Pope had thus made the New World an Iberian Catholic preserve. But other nations of Europe soon disputed any idea of exclusive rights, among them the French, the Dutch, and the British. It was not long before the hit-and-run raids of freebooters and buccaneers became a more orderly occupation of defensible territories neither Iberian nor Roman Catholic. It was among these Protestant enclaves that the work began of persuading by preaching the good news of justification by faith in the work of Christ.

In 1555, Admiral Coligny dispatched to Brazil a number of French colonists, settling on an island in the beautiful bay of Rio de Janeiro which still bears the name Villegagnon, for the French leader.[9] The Huguenot workmen in the party proving the best workmen and colonists, Villegagnon sent to Paris and Geneva for more Huguenots. Calvin dispatched a party of Swiss Protestants with two Reformed pastors to Brazil, and they arrived at Rio in early 1557. One of their number, Jean Lery, preached to Brazilian Indians in the hinterland. Villegagnon renounced his Reformed allegiance and engaged in a persecution of Huguenots to compel them to revert to Catholicism. Several Huguenots were martyred thus.[10] In 1560, the Portuguese blockaded Rio de Janeiro, and destroyed the French colony completely.

Some seventy years later, the Dutch sent out a colonizing expedition to Brazil, seizing part of Pernambuco northeast, on the coastal bulge. Several Reformed ministers arrived with the colonists, and a couple of them attempted to win the local Indians to the faith. The leader of the expedition was the able Count Maurice, but he received little backing in his plans, and this colony was driven out by Portuguese forces also.[11]

Neither of these abortive enterprises was a mission in the evangelical sense. These early Calvinist efforts were subordinated to military and commercial objectives, and perished with their sponsors.

The Dutch and British were successful in colonizing the Guianas on the northern South American mainland; and the British, French, Dutch and Danes penetrated the Hispanic domain of the Caribbean to set up island colonies, peopling them with African slaves. It was in these island enclaves that Protestant evangelism began.

Hispanic evangelization arose from the Counter-Reform in Spain, with its well-organized attempts to re-conquer Europe and conquer the world for the Papacy, the Society of Jesus with matchless discipline and the Inquisition with powers of persuasion being backed by the Council of Trent. It was promoted by political power.

The evangelistic penetration of the Caribbean and the Guianas resulted from those strange movements of the Holy Spirit, the First and Second Evangelical Awakenings which were neither planned by churchmen nor promoted by any government concerned. The evangelization resulted from voluntary action of dedicated disciples, as in the Acts.

In the spring of 1727, there was an extraordinary effusion of the Holy Spirit on a company of Moravian exiles living at Herrnhut, in the Zinzendorf estate in Germany. Out of this revival came the unprecedented missionary thrust of the Moravian Brethren, far in advance of the missionary movements of the late eighteenth century.[12] Moravian pioneers began to preach in Russia, India, South Africa, West Africa, the West Indies, and North and South America.

The first Moravian mission was sent to the slaves of the Danish West Indies, to St. Thomas in the Virgin Islands, in 1732.[13] Each inhabitant for half a century had been required to attend Sunday services at drumbeat, but nothing was done for the spiritual welfare of the slaves who were subjected to such stringent regulation that an insurrection began in 1733.[14] The Moravians faced a frightening death rate.

In 1735, the Moravians established a mission in Dutch Guiana, then more extensive in area.[15] They tried to win the Arawak Indians as well as plantation Negroes and bush Negroes. Converts were made among the Negroes of the plantations, but work among the bush runaways ceased, and Indian work was restricted. Missionaries in the main were self-supporting, running a business house in Paramaribo.

The Church of England followed the planters to Jamaica, but most slave-owners were very reluctant to allow their slaves to be baptized or given Christian instruction, for fear of making them discontented and so provoking slave insurrections.[16] In 1754,[17] two Anglican plantation-owners invited the Moravians to minister to four hundred slaves, presenting the pioneers with a plot of ground for their aid. Moravians pioneered in other British islands also.[18]

In the course of the American revolution, various loyal dissidents made their way to the West Indies, among them several Negroes[19] who had supported royal forces against the patriots. One such was George Lisle—sometimes spelt Liele—who began preaching to Jamaican slaves about 1784 and was assisted by a number of local preachers, somewhat superstitious and illiterate, Moses Baker in particular of excellent character. White plantation society continued for decades to hinder the work of evangelism in the plantations, ever objecting to the betterment of slaves.

The condition of the working population of the Protestant Caribbean was much the same as that of the working people of the Latin American mainland and islands, even though superficially 'evangelized' by their exploiters.

2

AWAKENINGS AND PIONEERS, 19th Century: I

The upheavals of the late eighteenth century, especially
the American and French Revolutions, were followed by a
decline in Christian witness so serious that, in the judgment
of Kenneth Scott Latourette, it seemed as though Christianity
became 'a waning influence, about to be ushered out of the
affairs of men.'[1] Even in the dynamic society of the United
States, the plight of the churches was desperate, the Anglican
Bishop of New York (for example) considering the situation
hopeless and simply ceasing to function.

The spiritual preparation for a worldwide awakening began in Great Britain seven years before the outpouring of
the Spirit there.[2] Believers of one denomination after the
other, including the evangelical minorities in the Church of
England and Church of Scotland, devoted the first Monday
evening of each month to pray for a revival of religion and
an extension of Christ's kingdom overseas; this widespread
union of prayer spread to the United States within ten years
and to many other countries, and the concert of prayer remained the significant factor in the recurring revivals of
religion and the extraordinary out-thrust of missions for a
full fifty years, so commonplace it was taken for granted.

The revival of religion, the second great awakening, began in Britain in late 1791, cresting in power among the
Methodists who seemed unafraid of the phenomena of mass
awakening. It was also effective among the Baptists and the
Congregationalists, though manifested in quieter forms; it
accelerated the evangelical revival going on among clergy
and laity of the Church of England.[3]

At the same time, the principality of Wales was overrun
by another movement of revival, packing the churches of the
various denominations and gathering unusual crowds of many
thousands in the open-air.[4] And phenomenal awakenings extended the work through the kingdom of Scotland, raising up
such evangelists as the Haldanes,[5] and pastoral evangelists
such as Chalmers in Glasgow and MacDonald in the North.
A reviving rescued Ulster from an Arian heresy.

This period of revival in the United Kingdom brought forth the British and Foreign Bible Society, the Religious Tract Society, the Baptist Missionary Society, the London Missionary Society, the Church Missionary Society, and a host of auxiliary agencies for evangelism. It produced also some significant social reform, even in wartime, including the movement for the abolition of the slave trade.[6]

In the United States and in British North America, there were preparatory movements of revival in the 1780s that raised up leaders for the wider movement following. Then sporadic revivals commenced in 1792. Isaac Backus and his friends in New England adopted the British plan for a general Concert of Prayer for the revival of religion and extension of Christ's kingdom abroad. Prayer meetings multiplied as church members devoted the first Monday of each month to fervent intercession.[7]

In 1798, the awakening became general.[8] Congregations were crowded and conviction was deep, leading to numerous thoroughgoing conversions. Every state in New England was affected, and every evangelical denomination. There were no records of emotional extravagance, and none among the churches of the Middle Atlantic States, where extraordinary revivals broke out in the cities of New York and Philadelphia as well as in smaller towns. In the western parts of New York and Pennsylvania, there were more startling displays; and in 1800, extraordinary revival began in Kentucky, long after its manifestation east of the Alleghenies. Among the rough and lawless and illiterate frontiersmen, there were extremes of conviction and response. It cannot be denied that the revival transformed Kentucky and Tennessee from an utterly lawless community into a God-fearing one. Soon the general awakening spread southward into Virginia, Carolina and Georgia, attracting crowds so great that no churches could possibly accommodate them, hence five, ten or fifteen thousand would gather in the forest clearings. The Negroes were moved equally with the whites.

Revived Americans duplicated the formation of various evangelical societies in Britain, founding the American Bible Society, the American Tract Society, the American Board of Commissioners for Foreign Missions, the Foreign Mission of the American Baptists, and society after society. The order and extent of missionary organization reflected in some measure the degree of involvement of denominations in the Awakening.[9]

The awakenings raised up evangelists on the American frontier, sent the Haldanes up and down to revive Scotland, produced Hans Nielsen Hauge to transform Norway and provoked revival and evangelism in England, Germany, Holland and other European countries, directly equipping churches with Sunday Schools, home missions, city missions and the auxiliaries taken for granted today.

John Wesley's adjutant, Dr. Thomas Coke, inadvertently disembarked in the West Indies when his ship was driven off course en route to Nova Scotia in 1785.[10] He spent six weeks in the Leeward Islands, preaching to all who would listen. A year or so later he returned, revisiting Antigua and other Leeward Islands, St. Vincent and the Windwards, as well as Tortola in the Virgin Islands, where fifteen hundred were added to the local society within six years. The hostility of the planters prevented a beginning in Barbados. In late '88, Coke again landed in Jamaica and continued into early 1789 preaching to whites, blacks, mulattoes and quadroons.

Wesleyan missionaries who followed him found mixed-bloods most responsive to the Gospel.[11] Societies were set up in Kingston and other towns, and an influx of converts sought instruction in the Word.[12] Missionaries and workers were arrested by the authorities as persecution continued, but by 1808 there were three circuits in Jamaica, while five constituted the Antigua district and four St. Christopher's.[13]

In 1814,[14] in response to urgent calls for help from Lisle and Baker, the Baptist Missionary Society sent out British missionaries to Jamaica. Undismayed by persecution, they joined forces with the black evangelists in evangelizing the slaves in the plantations. Baptist chapels, both missionary and independent, multiplied throughout the country and bore the brunt of the persecution in the plantations.

The Jamaican Assembly passed legislation disallowing Christian instruction of slaves by any but the Established Church, so, for eighteen months, the converts of Baptist and Methodist preaching were deprived of teaching until the Government in London nullified the law.[15] Prosperity in the chapels followed Waterloo and the coming of peace, when revival was renewed in the Mother Country.

The Wesleyans reported a quickening in their Jamaica circuits,[16] the same being reported in Antigua, St. Vincent, Tortola and other islands, each missionary commenting on the need of vigilant discipline in view of the temptations of slave society, with its disregard of family ties.

And so it was that in 1829 nearly a thousand slaves were added to the West Indian circuits, even at a time of renewed persecution.[17] The St. Ann's chapel was destroyed by a mob, and for preaching the Gospel, Joseph Grimsdall was incarcerated in a fetid dungeon, dying of a fever thus contracted. Isaac Whitehead, a missionary in that district, was confined in the same dirty cell, and yet another, Joseph Orton, was imprisoned there, both suffering injury to health.

The plantation owners, very fearful of developments in London which heralded the emancipation of the slaves, did all that they could to prevent evangelization of the blacks. Despair began to afflict the persecuted plantation workers. At the end of 1831 began a slave insurrection which was crushed with wild ferocity.[18] Missionaries were threatened or arrested, and great numbers of slaves lost their lives. Martial law lasted five weeks. A Colonial Church Union was formed by the plantation owners, its avowed purpose being the expulsion of all 'sectarian missionaries' from the island. It over-reached itself, the Governor in council upholding the rights of dissenters to evangelize.[19]

The Baptists again bore the brunt of the persecution, a number of their chapels being destroyed, and the slaves responded by joining the Baptist churches by the thousands. In spite of the rage of the planters, Baptist and Methodist chapels were rebuilt by colonial funds set aside by the new Governor, who followed directions from London.

Emancipation came in 1834, followed by apprenticeship which expired in 1838.[20] Three-quarters of a million slaves in the West Indies were affected. At midnight, 31st July 1834, the chapels in Jamaica and the other islands were crowded by rejoicing people, and the day of liberation—far from being one of bloodshed as predicted—became a day of order, reverence and rejoicing.

The British Parliament, in altruistic statesmanship, paid the slave-owners twenty million pounds compensation. Baptist missionaries criticized abuses of the apprenticeship system.[21] William Knibb, one of their number, bought out landed estates to sell in small parcels to freed slaves, and other evangelical missionaries helped their followers.[22]

What followed was a folk movement into the Baptist and Wesleyan and other denominations which lasted until 1840. The influx brought many superficially interested people into the churches, hence there was a decline in the years that followed, in Jamaica and elsewhere.

Meanwhile, the Moravian work in Barbados enjoyed 'a widespread revival of religion' in which the membership rose to fifteen hundred, a new church being built.[23] Reports of occasional local revivals in various islands were made by Wesleyan missionaries.[24] Both Methodists and Baptists at this time were being moved by spiritual revivals in their home constituencies, hence they were revival-minded.

     *   *   *   *

The major events of the nineteenth century in the Latin American countries were the revolutions which set these colonies free from the paternal rule of Spain and Portugal, a political revolution which was followed by a measure of social revolution, falling far short of American liberties. The storm of rebellion against Spain broke during the second decade of the nineteenth century. San Martín led the revolutionary forces in Argentina and Chile, and up the coast to Peru. Bolívar directed the forces of revolution in Venezuela, Colombia and Ecuador, meeting San Martín in Peru.[25] Meanwhile, Mexican independence was secured by rebels between 1810 and 1821.

The revolutionary movements were not directed against the Roman Catholic Church. In fact, many of the native-born priests were ardent revolutionists, although their higher clergy supported the Spanish metropolitan government; the struggle between creoles, or native-born, and gachupines, or Spanish-born, was sharp in all sectors of the Spanish colonial society, and this was true within the Church.[26]

Developments in Brazil seemed more evolutionary than revolutionary.[27] The Portuguese royal family had already fled to Brazil in 1807 and, in 1822, Dom Pedro proclaimed its independence and was crowned emperor, being in 1831 succeeded by Dom Pedro II, an enlightened ruler.

The Roman Catholic Church in Spain and Portugal had lost its militant zeal.[28] In the nineteenth century, Iberian Catholicism produced no major new orders, as did France; and in Latin America, Roman Catholicism developed no new thrusts; it was regarded as mainly reactionary.

It must not be forgotten that 1781 was the date of the last live incineration of a 'heretic' in Spain, and that in 1816 the Pope finally prohibited the use of torture by the Holy Inquisition anywhere.[29] In view of such a record, the open penetration of the overwhelmingly Roman Catholic dioceses by the private enterprise of a single pioneer was a most unusual happening.

Both the United States and the United Kingdom were very popular in Latin America at the time of the revolution. The former had won their independence and served as a shining example to be followed by the southern colonies. The latter had helped deliver Portugal and Spain from Napoleon's fist, and British commerce was more than welcome.

In London, there occurred a chain of events which was to bring to Latin America a remarkable Scotsman.[30] King George III heard that a Quaker was successfully teaching several hundred boys singlehandedly in a school in Borough Road; so the King called for his coachmen and visited the school to ascertain how such a feat was accomplished.[31] 'By the same principle,' replied Joseph Lancaster, 'that thy Majesty's Army is kept in order.' Lancaster had devised a scheme whereby he had taught a group of boys their first year subjects; then he taught them second year, while they passed on their knowledge to an incoming first year class; next he taught them third year, while they taught second, and second taught first. Out of this developed the Royal Lancasterian Society and its monitorial education. In 1814, it became the British and Foreign School Society.[32]

These developments were part of the social gains of the period of the Second Evangelical Awakening, 1792 onwards, happening during the life-and-death struggle with Napoleon. The project expanded by leaps and bounds. The monitorial system was very poor, permitting no asking of questions and no development of personality; it was a kind of mass-production education, but it was better than no system at all and a necessary stopgap on the way to popular education. Lancaster was spoiled by his success, and spent money recklessly, running into debt and suffering arrest.[33] The British and Foreign School Society decided to promote the Lancasterian system without Lancaster; and its founder left in disgust for the United States, where he was given a reception by the House of Representatives, and founded his Lancasterian schools in several American cities.[34] He even visited Venezuela on the invitation of Bolivar.[35]

James Thomson, born in Galloway in 1781, a product of the revival in Scotland, became co-pastor with one of its greater figures, James Haldane, in Edinburgh.[36] Thomson moved to London and became interested in the British and Foreign Bible Society and the British and Foreign School Society, ardently supporting the cause of Bible distribution and taking training in the Lancasterian methods.[37]

Thomson set his sights on Latin America as early as 1817.[38] He knew that to present himself there as a Protestant missionary would result in expulsion. He was aware that the revolution in the former Spanish colonies had created a need for elementary education, hence his training in the Lancasterian system was ideally useful, even more so in that it used the Holy Scriptures as a textbook.

Lancaster's work in London was known to the Latin American revolutionaries, for both Bolivar and Miranda had visited the Borough Road school.[39] So, when Thomson arrived in Buenos Aires on 6th October 1818, after a three months's voyage from Liverpool, he received a very cordial welcome from the Argentine government.[40] There was much support also from three thousand British residents who had far-reaching influence in the country's commerce in spite of the defeat of a British force there in 1807.

A majority of the Argentine people were 'a melancholy sea of illiterates' at the time, and the more enlightened of leaders were determined to do something about education. As early as 1810, the military hero, Manuel Belgrano, had advocated a system of primary education both compulsory and free.[41] A Chilean priest established the first English-model monitorial school in what later became Uruguay just before Thomson's arrival.[42] Thomson offered his services to the Buenos Aires cabinet, and on 17th August 1819 he was appointed to operate a primary school, a salary of a thousand pesos being allotted.[43]

Thomson devised lesson materials from the Old and New Testaments, and the government introduced them into the other public schools. Thomson's monitorial school held in the premises of a Franciscan monastery proved successful, and, by 1820, Thomson had become director of all schools in the muncipality.[44] Thomson made lasting friends among the Franciscans, Don José Catala being his collaborator-in-chief. Thus Thomson was enjoying the support of the rich, the attendance of the poor, and the approval of the clergy.[45]

Despite the opposition of some clergy suspicious of a Protestant and of some teachers required to re-study their methods, Thomson succeeded in establishing a monitorial system of education, and was awarded honorary citizenship in the United Provinces of the Río de la Plata, the highest recognition that the Argentines could grant.[46] Undoubtedly, Franciscan goodwill contributed to his success, on which President Rivadavia built well for a number of years.

Uruguay, at that time, was under the control of General Lecor, a Brazil-based Portuguese who had commanded a British division under Wellington. Thomson in 1820 visited Montevideo, and sent his friend Catala to help set up the monitorial schools in Uruguay, in which a chapter of the Bible was authorized to be read each day.[47] The system was a success, but opposition was forthcoming.

In 1813, Santiago de Chile had a population of 50,000, but only seven schools with a total of 664 pupils.[48] In 1821, the government of Bernardo O'Higgins secured the services of James Thomson, who opened the first monitorial school on 18th September with two hundred pupils. A Lancasterian Society was founded with impressive backing from leaders in church and state.[49] A year later, O'Higgins declared the Scot an honorary citizen of Chile.

San Martín's liberation troops occupied Lima, capital of Peru and cultural heart of Spanish America, in July 1821. James Thomson was invited to Peru, and arrived in Lima a year later.[50] San Martín set him up as director of public education, but there were those who blocked every move made by Thomson until Congress appointed an enterprising priest, José Francisco Navarette, to assist him. The dining room of the Colegio Santo Tomás was equipped for pupils. Unfortunately, San Martín had already left Lima, and the royalist Spanish army recaptured the city in mid-1823, but they left Thomson's school untouched.[51] Then Simón Bolívar landed at Callao with two thousand men, and his regime in Lima declared its support of the Lancasterian system. In 1824, the Spanish army again occupied Lima, but left the Scotsman free to teach, which he did without regular salary. The Spanish army was soon defeated. Thomson achieved his objective, the establishment of a central school in Lima and daily use of the New Testament as principal textbook, with the training of teachers to continue the work.

Thomson arrived in Bogotá, capital of Colombia, at the beginning of 1825. There he found that the monitorial school had already been established, hence there was no need for him to initiate one. Thomson instead devoted his talent and time to the formation of a Bible Society, and in this project he successfully enlisted leaders in church and state, who agreed that it was in accord with the laws of Colombia and of the Roman Catholic Church also to establish a Colombian Bible Society to print and circulate the Scriptures, in the native tongue and in approved versions.[52]

It is obvious that Thomson was interested not only in the establishment of schools but in the distribution of the Holy Scriptures. He found a soil prepared for Bible study by the influence of Illuminismo Católico (Catholic Enlightenment) in Spain of the latter third of the eighteenth century.[53]

While James Thomson was involved in school promotion in Argentina and Chile, he kept in unofficial touch only with the directors of the British and Foreign Bible Society, often reporting his activities and giving advice on translations as well as requesting supplies of Spanish Scriptures. It was not till 1824, when he faced financial crisis in Peru, that he requested appointment as an official agent of the Society.[54]

Later critics of his work considered his dual interest in primary education and Bible distribution as 'a master work of hypocrisy,' but this opinion was not held by his Roman Catholic collaborators at the time, or by modern writers.[55]

Thomson had been in Argentina more than a year before he engaged in Scripture circulation. He left behind him a local Bible Society supported by British residents; by 1825, a thousand Bibles and two thousand Testaments had found their way into the country.[56] Likewise in Chile, Thomson experienced no hindrance to the circulation of Spanish New Testaments. In Peru, Thomson received a shipment of five hundred Spanish Bibles and five hundred Spanish Testaments and was sold out in two days.[57]

Thomson persuaded the Bible Society to help produce a translation of the Gospels into Quichua, but the manuscript was lost in the vicissitudes of war and fifty years passed before any Quichua portions were published; Thomson also encouraged a translation into Aymara.[58]

In Guayaquil, Thomson found a misdirected shipment of Spanish New Testaments, and made good use of them in Ecuador and Colombia.[59] However Pope Leo XII had issued an encyclical which condemned the Bible Society for translating the Scriptures into the vulgar tongues and urged the bishops to keep their flocks away from such poison.[60] This caused a setback in Thomson's work and that of his friends.

The versions of the Scriptures preferred by the Society were either the translation by Padre Scio or that by Torres Amat,[61] both licensed by the appropriate church authorities. They omitted the notes which the Church concerned deemed necessary to counteract direct private interpretation. Soon even the Colombian Bible Society began to wither away as the heat of clerical disapproval blasted its activities.

What of Thomson's work in the monitorial schools? In the Buenos Aires district, the government supported twenty Lancasterian schools for boys and girls seven years after Thomson departed.[62] In 1829, Juan Manuel de Rosas gained power and became dictator of Argentina. He gradually but thoroughly eliminated any progressive ideas in education, and in a score of years the reforms were blotted out.[63]

In Chile, Thomson was succeeded by Anthony Eaton, a Lancasterian pedagogue. Not long afterwards, Eaton was invalided to England, the direction of the work also suffering because of increasing objections by reactionaries,[64] another factor being the fall from power of Bernardo O'Higgins who had been moving too fast in reforming Chilean society. In exile in Peru, O'Higgins became a Franciscan, and late in life addressed an appeal to Pope Gregory XVI urging that the Scriptures be widely diffused, the clergy relieved of the vows of celibacy, and an effort be made to unite the Roman, Greek and Anglican Churches, an Ecumenical Council to be called to approve these measures.[65]

The monitorial schools established in Peru lasted much longer.[66] In 1850, President Ramón Castilla allowed every teacher to adopt whatever teaching method he preferred, monitorial teaching being no longer obligatory. But even in the 1870s, monitorial methods were in use. It was much the same in Colombia, Mexico, and elsewhere.

The expert, Dr. Donald R. Mitchell, has rightly called the work of James Thomson[67] 'an impressive achievement.' Unknown, he enjoyed the friendship of Rivadavia in Buenos Aires, O'Higgins in Santiago, and San Martín and Bolívar in Lima. His contribution to primary education lingered in effect as long as monitorial education served as a stopgap measure throughout the western world. His contribution to Bible distribution lasted until papal policy made the Bible a proscribed book for Roman Catholics in Latin America. A modern Roman Catholic writer, the Franciscan Antonine Tibesar, has pointed out that, in the light of Vatican II, the Catholic collaborators of Diego Thomson in Latin America were a hundred and fifty years ahead of the priesthood in Europe.[68] It is also a fact that James Thomson lacked the organized support of the British and American evangelical Churches and Societies who could have found ways of giving more substantial aid. The evangelization of Latin America by means of the Sacred Scriptures was made to wait another opportunity, after the Awakening of 1858.

3

AWAKENINGS AND PIONEERS, 19th Century: II

Meanwhile, the first and second waves of revival in the early nineteenth century had run their course in the West. Inevitably, there came about a decline in the spirituality of the Churches affected by the 1800 Awakenings. Not only was the attack of unbelievers renewed, but anti-evangelical notions claimed a following in the Anglican, Lutheran, and Reformed constituencies, and even among Baptists—taking the form of non-cooperation with other Evangelicals.

In the autumn of 1857, there were signs of an awakening, success in revival and evangelism in Canada, and an extraordinary movement of men to prayer in New York City that spread from city to city throughout the United States and over the world.[1] Churches, halls and theatres were filled at noontime for prayer, and the overflow filled churches of all denominations at night as a whole nation turned to God.

The same movement also affected the United Kingdom, beginning in 1859 in Ulster, the most northerly province in Ireland; about ten per cent of the population professed an inward change as well in Wales and Scotland, and a great awakening continued in England for years. Repercussions were felt in many other European countries.[2]

Phenomena of revival were reported in countries around the world, including both South Africa and India, during the decade that followed the awakening in the sending countries: wherever an Evangelical cause existed, a revival resulted; and the effects were felt for a lifetime.

The 1858-59 Awakenings extended the working forces of of Evangelical Christendom. Not only were a million converted in both the United States and the United Kingdom, but existing evangelistic and philanthropic organizations were revived and new vehicles of enterprise created. The Bible Societies flourished as never before, Home Missions and the Salvation Army were founded to extend the evangelistic and social ministry of the Revival in a worldwide mission. The impact on the Y. M. C. A. organization was noteworthy,[3] and a missionary recruitment of university students followed.

Out of the 1859 Awakening in Britain arose a phalanx of famed evangelists—aristocrats and working men. Spurgeon built his Tabernacle on the crest of the movement. The War between the States (in which there was extraordinary revival and evangelism) delayed the emergence of great American evangelists from the 1858 Awakening, though Moody himself served his apprenticeship in that movement in Chicago, and extended its impact and methods for forty years.[4]

It is noteworthy that the years of revival in the United States and elsewhere were followed by a missionary thrust. The Awakening of 1858-59 onwards provided the enterprise and also the volunteers for the invasion of the vast southern continent and the countries of Central America.

Not all of non-Roman Christendom was involved. High Church parties in some Churches of the Reformation still advocated a recognition of Rome's prior claim. Precisely those denominations most revived in the Awakening seemed to develop a concern for the unevangelized millions to the south, and assessed the need more in keeping with opinions expressed by twentieth century experts of both faiths.

In 1862, an Anglican Evangelical, W. H. Stirling, became superintendent[5] of the South American Missionary Society, seven years later being made Bishop of the Falkland Islands diocese with oversight of all the continent, except Guiana. This missionary society resulted from abortive expeditions in the Southlands by a former commander of the Royal Navy Allen F. Gardiner. Thrice in the 1840s, he tried to pioneer fallow fields, in Patagonia, Bolivia and Tierra del Fuego. At mid-century, as one of a party of seven, Gardiner landed on the shores of Tierra del Fuego, but within a few months the whole party died of starvation and exposure.[6]

Far from daunting the Anglican Evangelicals, the death of Gardiner spurred them to renewal of the mission.[7] In 1859, a party of eight were killed by Tierra del Fuegans. Continued efforts resulted in success. Charles Darwin was greatly impressed with the results of the mission's work among the primitive people in Tierra del Fuego whom he had previously declared to be hopelessly degraded, and he became a financial contributor to the work until the year of his decease.[8]

Bishop Stirling itinerated incessantly over the territory of the republics, supervising the chaplaincies of the Church of England, and sponsoring attempts to reach the Indians and to witness to nominal Roman Catholics.[9]

Immigration helped to open closed doors in the southern republics of South America, and revived evangelical laymen and ministers took advantage of the opportunity. It was not long before the tiny evangelical communities were engaged in witnessing to their fellow-citizens.

Already the British colonists in Argentina and Uruguay were being served by Anglican and Presbyterian chaplains. After the 1860 British revivals, there came a change of pace. Anglican parishioners took over their own support, as did the Scottish emigrants. In the wake of the Welsh Revival of 1859, a Welsh colony was founded in the province of Chubut in Patagonia, cared for by Welsh-speaking ministers. The Waldensians settled in Uruguay and Argentina as farmers, and maintained both piedmont dialect and evangelical faith.[10]

There was an echo of the work of James Thomson in the Argentine. Domingo F. Sarmiento, who was aware of the impact of Lancasterian education, was driven to Chile as an exile.[11] He returned to Buenos Aires, but in 1865 was sent to the United States as Argentine ambassador. Then Sarmiento became president in 1868. Determined to set up a stronger system of normal schools, from the United States he recruited a number of dedicated teachers, of whom sixty of the sixty-five pioneers were evangelical by personal conviction, the remainder dedicated Roman Catholics.[12] The same forces of reaction which had opposed Thomson now opposed Sarmiento and his proteges, the Bishop of Córdoba excommunicating the parents of those who patronized the new schools, the Bishop of Salta following suit. Sarmiento dismissed one and suspended the other. The work of the educationalists was eminently successful, and raised the literacy rate in Argentina 25% in twenty-five years.[13]

Evangelical interest in the Latin American Republics was by no means confined to helping Protestant immigrants. In Chile, in the 1860s, a liberal government came to power, interpreting the national constitution to sanction Protestant evangelism.[14] So Spanish-speaking churches were organized in Valparaiso and Santiago. In the same decade,[15] the first Spanish sermon by a Protestant was preached in Argentina, and the churches began to experience slow growth.

Thus far, in temperate South America, there had been no movements of the Spirit that could be called revivals or awakenings. The pioneering was hard and slow, subjected to unrelenting persecution on the part of the dominant Church which tolerated only ethnic action by foreign chaplains.

A Presbyterian historian has declared that there was no episode more dramatic than the revival and ingathering in the Chilean port of Constitución south of Valparaiso in 1884. Alberto Vidaurre, a postmaster, was converted that year through reading a Bible. He became an impassioned orator in the proclamation of Scripture and gained the sympathies of the townsfolk within a short space of time. The group appealed to the Presbyterians for help and a commission of inquiry was sent south. It reported:[16]

> Even with our Saxon caution, we could not reject the evidence of a visitation from on high. The whole town was moved; there were proofs on every hand of a sincere repentance and faces showed the joy of those who are saved by Christ. We could not establish exact criteria of Sr. Vidaurre, but we dare not withhold our support in the presence of a work in which the Holy Spirit accompanies its preaching.

Within a year, the Constitución church was larger than any other Presbyterian congregation except the church in Valparaiso. Alas, the caution displayed among the foreign missionaries who distrusted things Chilean and were afraid of spontaneous movements helped to stifle the revival.[17]

Bolivia and Paraguay remained closed to evangelistic witness for many years, until a long delayed exploration of the Chaco wilderness was made by Anglican pioneers of the South American Missionary Society.[18]

Before the mid-century, the American Seamen's Friend sent a chaplain to Callao, port of Lima, in Peru.[19] Between 1860 and 1864, the American and Foreign Christian Union placed missionaries in Peru.[20] But it was not until 1888 that a real footing was gained by Francisco Penzotti as agent of the American Bible Society, a Methodist missionary who built up a congregation in Callao and suffered imprisonment for his Bible distribution and his evangelism; he was not released until 1891, when the legal battle for the toleration of Protestantism was practically won.[21]

About this time, beginnings were made in Colombia, not many converts being made by the Presbyterians or other pioneers.[22] Schools were opened in Bogotá and provincial cities, and thus a foothold was gained in tropical America. Entrance by evangelical missionaries to Venezuela and to Ecuador followed much later. Resistance to evangelization seemed to bear relation to proximity to the ancient seats of Spanish viceregal power, strongest in the tropics.

The first Protestant church building in Latin America had been erected by Anglicans in 1819[23] in Rio de Janeiro. The Bible Societies[24] had early shown an interest in Brazil. The British and Foreign Bible Society shipped many of the twenty thousand Portuguese New Testaments printed during its first decade to Brazil, and thousands of Bibles were sent to British merchants in the coastal cities in years following. The American Bible Society, from its inception, sent New Testaments and Bibles, and—after the mid-century—used agents appointed to work in Brazil, the veteran H.C. Tucker distributing nearly two-and-one-quarter million Scripture portions during forty-four years of work[25]

Just before the 1858 Awakening, there was penetration of the Empire of Brazil, ruled by the enlightened Pedro II. A Scottish physician, Robert Reid Kalley, had achieved a remarkable success as an evangelist among the people of Madeira, hence severest persecution arose, forcing him to move to Brazil where he was joined by Madeiran believers. A papal legate appealed to the Government of Brazil to expel Dr. Kalley, but, instead of being ousted, the Scotsman acquired the personal friendship of Dom Pedro II himself. His work in the Empire was equally successful, and in 1858 he formed his converts into a congregation of simple order, the forerunner of an evangelistic Congregational Union of Churches, more akin to the Baptists in practice.[26]

In 1859, backed by the prayers of revived Presbyterians, Ashbel Green Simonton arrived in Brazil as a missionary of the Presbyterian Church in the U.S.A., and formed a congregation in Rio de Janeiro in 1862. His brother-in-law, Alexander Blackford, planted churches in São Paulo.[27] A presbytery was formed in 1865. José Manoel da Conceição, long dissatisfied as a Roman priest[28] was converted and soon became an outstanding evangelist in the cities and the inland towns. Great crowds gathered to hear him, and he planted here and there little congregations directed by their natural leaders. On one occasion, he was stoned and left for dead; but when he recovered, he wiped the blood from his face and returned to the market-place to continue his preaching, so causing a panic among his persecutors who thought that he had risen from the dead.

German immigration to Brazil was already extensive, but it was only in 1860 that German missionary societies began to develop an interest, the Basel Missionary Society sending out pastors in 1861 to gather congregations.[29]

General A.T. Hawthorne, Army of the Confederate States of America, one among many who found an oath of allegiance to the United States distasteful, visited Dom Pedro II in Rio, and was so encouraged by the friendly reception that he induced numbers of Southerners to move to Brazil, some settling in Campinas. Hawthorne called for Texan and other Southern pastors to care for the immigrants.[30]

American Methodists had worked in Rio de Janeiro for half a dozen years between 1836 and 1842. Immigrants of Methodist affiliation coming from the Confederacy drew a number of Southern Methodist missionaries into Brazil, their work beginning in 1867.[31]

In the late 1860s, immigrants of Baptist affiliation began to settle in Brazil, but a dozen years passed before a pastor was sent, followed by missionaries to the Brazilians.[32] The Baptists concentrated more upon evangelism and less upon educational institutions than did Methodists, and grew more rapidly.[33] They became strongest in Rio de Janeiro.

Between 1859 and 1864, an abortive attempt was made to establish an American Protestant Episcopal mission in the Brazilian Empire. A quarter of a century later, Rio Grande do Sul was entered by Morris and Kinsolving.[34]

Each Protestant denomination established schools, and evangelical institutions sprang up in Recife, Rio de Janeiro, São Paulo, Campinas and Pôrto Alegre. The most famous was the Escola Americana founded by G. W Chamberlain in São Paulo, becoming Mackenzie Institute, then Mackenzie University.[35] Fernando de Azevedo, in his outstanding work on Brazilian culture, declared that these schools [36]

> ... helped to change the didactic processes, influenced by the imported ideas of North American pedagogical technique, and for a long time they were to be among the few innovating forces in education—those living forces which keep the temperature of spiritual institutions from a kind of moral cooling off due to uniformity and routine.

Reports of pioneer missionaries are difficult to check, and Brazilian census figures are hard to interpret. Thirty years after the 1858-59 beginnings, there were sixty-three churches and three thousand members among Presbyterians, twenty churches and 350 members among Methodists, five churches and 250 members among Baptists, and three with the same total of membership among Congregationalists— four thousand Evangelicals in Brazil plus ethnic Germans.[37]

The invasion of Mexico by American troops during the war of 1846-48 gave the American Bible Society widespread opportunity of distributing Spanish Bibles and Testaments among the Mexican people.[38] It is significant that in the areas where the Bibles were distributed there lingered a tolerant attitude to the proclamation of the Gospel.

The writing of a liberal constitution in 1857, with the rise to the presidency of Benito Juárez, provoked a widespread movement in the direction of evangelical religion. For example, a number of priests disillusioned with Roman religion organized 'the Church of Jesus' which afterwards merged with the Protestant Episcopal Church.[39]

The first Protestant communion was shared in Mexico in 1859.[40] In 1860, the American Bible Society sent thence an agent, who was followed by James Hickey, an Irish convert who gathered a congregation in Monterey.[41] Then Melinda Rankin, founder of a school for Mexicans on the Texas side of the border, moved to Monterey in 1865.[42] She was soon followed by various missionary societies, but Presbyterian, Baptist, and Methodist missionaries encountered fiercest opposition from Roman priests.

Despite persecution, converts were won from among the mestizo masses rather than the upper class of an educated Spanish elite or the lower class of Indian peasants. Twenty years after the opening of Mexico, there were about twelve thousand evangelical communicants in the country, meeting in nearly four hundred congregations, small and smaller, with less than fifty foreign missionaries and about as many foreign workers, and a hundred or so national preachers, ordained or unordained.[43]

During the 1880s, persecution of Protestants continued in Mexico. On 7th August 1887, the Rev. Abraham Gómez was murdered along with two members of his Presbyterian church in Ahuacuatilan, in the state of Guerrero. The day before, a priest (the Rev. Jesús Vergara) appealed to his congregation at mass 'to make an example of the minister of Satan,' assuring them of the protection of the chief of police in killing him. Assault was made on the Evangelicals, so the pastor with six brethren appealed to a local judge for the protection of the law. Five were arrested, and the judge ordered the ringing of the church bell to summon two hundred people, instructing them to attack the Evangelicals, which they did with pistols and machetes, hacking the body of Abraham Gómez to pieces.[44]

4

CARIBBEAN AWAKENING, 1860

The parabola of the West Indies stretches from southern Florida through the Greater Antilles (including Jamaica) and Lesser Antilles (including Trinidad) to the north coast of the continent of South America. The Bahamas, Jamaica, and various of the Leeward and Windward Islands were Anglo-African in population, similar to the plantation folk of the southern United States.

The impact of the 1858-59 Revival was felt immediately in the British West Indies among emancipated slaves and their children who had suffered spiritual decline following a first blessing after their Emancipation, Baptist members having dwindled from 40,000 to 20,000 in twenty years.[1]

Primarily through the influence of the American Revival of 1858, awakenings began in the Bahamas, in Jamaica, in the Leeward and Windward Islands before the 1859 Revival had spread throughout the British Isles. There were, for example, 'gracious outpourings of the Spirit' in Barbados before the end of 1858.[2]

In Jamaica, there had been much prayer for spiritual revival as the news of the 1858 Awakening farther north had been told. By 1860, there was a confident expectation in the hearts of many that the year would not close without a signal blessing; but no one anticipated such 'copious showers.'[3]

Among a population engrossed in work in the fields, the noonday prayer meetings of the 1858-59 Revival elsewhere became 'peep of day prayer meetings' in the plantations. The movement followed the pattern of earnest prayer, conviction of sin, then outright conversions of outsiders.[4]

In September 1860, a remarkable evangelical awakening began in a Moravian chapel and spread throughout the whole island.[5] Beginning in the southwest, it moved congregations of every denomination in the parishes on the north coast and south coast, in the west and in the east, from Montego Bay to St. Thomas, from St. Ann's Bay to Savanna-la-Mar. The movement lasted a couple of years in intensity, and was effective for a generation.

The work began in St. Elizabeth Parish, in the southern part of the western county of Cornwall, commencing among the Moravians, and spreading in the Church of England, and moving among the Baptists.[6] The parishes of St. Elizabeth, St. James, Hanover and Westmoreland were soon stirred. Eastwards, the movement touched Mandeville, an inland town in the parish of Manchester; it spread along the coast to villages and hamlets, everywhere causing a sensation.

The Rev. Theodor Sonderman, a Moravian missionary, kept a journal of events which gave a glimpse into the beginnings of the movement. When he visited Clifton, he was told that a meeting was going on, so he rode on until he met a crowd of people, some weeping for joy, others under deep conviction, and others bewildered by the events. He tried to allay the excitement, but while engaged in prayer, his own feelings overpowered him and he felt it wise to leave them to the direction of the Holy Spirit.[7]

On Friday 28th September 1860, a typical meeting began at nine o'clock. A verse was sung, and opening prayer was offered.[8] There was no occasion to call on anyone to pray, for no sooner had one finished than another began. Little children took part in it. When one little boy began to pour out his soul before God, a trembling seized the company. Tears were shed, cries for mercy were heard, and groans from the hearts of hardened sinners. A little girl lifted up her voice in prayer in earnestness, fervency and fluency. Then the Spirit came 'like a rushing mighty wind'—to quote the German missionary. Strong men trembled on their knees as though shaken by an invisible power. Weeping was so general and so incessant that the missionary feared it would overstep the bounds of order. The meeting broke up at twelve, but the people reassembled at the schoolhouse to continue while the missionary conversed with those distressed.

Next day Sonderman reflected that he might as well have attempted to stop the river in its course as to stem the stream of the outpouring of heart, yet that day, quiet order and utter decorum prevailed in the church.

The prayer meetings spread to nearby districts.[9] The great feature of the awakening was prayer, and 'such prayer' it was. People whose lips seemed only accustomed to curse and swear now prayed as if this had been the daily employment of their lives. The prayer meetings seemed to generate a supernatural power which won a multitude to reformation of living, and frightened others into temporary conformity.

In its beginnings, the revival was regarded by Christian people as a work of God, yet it was spoken of with fear and trembling. Ministers were at once startled, awe-stricken, yet filled with gratitude by the manifestation of the wonder-working power of God. Fear fell upon the people, yet joy possessed many hearts. Some believers declared, 'Minister, we been praying for revival of religion, and now God pour out His Spirit we all 'fraid for it.'[10]

In a prayer meeting held in a notoriously wicked place, two young women were struck down as if by lightning, one confessing her life of abandon.[11] Then two young men were struck dumb, one writhing in agony.

A Moravian minister noted that the work in St. Elizabeth awakened very many from their sleep of religious formality and prostrated many ungodly persons. In four weeks, he had conversed with 315 inquirers, and the movement was still potent in stirring the multitudes.[12]

In early November, a minister journeyed to Montego Bay to preach a Sunday sermon. From five o'clock on Saturday evening onwards, there came a stream of inquirers. The whole town was in a state of excitement, in market-place and store, all classes discussing it, the market people and merchants, the planters and field-hands, some mocking and some praising God.[13]

After preaching a sermon in Bethel Town, a missionary proposed a dawn prayer meeting for Monday morning. Five hundred people attended. Another meeting was announced for Monday evening, presided over by a local preacher.[14] At the end of the service, as the last petition was offered, 'the Spirit was poured out and the mighty revival movement had commenced in real earnest.' The people would not leave the chapel. The missionary was alerted, and returned on the Wednesday evening to witness unforgettable scenes, with as many as a hundred hardened sinners prostrated at once. A dozen couples 'living in sin' asked the church to publish the banns for their marriages.

A justice of the peace, G. W. Gordon, participated in the movement in the absence of the missionary.[15] At 11 a.m., a congregation of twelve hundred filled the Mount Carey chapel and stood outside. About seven hearers were prostrated, causing a sensation which was subdued by the leadership. In three little places, in the absence of the minister, there were three thousand sinners awakened. This seemed typical of happenings throughout the island.

Apparently there was spontaneous confession of sins. No one asked anyone in the congregations to confess anything but, when penitents began to pray, they poured out everything before God in audible prayer, utterly indifferent as to the consequences. In some places, disclosures were made that were truly astounding, some even horrible.[16]

A missionary in Clarendon commented that there were many who doubtless lacked sympathy with this movement, but the results were so astonishing and so wonderful that they were awed into silence.[17] A few scoffers were besieged by the prayers of their friends so that they had no rest from their importunity to cease their rebellion against God.

The conversion of the most vile and abandoned characters was followed by their untiring ministry on behalf of others. New converts by the hundreds went from house to house all day long and often at night, entreating sinners to repent.[18]

The Anglicans shared in the Awakening.[19] There were those whose culture separated them from the masses, but there were also multitudes of praying people in the parish churches, and the movement soon affected them also. The High Church S.P.G. took little note of the movement, but in 1861 the Home and Foreign Missionary Society was started to open scores of mission stations in the island and to share in Anglican mission work in West Africa.[20] In many cases, members of African race in the West Indies rendered a 'notable service' in building up the African Church in West Africa, according to Bishop Stephen Neill.[21]

The Baptist churches were packed to capacity. Among them, the movement crested during the last quarter of 1860 and continued in power throughout 1861. Beginning with the prayer meetings, the Revival soon became an awakening of the masses with conviction of sin, painful penitence, and outright conversions. One characteristic of the movement was that 'the world hates it.'

> Chapels became once more crowded. There was a widespread conviction of sin. Crime diminished. Ethical standards were raised. There was renewed generosity. Old superstitions which had reasserted themselves once more declined in power. As the movement spread, unhealthy excitement and religious hysteria showed themselves in places, but the testimony of almost all observers of whatever denomination was that the (1860) Revival did permanent good.[22]

One of the senior Baptist missionaries on the island, the Rev. John Clark, described the impact of the Awakening upon Savanna-la-mar in Westmoreland, at the western end of the country. Almost every morning, meetings for public prayer and reading the Scriptures were held in private houses,[23] from fifty to a hundred readily attending. Very large numbers were giving their names to be published for marriage, and separated couples were leaving paramours and coming together again. Many were seeking admission to church membership, including more young people than had ever been seen in thirty years of service. Backsliders were seeking pardon and re-admission. The rum shops were much less frequented and the noise of quarrelsome and tipsy patrons on the roads was no longer heard.

The Baptists in Jamaica, with threescore churches in the Union and about twenty unaffiliated, reported more than six thousand baptized or restored to fellowship, another six thousand applying for baptism and fellowship. The Revival was regarded as of incalculable value. Before 1860, the membership of the churches had been declining, reduced from thirty thousand in 1840 to twenty thousand in 1860. The Revival raised the figure to above twenty-five thousand.[24]

A Congregationalist minister was convinced that the work was of God by the fact that it closed the rum shops and the gambling houses, reconciled long-separated husbands and wives, restored prodigal children, produced scores of banns to be read for marriage, crowded every place of worship, quickened the zeal of ministers, purified the churches, and brought many sinners to repentance. It also excited the rage of those ungodly people whom it had not humbled.

The Congregationalist churches planted by the London Missionary Society thus shared in the Awakening. So great was the improvement of their Jamaican churches that the L.M.S. in 1867 decided to withdraw from the field.[25]

The missionaries of the United Presbyterian Church of Scotland reported gladly on the results of the 1860 Revival — 'the most remarkable and encouraging that have ever come from Jamaica.' Church membership rose from 4299 to 5561 as 1326 converts admitted to the Church maintained a consistent deportment, with very few exceptions.[26] At the end of 1860, there were 1928 candidates waiting to be admitted to membership, a year later another 1703. In all twenty-six congregations, church attendance had reached a total of 10,420, signifying a healthy outreach.

From October 1860 onwards, the Methodist circuit at Montego Bay was experiencing unusual revival, marked by 'strong crying with tears,' sinners wailing aloud for mercy and many people prostrated by conviction.[27] Eight hundred regular members welcomed 547 professed converts on trial. There was a strong movement in Lucea. An unprecedented movement was reported from the hitherto discouraging Brown's Town circuit.[28] Around St. Ann's Bay, a revival had suddenly begun in the Wesleyan congregations, with 150 on trial and a regular membership of 500 or so.[29] This was typical of the north coast circuits.

On the south coast, the circuits were likewise moved. Clarendon churches were crowded to excess, 400 on trial and a membership of 800.[30] Daily prayer meetings were held also in Spanish Town, with the same kind of results, 120 converts on trial with a regular membership of 650. Some people were prostrated for days.[31]

In early 1862, it was reported that Kingston Methodists (3159 in 1861) had added 708 to membership with another 82 still on trial; Montego Bay (807) had added 708, with 220 on trial; Spanish Town (655) had added 210, with 126 awaiting transfer.[32]

In early 1863, the Kingston Methodists reported that a holy fire was still burning, though the leaders were weary in well-doing.[33] In Montego Bay, the ministers were well-satisfied that a goodly number of the newly converted had joined the membership.[34]

Sales of Scripture from the Kingston depot had averaged 4700 a year, but 20,700 were issued during the extraordinary revival of the years 1860 and 1861.[35] The salient peculiarity of that sudden awakening was the insistent demand for the Word of God. It preserved most of the people from excess and extravagance, and in many cases it deepened the sense of sin into a new life.

In a certain meeting,[36] a man objected to the reading of the Scriptures and proposed that the singing be continued. Curiosity led to inquiries. It was found that this married man was an adulterer who had led many younger women into sin, hence his preference for singing rather than the reading of the convicting Word.

Throughout 1861, the Baptists and Congregationalists, Methodists, Moravians, and Presbyterians reported many accessions to their memberships, Anglican communicants increasing meanwhile.

During the awakening period, every place of worship had been crowded to excess, and nearly all the population desired to hear the Good News of Christ proclaimed. Quarrelsome folk became quiet, drunkards became abstainers, swearers feared to utter an oath, the unclean forsook licentious living and thousands were united in marriage. Reading the Bible, praise, prayer and preaching became the order of the first period of the Awakening.[37]

It was recognized that the larger part of those awakened continued quietly in their Christian profession.[38] A lesser number became careless, and some returned to the sins from which it had been hoped that they were rescued. The noisiest converts, as in Ireland, proved in many cases to be the least persevering.

When the excitement passed away, though numbers fell back into superstition and immorality, two-thirds of the converts at Brown's Town stood faithful. And this may be considered typical.[39]

After nine month's experience of the 1860-61 Awakening, a senior missionary reported that there was much over which to rejoice, much about which there was anxiety, and much about which to lament as the work of the Enemy.[40]

The 'unhealthy excitement and religious hysteria' cited by Dr. Ernest A. Payne were understandable in a population of recently liberated slaves.[41] It contrasted with the utter lack of extravagance of any kind in the 1858 American Revival, and in most other places across the Atlantic.

The Moravians, among whom the 1860 Revival had begun, were convinced that the movement was thoroughly genuine, even though for some months it was disfigured by excesses 'no worse than those which occurred in England during the Evangelical Revival.'[42] Convicted sinners were sometimes struck deaf and dumb, but on other occasions they gnashed or screamed or tore their clothes. Some were speechless for a couple of weeks, others unconscious for days. Other penitents refused food, and a few reportedly snapped and twitched. It was not a fear of hell but a sense of sin which brought about distress. Remarkable visions were often told by various people.

A Methodist historian complained that extravagance and antinomianism arose among native revivalists.[43] This was part of the counterfeit revival, a phenomenon regarded as almost inevitable by Jonathan Edwards, who felt that every work of God would be accompanied by satanic counterfeit.[44]

The unaccountable prostrations were often followed by terrific contortions of the body, jumping, shouting and wild actions. Such counterfeits were followed by a revival of the African superstition, obeah witchcraft, and the rise of local prophets dedicated to rooting out this superstition. Where the madness of 'myalism' was not quickly checked, it did fearful mischief among ignorant and superstitious people. Where ministers opposed the fanatics, they were denounced as hinderers of God's work.[45] Soon the wave of counterfeit revival spent itself, and there was a relief from excesses.

The white plantation society of Jamaica was not noted for its piety, rather the reverse. A returned governor had told a British audience: 'In short, gentlemen, there are just two classes of people in Jamaica, black Christians and white devils.' [46] The blacks were 'a people neglected, a people wronged, a people burdened,' according to G. W. Gordon.[47]

Five years after the outbreak of the Jamaican Revival of 1860, an uprising provoked by widespread discontent due to spreading poverty, increased taxation, land hunger and injustice occurred at Morant Bay, in which the chief magistrate of the parish among a score of European people was killed. Martial law was proclaimed by Governor Eyre and the local rising was ruthlessly suppressed, its principal instigator being hanged, to the applause of the planters but the dismay of many missionaries. Indignation among the missionaries' friends in Britain led to the recall of the Governor and to a change of government.[48] Grant, the new governor under the Crown, achieved a remarkable reorganization of the colony, and the economy improved as well as the administration.

The immunity from trouble of masses of people in large districts during the negro rising of 1865 was ascribed by those on the spot to the influence of Bible reading.[49]

Other West Indian islands were affected by the Revival. On Antigua, St. John's circuit boasted 109 new members with 76 on trial. The Tortola circuit reported in 1861 'an outpouring of the Holy Spirit,' with 229 new members and 74 converts on trial.[50]

For reasons of success, the London Missionary Society also withdrew from other West Indian islands at this time. The Awakening of 1860 rekindled the zeal of Trinidad Negro Christians descended from rebel slaves who were removed from the Carolinas by the British in the War of 1812. In the following decade, Canadians started their missionary work among East Indians working the Trinidad estates.

News of the Revival in Jamaica brought about a reviving in Belize, an enclave of Indian, Negro, Mestizo and a few British people on the Caribbean coast of Central America, the Wesleyans adding 379 members and placing 76 on trial, and the Baptist cause prospering.[51]

More isolated was a similar enclave on the Caribbean coast of Nicaragua, known as the Mosquito Coast, whose local king enjoyed some measure of British protection. At mid-century, the Moravian missionaries built a church in Bluefields, and gathered congregations along the coast.[52]

In 1881,[53] a great awakening began in the Bluefields area. Resembling the Jamaican revival of two decades earlier, it began simultaneously in the town of Bluefields and at Pearl Lagoon.[54] Excitement arose in Sunday services, despite the restraint of the missionaries; and next day every house in Bluefields was affected, all classes of people being stirred. Bands of Indians at work in the forest, away from mission stations, were seized by an overpowering conviction of sin. At mission stations, children knelt and prayed for pardon. The movement spread quickly like an epidemic. As earlier in Jamaica, there were unusual manifestations, trembling, groaning and refusing food, some prostrated to the ground, a number convulsed. Visions and dreams were reported. In the meantime, the German brethren kept calm and sought to help all who were in distress of body and soul.

In spite of the excesses, the strange visitation produced much good. As a result of the Awakening, Indians, Negroes, Creoles and Mestizos felt the power of the Spirit in their lives and responded by repentance and restitution of wrongs. Tested by time, the conversions proved to be genuine, and few fell away.[55] A result of the Awakening was the adding of fifteen hundred communicants to the thousand already on the rolls at the beginning of the year, a 150% increase in a matter of months. Ten years later came a decline.

In 1894, the Mosquito Coast was incorporated into the Republic of Nicaragua, causing much dislocation of social life as the medium changed from English to Spanish. It was complained that the Nicaraguans, contrary to a negotiated treaty, occupied the Mosquito Reserve,[56] and the presence of soldiers at Bluefields caused both unrest and disorder. Many of the evangelical Christians fled, and some churches were on the verge of ruin. Lamplight services were given up, for no decent woman cared to walk the streets after dark. Recovery came after many years of turmoil.

Beyond the shores of the Caribbean, on the mainland of South America, the Guianas shared something of the ethnic and cultural background of the West Indies. Their population was a mixture of slave or bush Negro and aboriginal Indian, a strain of East Indian settlers added, with a thin veneer of colonial European civilization. Anglicans, Congregationalists and Methodists in Guyana, the British colony, shared in the spiritual prosperity of the mid-century revival. The London Missionary Society then decided, in 1867, to withdraw from Guyana for the reasons given in the West Indies, that their churches had matured.[57]

Between ten and twenty thousand Bush Negroes (runaway slaves) lived in the hinterland of Surinam, the Dutch colony. Lapsed from whatever Christian teaching they knew, they sacrificed to Gran-Gado (the great God), Maria and Jesi as well as the spirits of animism.[58]

About the time of the 1858 Revival, a Bush Negro named Adiri became subject to strange visions and dreams, often a means of divine enlightenment in the absence of Scripture. Adiri had been born in Paramaribo in 1830, the son of the third marriage of his mother, Ademsi.[59] In his early teens, the family settled among the Bush Negroes at Maripastoon, sharing in the witchcraft so prevalent around them. Adiri began to resist the demon possession of his people, and was persecuted and then tortured—manacled hand and foot for three months at a time—to make him conform. Visions persisted, until at last he cried to God for salvation.

In his vision, he was commanded to visit the missionaries at Paramaribo, where Moravians taught him to read and to write. He returned to Maripastoon and built a chapel there, challenging the fetish worship. From 1861 onwards, the place was overcrowded.[60] A kinsman became pastor as he itinerated in the hinterland. He was baptized in 1863, when his name was changed to John King.

Calker and Bramberg, the first missionaries to visit the village of Maripastoon, found that every trace of heathenism had been effaced, men and women decently dressed, order and prosperity prevailing within a Christian community. So the folk movement spread through the preaching of the Word to many parts of Surinam, thousands being converted.

5

MISSIONARY RESURGENCE, 1890—

A quarter of a century after the outbreak of the 1858-59 Revival in the English-speaking world, while the forces of evangelism and renewal were still pulsating strongly in all the Protestant denominations, there came a resurgence of missionary interest in the churches, more particularly in the ranks of Christian students.

The recognized leader of Evangelicalism in those days was the humble yet dynamic Dwight L. Moody, and it is significant that—although he lacked an education himself— it was his compelling influence upon the more sophisticated youngsters that stimulated them to action.

Moody's historic preaching mission at the University of Cambridge in 1882 was soon followed by a movement among British students in the years following when the Cambridge Seven volunteered for China.[1] In 1884, Moody chaired a conference for American students, and out of that gathering in Massachusetts came the Student Volunteers, with their slogan of 'the evangelization of the world in this generation.' In half a century, more than twenty thousand volunteers from the world's universities reached the mission fields as evangelists, doctors, educators, nurses and the like.[2] The great majority of these missionaries sailed for the mission fields of Asia and Africa, and only a minority went to Latin America, which remained comparatively neglected.

Nevertheless, in Canada and United States, the interest in the lands to the South was re-kindled, and many people projected their prayers upon the closed or partly-opened countries of the Caribbean and South America. Cuba and the United States of Mexico loomed largest in the minds of the North Americans.

It was in 1898 that the United States became involved in war with Spain over the remaining Spanish colonies in the Caribbean. But the missionary interest long preceded this development of American imperialism, if such it was. The missionary literature of the eighties and nineties gave more and more space to the needs of Latin America.[3]

Bishop Stephen Neill has observed that most American Protestants have lacked hesitation about proselytizing in nominally Roman Catholic countries, treating such efforts as missions just as much as the missions in non-Christian countries. They have regarded Mexico, the Caribbean, and South America as mission fields. Where the Anglicans and Lutherans generally restricted their operations to people of their own affiliation, the Presbyterians, Methodists, and Baptists and other groups entered Latin America with the express purpose of converting Roman Catholics.[4] He added:

> For this there is a measure of justification. Roman Catholic writers admit that the conversion of many of the aboriginal peoples was superficial in the extreme; and in recent years the shortage of priests has been such that for many of the inhabitants there is extremely little chance of any real instruction in the tenets of the Roman Catholic faith.

One might add that the concerned American and other Protestant societies attributed the superficial conversions to a sad neglect of preaching the Word.

Fifteen years after the American 1858 Awakening, there was only one Evangelical congregation in Mexico City, with seventy-five communicants.[5] Twenty years later, in 1894, a 'large native memmbership' met in eighteen such churches, and throughout Mexico there were 385 churches meeting in 469 congregations.[6] But, in that previous year, there were no less than 58 Evangelicals murdered for their faith.

The year 1894 proved significant in the history of the Mexican Evangelicals, for that year the first missionary conference was held at Toluca; the National Evangelical Convention—continued throughout the twentieth century—was instituted, and D. L. Moody preached in Mexico.[7]

Meetings of the first General Missionary Conference in Mexico that year were devoted to the study of the Spirit of God as revealed in the Acts of the Apostles.[8] A hundred and forty workers representing a dozen societies met with the warm-hearted Moody and Sankey. The Methodist, John W. Butler reported:

> There came upon the assembly one of the richest baptisms of the Holy Ghost it has ever been our privilege to experience. During the singing of the second hymn, without any indication from any in the room, people began to . . . speak words of personal encouragement to each other.

Moody also addressed an evangelistic service at the Teatro Nacional, holding rapt attention. According to high Mexican authorities, Moody's ministry at the 1894 National Evangelical Convention and other gatherings resulted in a great revival in the Church, with many seekers added.[9] In those days, the national ministry was small in numbers but it caught the fire of revival and took it to the churches.

Among those national ministers stirred up by Moody's visit to Mexico were Vicente Mendoza and Arcadio Morales. Mendoza, a Methodist, became a talented evangelist with an influence upon younger folk, and he was later instrumental in a gracious revival which moved the Evangelicals in the capital city a dozen years later.[10] Morales, a Presbyterian, also became a powerful evangelist and was known as 'the Moody of Mexico' in the early twentieth century.[11]

At the time of the 1858 Revival, an agent of the American Bible Society trying to circulate the Scriptures had been murdered in Central America.[12] In the 1880s, Presbyterian missionaries opened a work in Guatemala City, their travel there paid by the President of that Republic.[13] In the 1890s, the Central American Mission founded by C. I. Scofield sent its first missionaries to the Central American republics. In 1899, a permanent station was opened in Guatemala. In 1896, work was begun in Honduras. That year also, work commenced in El Salvador. Nicaragua was entered at the end of the century. In 1891, the pioneers entered Costa Rica.[14] Even in 1895, there were about thirty missionaries with seventy national workers and three thousand members of the various denominations in Spanish-speaking Central America.[15] The decade was one of pioneering.

In the English-speaking enclaves, there was an older and more flourishing enterprise.[16] In British Honduras, more than two hundred Methodist local preachers were reported, with two thousand members, besides Anglican and Baptist followings; and in the Mosquito Coast of Nicaragua there were more than five thousand Moravians, while in a tinier Anglo-African enclave in Caribbean Costa Rica was found a Jamaican-related Baptist congregation.

In the mid-nineties, the Baptists in Jamaica numbered forty thousand members, meeting in congregations which averaged over two hundred in strength.[17] Other Protestant denominations claimed sixty thousand members, the Roman Catholic communion 12,500 baptized. Thus there remained a huge missionfield of four hundred thousand unevangelized.

Missionaries regretted to admit that the people seemed or ly superficially evangelized.[18] Sexual laxity was regarded as appalling, and sixty per cent of children were born out of wedlock. Yet Jamaica flourished in contrast with Haiti, for in the British island were many who lived exemplary lives according to the highest Christian standards.

Evangelical missions in the nearby island of Hispaniola, including the Dominican as well as the Haitian republics, were manned by Baptists (Jamaican, British and American) and Methodists, with some Anglican missionaries, but no more than twenty-four hundred[19] were gathered in churches. In Haiti, where Christo-paganism and pagan superstition permeated the population, observers in the 1890s reported 'commercial bankruptcy, physical squalor, moral rotten-ness, intellectual stagnation and spiritual deadness' in all parts of the black republic.[20]

A civil engineer, Alberto J. Díaz, working with the help of his family and the American Foreign School Association, succeeded in 1882 in opening four Sunday Schools in Havana. Within the span of a year, Díaz baptized 130 or so Cuban converts.[21] Cuba seemed to evidence more desire for the freedom of religion than did its mother country.

Given such a promising lead, Southern Baptists entered Cuba and in little more than two years baptized 1100 people. It was said that eight thousand had applied for membership. Díaz being a Spanish-speaking American citizen, some of the more naive thought that evangelical membership was coincident with North American citizenship, hence only the truly converted were received.[22] Thorough instruction was given all inquirers.

By 1896, the Home Mission Board of the Southern Baptist Convention had sent two dozen missionaries to Cuba and twenty-seven hundred church members had been enrolled. Díaz ministered in Havana in a location seating 3000 but without a sign to advertise its activities.[23] Díaz himself had suffered imprisonment six times for preaching the Gospel, as when the Cuban hierarchy decided to promote Columbus to sainthood, which provoked Alberto Díaz to say that he respected Columbus as discoverer of Cuba, but did that by itself make him a saint? For 'disrespect to a saint,' he was imprisoned, but was released when the proposal fell through. Díaz welcomed persecution and observed that it always increased membership and deepened consecration, which was true elsewhere in restive societies.

Then came the Spanish-American War.[24] Alberto Díaz was careful to dissociate himself from the hostilities, but numbers of his congregation enlisted in a Cuban regiment fighting for liberty, and Díaz formed a society for relief of both Cuban and Spanish sick and wounded. The vicissitudes of war scattered the flock, so that fifteen hundred converts only continued to meet, but with the coming of peace the work recovered, several denominations entering the island at the turn of the century.

At the time of the Revival of the 1860s in Britain, a layman engaged in British trade bought himself a farm and set out to give the needy Puerto Ricans instruction.[25] He died of smallpox, but a convert, Antonio Badillo, carried on this work of Heiliger. The circulation of the Scripture was then forbidden, and Badillo was hailed before officials who tried to find where his Bible was hidden. He memorized Bible verses, and built up a following.

Until 1898, Puerto Rico was closed to Evangelical work, a chaplain of the Anglican Colonial and Continental Society serving British and other sailors being the only missionary. Religious services in the island were poorly attended, and despite a compulsory school attendance law (a dead letter), illiteracy claimed no less than 87%.[26] On the defeat of Spain, Protestant missionaries entered the island, establishing a comity of operation immediately, Baptists, Presbyterians and United Brethren making the most progress.[27] Badillo's group made contact with the Presbyterians to see whether they preached the same Word; they soon united.

Trinidad, close to the South American coast, possessed a Roman Catholic majority, but the Church of England had built up a diocese after disestablishment, and was baptizing besides a hundred East Indians annually in the 1890s.[28] The Canadian Presbyterians in the 1860s had also developed a work among the East Indian population.[29] In Barbados, the Anglican establishment long continued and membership was high compared with that of other Protestant fellowships.[30]

In British Guiana, the Anglican establishment continued until the end of the century, and claimed twenty thousand communicants in the 1890s.[31] There were other Protestants, including the Moravians, who in nearby Surinam cared for thirty thousand members, half the population being the fruit of the earlier evangelical awakening.[32] Other Protestants numbered ten thousand, Roman Catholics thirteen thousand, and there were Hindus and pagans.

In the 1890s, northern South America was still a pioneer territory. The first resident Protestant missionary, agent of the American Bible Society, had arrived in Venezuela in the late 1880s.[33] Bible classes were held in his house, and a number of Venezuelans became regular attenders. Plymouth Brethren commenced a mission in Caracas in 1883. Before the end of the century, the Presbyterians opened a mission in Caracas also.[34]

About the same time, Presbyterian missionaries working in Bogotá and other cities in Colombia were facing difficult times on account of political strife, having been cut off from base and supplies for nine months, and evening meetings in the port of Barranquilla were impossible because of martial law.[35] As in Venezuela, there were few converts.

A new concern for tropical South America arose from a series of meetings held in Kansas City by Dr. H. Grattan Guinness, the Irish revivalist of 1859 who became such a promoter and organizer of foreign missions. In a meeting of a dozen men, six volunteered for service and the other six offered to maintain support, the result being the Gospel Missionary Union.[36]

Ecuador, at that time, was a citadel of intolerance, but in mid-1895 there was an uprising against clerical tyrrany and a liberal government took office under Eloy Alfaro, introducing a measure of toleration and adopting projects for civil liberties and popular education.[37] To Ecuador went the Kansas City volunteers, W. E. Reed and Jerome Altig, thus establishing a missionary foothold.[38] Pioneers of Christian and Missionary Alliance projects settled in Quito in 1897. Persecution was so severe that local police were called on to save the missionaries from a violent death.[39]

The world-ranging William Taylor, after a remarkable revival and evangelistic ministry in Australia, South Africa and India, had started educational mission projects in Lima and Callao in Peru, but after seven years or so, the work languished.[40] In Peru, when Penzotti was imprisoned, his place was taken by a Peruvian convert, José Q. Illescas. In 1891, an outstanding Methodist, T. B. Wood, arrived in Callao and embarked upon a project of penetration by means of secular education. His school doubled and trebled and quadrupled in enrollment.[41] In 1893, a Plymouth brother, Charles Bright, reached Lima, and out of his evangelism grew the largest congregation of Lima, Iglesia Maranata, of the Iglesia Evangélica Peruana.[42]

That same year, three Englishmen arrived from Grattan
Guinness's College in London and laid the foundations of a
work later known as the Evangelical Union of South America,
an enterprise that spread within a few years north to south
and inland to the ancient Inca capital of Cuzco.[43] In 1897, Dr.
Harry Grattan Guinness visited his Harley College men and
held prayer meetings in the mornings, scripture teaching in
the afternoons and gospel preaching in the evenings, in which
there was unusual revival of believers, and numbers came
forward nightly for counsel, a majority of students in the
mission high school professing conversion. All the converts
were bilingual, and T. B. Wood was delighted that neither
defection nor backsliding followed.[44]

Luke Matthews had itinerated in Bolivia as a colporteur
in the late 1820s.[45] It is likely that Matthews was murdered
somewhere in the Andes. In 1876, Joseph Monguiardino
commenced a South American tour of unparalleled scope.
In 1877, he visited Bolivia and sold a thousand copies of the
Scriptures, but was waylaid and murdered. The authorities
forced those who had stoned him to death to carry the corpse
to a town some miles away, where the priest refused burial
within the town limits.[46] Penzotti and Milne visited Bolivia
as colporteurs in the 1880s.

The law of the land proclaimed that conspiring to practise
any form of religion other than the established Church was
treachery punishable by death.[47] But, in the 1890s, another
colporteur, J. B. Arancet, established residence in La Paz.
An Irishman, from a Brethren assembly in Dublin, William
Payne, took up residence in Bolivia. In 1898, Canadian
Baptists succeeded in gaining a foothold.[48]

Meanwhile, W. B. Grubb had penetrated the Gran Chaco
of Paraguay, making friends with the hostile Lenguas, the
impressed Paraguayan Government naming him Pacificador
de los Indios.[49] He gathered a Lengua congregation. The
remainder of Paraguay was destitute of evangelical witness.

In 1897, the Valparaiso Bible Society sold 12,000 books,
including two thousand Bibles.[50] In Chile, the Presbyterians
and the Methodists each had four hundred members and a
thousand Sunday School pupils. Among the immigrants to
Chile, the German Baptists enjoyed a period of revival in
the nineties.[51] Some of their meetings continued all night,
and several bilingual young people were converted and soon
started services for their Spanish-speaking friends.

Across the Andes, there were significant developments in Argentina. British engineers were building the Argentine railways and the Plymouth Brethren found great opportunity among English-speaking people who were forced to seek informal fellowship.[52] When they reached out to the Spanish-speaking masses, these Hermanos Libres took a leading role in the evangelical movement. Methodists were still extending their stakes, and had established local schools and a theological seminary.[53] The Salvation Army entered Buenos Aires in 1890.[54] Thus far, there was no report of any movement resembling a revival. The same was true of Uruguay, where American Methodists pioneered.

In 1889 came the collapse of the Empire in Brazil, the abdication of the popular Dom Pedro II, and the separation of church and state. Brazil entered the 1890s with hope of further progress. Apart from the ethnic Germans, the Presbyterians were the largest denomination, but Baptists were growing rapidly.[55] The Presbyterians turned over the work in Rio Grande do Sul to Protestant Episcopal clergy, and L. L. Kinsolving was consecrated bishop in 1900.[56] Other denominations extended their operations, and the Y.M.C.A. founded its first association in South America. The Bible Societies accelerated the distribution of the Scriptures.[57]

It is noteworthy that the only outpourings of the Spirit in the reviving of believers and the awakening of communities thus far in the whole area from the Rio Grande to Cape Horn had occurred in places where the language was English or German and a knowledge of the Scriptures was imparted. In the Spanish and Portuguese-speaking communities, there was an absence of such movements of prayer and conviction of sin, and consequent outreach to the community.[58]

As was the case with Bishop James Thoburn in India, the pioneer Methodist missionary, T. B. Wood, made a striking prophecy of coming revival at the turn of the century. The Evangelicals everywhere were faced with a difficult struggle, but the veteran had seen a local revival unparalleled in the memory of his constituency,[59] so he predicted:[60]

> The signs of the times point to the coming of great sweeping revivals. All the work thus far is providentially preparatory to them. And when they once get started among these impulsive peoples, the mighty changes that will follow fast and far throughout this immense, homogeneous territory promise to surpass anything of the kind hitherto known.

6

THE FIFTH GENERAL AWAKENING

The worldwide Awakening of the early twentieth century came at the end of fifty years of evangelical advance, following the outpouring of the Spirit far and wide in 1858-59 and the 'sixties. Thus it did not represent a recovery from a long night of despair caused by rampant infidelity, as was the case in the days of Wesley. It seemed, rather, a blaze of evening glory at the end of 'the Great Century.'[1]

It was the most extensive Evangelical Awakening of all time, reviving Anglican, Baptist, Congregational, Disciple, Lutheran, Methodist, Presbyterian and Reformed churches and other evangelical bodies throughout Europe and North America, Australasia and South Africa, and their daughter churches and missionary causes throughout Asia, Africa, and Latin America, winning more than five million folk to an evangelical faith in the two years of greatest impact in each country. Indirectly it produced Pentecostalism.

Why did it occur at the time it did? The ways of God are past finding out. One can only surmise. A subtler form of infidelity had arisen, a compromise between Christianity and humanism. A more sophisticated interpretation of human conduct, inspired by Freud, spoke of God as an Illusion.

The prescient wisdom of its Author may also account for the sudden spread of the Revival of 1900-1910. Within ten years, the awful slaughter of World War I had begun and a gentler way of life passed into the twilight of history.

Arnold Toynbee, reminiscing, recalled the trauma of the time, when half his classmates perished in battle. Oneself was a child when the news of the Battle of the Somme threw every family in his native city into mourning for the finest of their fathers and sons and brothers killed in action.[2]

The Awakening was a kind of harvest before the devastation of Christendom. It was Sir Edward Grey who lamented in 1914 that the lights of civilization were going out one by one, not to be lit again in his lifetime. The upheavals of war unloosed the times of revolution on mankind. A biographer of Wilbur Chapman observed:[3]

As we look back over these extraordinary religious
awakenings which . . . so quickened the churches and
so effectively pressed the claims of God upon the consciences of multitudes, we cannot escape the conviction
that God in gracious providence was reaping a spiritual
harvest before He permitted the outburst of revolutionary forces that have overwhelmed the world, impoverished almost every nation, produced economic and
social chaos, and stained with dishonor the pride of
Christian civilization.

In the history of revivals, it has often been noted
that such restoral periods are a warning of, and syn-
chronize with, impending judgment. The harvest is
gathered before the field is doomed to death.

The early twentieth century Evangelical Awakening was
a worldwide movement. It did not begin with the phenomenal
Welsh Revival of 1904-05. Rather its sources were in the
springs of little prayer meetings which seemed to arise
spontaneously all over the world, combining into the streams
of expectation which became a river of blessing in which the
Welsh Revival became the greatest cataract.

Meetings for prayer for revival in evangelical gatherings
such as Moody Bible Institute and the Keswick Convention
greeted the new century—not surprisingly.[4] What was remarkable was that missionaries and national believers in
obscure places in India, the Far East, Africa and Latin
America seemed moved at the same time to pray for phenomenal revival in their fields and world wide. Most of
them had never seen or heard of phenomenal revival occurring
on missionfields, and few of them had witnessed it at home.
Their experience was limited to reading of past revivals.

The first manifestation of phenomenal revival occurred
simultaneously among Boer prisoners of war in places ten
thousand miles apart, as far away as Bermuda and Ceylon.
The work was marked by extraordinary praying, by faithful
preaching, conviction of sin, confession and repentance with
lasting conversions and hundreds of enlistments for missionary service. The spirit of Revival spread to South Africa in
the throes of economic depression.[5]

Not without significance, an Awakening began in 1900 in
the churches of Japan, which had long suffered from a period
of retarded growth.[6] It started in an unusually effective
movement to prayer, followed by an unusually intensive
effort of evangelism, matched by an awakening of Japanese
urban masses to the claims of Christ, and such an ingathering

that the total membership of the churches almost doubled within the decade. Why did the Japanese Awakening occur in 1900? It would have been impossible four years later when Japan became involved in momentous war with Russia. Significantly also for the evangelistic follow-up of the general Awakening, the Torrey and Alexander team found that unusual praying had prepared a way for the most fruitful evangelistic ministry ever known in New Zealand and Australia,[7] and the unprecedented success of the campaigns launched Torrey and Alexander (and later Chapman and Alexander) on their worldwide evangelistic crusades, conventionally run but accompanied by revival of the churches.

Gipsy Smith experienced much the same kind of response in his Mission of Peace in war-weary South Africa, successful evangelism provoking an awakening of the population to Christian faith. Gipsy Smith extended his ministry.[8]

Meanwhile worldwide prayer meetings were intensifying. Undoubtedly, the farthest-felt happening of the decade was the Welsh Revival, which began as a local revival in early 1904, moved the whole of Wales by the end of the year, produced the mystic figure of Evan Roberts as leader yet filled simultaneously almost every church in the principality.[9]

The Welsh Revival was the farthest-reaching of the movements of the general Awakening, for it affected the whole of the Evangelical cause in India, Korea and China, renewed revival in Japan and South Africa, and sent a wave of awakening over Africa, Latin America, and the South Seas.

The story of the Welsh Revival is astounding. Begun with prayer meetings of less than a score of intercessors, when it burst its bounds the churches of Wales were crowded for more than two years. A hundred thousand outsiders were converted and added to the churches, the vast majority remaining true to the end. Drunkenness was immediately cut in half, and many taverns went bankrupt. Crime was so diminished that judges were presented with white gloves signifying that there were no cases of murder, assault, rape or robbery or the like to consider. The police became 'unemployed' in many districts. Stoppages occurred in coalmines, not due to unpleasantness between management and workers, but because so many foul-mouthed miners became converted and stopped using foul language that the horses which hauled the coal trucks in the mines could no longer understand what was being said to them, and transportation ground to a halt.

Time and again, the writer has been asked why the Welsh Revival did not last. It did last. The most exciting phase lasted two years. There was an inevitable drifting away of some whose interest was superficial, perhaps one person in forty of the total membership of the Churches. Even critics of the movement conceded that eighty percent of the converts remained in the Churches after five years.[10]

But there was a falling away in Wales. Why? It did not occur among the converts of the 1904 Revival, other than the minority noted. Converts of the Revival continued to be the choicest segment of church life, even in the 1930s, when the writer studied the spiritual life of Wales closely. Two disasters overtook Wales.[11] The first World War slaughtered a high proportion of the generation revived, or converted, or only influenced by the Revival, leaving a dearth of men in the churches; the coal mines of Wales were hit in the 1920s by tragic unemployment, which continued into the thirties in the Depression; and the class under military age during the war, infants during the Revival, espoused the gospel of Marxism. The Aneurin Bevans replaced the Keir Hardies in the party.

There was yet another reason. The Welsh Revival took scripture knowledge for granted, and preaching thus deemed superfluous was at a minimum. The Welsh revival constituency was ill-prepared for a new onslaught of anti-evangelicalism which captured a generation of otherwise disillusioned Welshmen. The province of Ulster moved into the place held by the principality of Wales as a land of evangelistic activities.

The story of the Welsh Revival has often been told. Most Christian people, including scholars, have been unaware of the extent of the Awakening which followed in the English-speaking world—in the United Kingdom, the United States, Canada, South Africa, Australia and faraway New Zealand.

The Archbishop of Canterbury called for a nationwide day of prayer.[12] Thirty English bishops declared for the Revival after one of their number, deeply moved, told of confirming 950 new converts in a country parish church. The Revival swept Scotland and Ireland.[13] Under Albert Lunde, also a friend of the researcher in later years, a movement began in Norway described by Bishop Berggrav as the greatest revival of his experience. It affected Sweden, Finland, and Denmark, Lutherans there saying that it was the greatest movement of the Spirit since the Vikings were evangelized.[14] It broke out in Germany, France and other countries of Europe, marked by prayer and confession.[15]

It is difficult to count converts in the Church of England, but, in the years 1903-1906, the other Protestant denominations (equal in membership) gained 10% or 300,000.[16]

When news of the Awakening reached the United States, huge conferences of ministers gathered in New York and Chicago and other cities to discuss what to do when the Awakening began. Soon the Methodists in Philadelphia had 6101 new converts in trial membership; the ministers of Atlantic City claimed that only fifty adults remained professedly unconverted in a population of 60,000. Churches in New York City took in hundreds on a single Sunday— in one instance, 364 were received into membership, 286 new converts, 217 adults, 134 men, 60 heads of families.[17]

The 1905 Awakening rolled through the South like a tidal wave, packing churches for prayer and confession, adding hundreds to membership rolls—First Baptist in Paducah added a thousand in a couple of months and the old pastor died of overwork. Believers' baptisms among the Southern Baptists rose twenty-five per cent in one year. Other denominations shared equally in the Awakening.[18]

In the Middle West, churches were suddenly inundated by great crowds of seekers. The 'greatest revivals in their history' were reported by Methodists in town after town; the Baptists and others gained likewise. Everyone was so busy in Chicago that the pastors decided to hold their own meetings and help one another deal with the influx. Every store and factory closed in Burlington, Iowa, to permit employees to attend services of intercession and dedication. The mayor of Denver declared a day of prayer: by 10 a.m., churches were filled; at 11.30, almost every store closed; 12,000 attended prayer meetings in downtown theatres and halls; every school closed; the Colorado Legislature closed. The impact was felt for a year.[19]

In the West, great demonstrations marched through the streets of Los Angeles. United meetings attracted attendance of 180,000. The Grand Opera House was filled at midnight as drunks and prostitutes were seeking salvation. For three hours a day, business was practically suspended in Portland, Oregon, bank presidents and bootblacks attending prayer meetings while two hundred department stores in agreement closed from 11 till 2.[20]

Churches of the various denominations, town or country, were moved from Newfoundland to British Columbia across Canada, in spontaneous prayer or ardent evangelism.[21]

Church membership in the United States in seven major Protestant denominations increased by more than two million in five years (870,389 new communicants in 1906) and continued rising.[22] This did not include the gains of the younger denominations of Pentecostal or Holiness dynamic whose rate of increase was considerably greater.

It is naturally difficult to estimate the gains in the Dutch Reformed Church in South Africa, for most converts therein already possessed family affiliation. The Methodist Church increased by thirty percent in the three years of revival.[23] No doubt, the same patterns applied in New Zealand, Australia and South Africa, all stirred by the Welsh Revival.

The writer has visited all the States of India, has addressed more than a million people there, and has lectured in twenty of their theological colleges, and to hundreds of missionaries and national pastors. And yet he encountered only one who knew of the extent of the Indian Revival of 1905-1906, a retired professor of theology. Yet the Awakening in India moved every province and the Christian population increased by seventy percent, sixteen times as fast as the Hindu, the Protestant rate of increase being almost double that of the Roman Catholic. In many places, meetings went on for five to ten hours.[24]

In Burma, 1905 'brought ingathering quite surpassing anything known in the history of the mission.' The A.B.M.U. baptized 2000 Karens that year, 200 being the average. In a single church, 1340 Shans were baptized in December, 3113 in all being added in the 'marvelous ingathering.'[25]

The story of the Korean Revival of 1907 has been told and retold. It is less well-known that the Revival came in three waves, 1903, 1905 and 1907—the membership of the Churches quadrupling within a decade, the national Church being created from almost nothing by the movement. Since then, the Korean Churches have maintained the impetus.[26]

The revival campaigns of Jonathan Goforth in Manchuria have been recorded and published, but the extent of the Awakening in China between the Boxer Uprising and the 1911 Revolution has not been apprehended. China's greatest living evangelist, survivor of the China-wide Awakening of 1927-1939, told the writer that he had not even heard of the Awakening (in every province in the 1900s) apart from the post-Boxer revulsion. Yet the number of Protestant communicants doubled in a decade to quarter of a million, twice that figure for the total Evangelical community.[27]

In Indonesia,[28] the numbers of Evangelicals, 100,000 in 1903, trebled in the decade of general Awakening to 300,000, and in subsequent movements of phenomenal power, the number of believers on one little island (Nias) surpassed the latter figure, winning two-thirds the population. Protestant membership in Madagascar increased sixty-six percent in the years of Revival, 1905-1915. And pioneering success was achieved in the newly-opened Philippines.

The Awakening had limited effect in the Latin American countries: unusual revival in Brazil, phenomenal awakening in Chile, with Evangelical membership in both countries starting to climb—until in our times it passed the number of practising Roman Catholics; pioneering continued in other republics with sparse results but promise of future harvest, since realised.[29]

The Edinburgh World Missionary Conference recognized that more progress had been made in all Africa in the first decade of the twentieth century than experienced hitherto. Protestant communicants in the African mission fields increased in 1903-1910 from 300,000 to 500,000, there having been many awakenings in various parts in those years.[30] But the full impact of the Welsh Revival was not felt until the war years, when phenomenal revival occurred among the Africans. In the next half century, the increase was double that of the general population.

It was most significant that the Awakening of the 1900s was ecumenical, in the best senses of the word. It was thoroughly interdenominational. The foregoing narratives have provided instances of Anglican, Baptist, Brethren, Congregational, Disciple, Lutheran, Methodist, Presbyterian and Reformed congregations sharing in the Revival. There is a total lack of evidence of any response on the part of Roman Catholic or Greek Orthodox communities, but this is not surprising, for it was so in the days of the Puritans, of Wesley, of Finney, and of Moody. Only in the mid-twentieth century, when their changing attitude to Scripture has accompanied a changing attitude to dissent, have heretofore non-evangelical church bodies been affected by evangelical movements.

During the Welsh Revival, there occurred charismatic phenomena—uncanny discernment, visions, trances—but no glossolalia. There was an outbreak of speaking in tongues in India in the aftermath of the Awakening. In 1906, there was speaking in tongues among converts of the Revival in Los Angeles, from which Pentecostalism spread widely.[31]

There is no telling what might have happened in society had not the First World War absorbed the energies of the nations in the aftermath of this Edwardian Awakening. The time, talent, and treasure of the people are pre-empted in any struggle for national existence, and what little is over is devoted to the welfare of the fighting men and the victims of war. This was the case in World War I, which dissipated the the social drive of the Awakening.

Even so, no one could possibly say that the Awakening of the 1900s in Great Britain or the United States was without social impact. In Britain, there was utter unanimity on the part of observers regarding 'the high ethical character' of the movement. The renewed obedience to the four great social commandments reduced crime, promoted honesty, inculcated truthfulness and produced chastity. Drunkenness and gambling were sharply curtailed. It was the same in the United States, for a wave of morality went over the country, producing a revival of righteousness. Corruption in state and civic government encountered a setback which was attributed by observers in church and state to the Great Awakening. For a dozen years, the country was committed in degree to civic and national integrity, until new forces of corruption triumphed again in the 1920s.[32]

In such awakenings, it seems that the individual response is much more immediate than the social response. The Methodists—then the largest denomination in the United States—declared in review that the public conscience had been revived, overthrowing corrupt officials, crossing the party lines, electing Governors, Senators, Assemblymen, Mayors and District Attorneys of recognized honesty. The people of Philadelphia 'threw the rascals out' and put in a dedicated mayor.[33] Washington Gladden, the 'father of the social gospel,' was assured that the general awakening was creating a moral revolution in the lives of the people.

In other countries, profound impressions were made but what was the social effect outside Western Protestantism? On mission fields, the missionaries multiplied their schools and hospitals. In twenty years, pupils in Christian schools in India doubled to 595,725; 90% of all nurses were Christian, mostly trained at mission hospitals. In China, missionaries pioneered secondary and higher education and laid the foundations of the medical service; the beginnings of the African educational systems and medical service were due likewise to the missionary impulse.

7

THE QUICKENING IN BRAZIL, 1905—

The opening years of the twentieth century found eager
Presbyterians, Baptists, and Methodists from the United
States engaged in aggressive evangelism in Brazil, aided
by British missionaries and by such interdenominational
auxiliaries as the Bible Societies and the Y.M.C.A.
Even American Protestant Episcopalians and German
Lutherans more and more were reaching out to nominal
Roman Catholics. Bishop Kinsolving in 1902 was bold to
declare that the Roman Catholic Church in the country had
repelled the people by its unchristian terms, its service in
an unknown tongue, the celibacy of its priests and the abuse
of the confessional.[1] It was much the same with Lutherans
in the South: their experience of a Catholicism so different
to that of Germany made them willing to evangelize the
friendly folk among whom their colonies were planted.

In 1903, a Capuchin friar in Pernambuco burned 214
Bibles in the presence of two thousand people, provoking
a leading newspaper in Recife to remark that the time had
passed for stifling human intelligence by fire, persecution
and violence 'reminiscent of the Inquisition which caused so
many evils to humanity, even yet awakening horrors when
called to mind.'[2]

Brazilian Freemasonry, more because of anti-clerical
antipathy than pro-Evangelical sympathy, supported this
protest vigorously. Dom Pedro II had lent the Freemasons
sympathy and support, and, although the movement among
the intelligentsia was secular rather than religious, it was
a providential means of opening Brazil and the Brazilian
mind to the Good News.[3] Many a missionary, evangelist,
pastor and teacher found freedom to propagate the simple
faith of the Apostles thereby. There were times when the
Freemasons armed themselves and threatened to shoot dead
any persecutor attempting to assault an evangelical preacher.
All the while, the Brazilian masses were being given an
opportunity of comparing the message of the New Testament
with the caricature otherwise presented.

Meanwhile, eager colporteurs continued to distribute the Scriptures throughout the States of the vast country. The Bible Societies were scattering a hundred thousand copies of the Scriptures annually.[4] So successful was such Bible distribution that Evangelical missionaries were often being greeted by spontaneously developed congregations of avid inquirers.[5] Audiences of hundreds met first-time visitors to interior towns; evangelical workers constantly exploring new territories found that the Word of God had run before them.[6] All this activity provoked intemperate denunciation of 'American Protestant impostors and Bible Societies.'[7]

Added to the positive factor of Bible distribution came a new wave of persevering prayer. Optimism rose and was greatly heightened when news arrived of the phenomenal revival in the little principality of Wales. All the believers were alerted to intercession. In Brazil everywhere, to this day, the popular hymn of petition for spiritual revival is 'Vem, visita Tua igreja, O bendito Salvador!'— 'Come, visit Thy church, O Saviour Divine!'— and the inevitable tune is the Welsh 'Ebenezer' to which the Welsh multitudes sang their theme song, 'O the deep, deep love of Jesus.'[8]

Of course, the movement to prayer began long before the news of the Welsh Revival reached Brazil. From the last few years of the nineteenth century, there were many services of intercession and many more regularly meeting prayer groups in operation all over the world.

Dr. W. G. Bagby, a Southern Baptist pioneer, reported 'a steady and blessed work of grace' about the turn of the century, 'attended by the blessing of the Holy Spirit.'[9] In January 1903, the Week of Prayer in Rio de Janeiro drew large gatherings to four evangelical churches in the city, each one overflowing.[10]

At the end of 1905, missionaries reported to the world 'A Religious Awakening in Brazil.'[11] A key figure in Brazil was the son of the most distinguished convert ever made in Brazilian evangelism till then, a University of Coimbra doctor of laws. Eliezer dos Santos Saraiva was the general secretary of the Young People's Societies (C. E.) of Brazil, hence in contact with the pastors of many churches. In the year 1905, reports of additions to the churches he received were 600 in the first three months, 1350 in the first six; and 3000 were added during the whole year, bringing the total of Evangelical communicants to 25,000. Undoubtedly, 1905 was a year of revival and evangelism.

Such an influx of untaught inquirers has often lowered the spiritual tone of the body of believers, but in Brazil in 1905 the opposite was true.[12] Instead of a decline, there was 'an apparent eagerness to more faithfully perform each duty.' The Sunday Schools were crowded with eager pupils seeking a knowledge of the Bible; and the preaching services were characterized by the same eagerness for God's Word.

In spite of the worst financial crisis in the history of the nation to date, money was being poured into the work by the Brazilians, and, as a result, many churches were not only paying their own pastors' salaries but supporting national evangelists sent out into the country.[13] Teams of young men conducted evangelistic services in the cities and towns and villages, voluntarily. Brazilian Young People's Societies played an important role in training the volunteers. Within three short years, seventy-five C. E. Societies had come into being with 2500 members.

A missionary observer happily complained that a map showing churches of the country would have to be revised every few months to show the location of all the meeting places. Chapels were springing up in country towns, but in cities the Evangelicals' edifices were beginning to vie in number with long-established state shrines. São Paulo held six evangelical churches, Rio de Janeiro many more, the Presbyterians alone[14] operating eleven preaching places in city and suburbs. And from the Amazon to the Parana, Evangelicals were in permanent, aggressive advance.

The manifestations of the 1905 Evangelical Awakening were the deepening of the spiritual life of believers, the increased religious activity of the membership, and the numerical growth of the Evangelical churches, but there was also included a significant social concern.[15]

Besides the various operations of evangelism, the more social enterprises of both missions and churches enjoyed financial support, the Y.M.C.A. and Evangelical hospitals and schools benefitting. Mackenzie University, chartered in 1891 as a college by the Regents of the State of New York and maintained by the Presbyterians, had graduated its first class in 1900.[16] There were tensions between its directors and the local pastors. But a Brazilian leader stated:[17]

> You people at Mackenzie do not parade your religion, but you made it felt and stand for it on any suitable occasion, and you are doing the best scientific training that is being done in Brazil today.

The Awakening of 1905 spread throughout Brazil much more slowly than in Wales, four hundred times smaller. But it spread both north and south and inland, and as far as the population had settled.

Farther north, in Pernambuco, a converted Jew named Solomon Ginsburg—described by Presbyterians as one of Brazil's greatest Baptist evangelists—had pioneered a work of church planting. In 1905, he reported the remarkable development of a spirit of prayer along with the flourishing of Bible classes and Sunday Schools.[18] Not least important in his mind was a spirit of unity and cooperation shown in the work of the various denominations in Pernambuco.

John R. Mott had visited Brazil in August of that year, telling the missionaries that if they were close to Christ, they would be close to one another.[19] Hence a bi-monthly prayer and fellowship meeting was arranged for all the missionaries. All this indicated a rising expectation of an awakening, of the imminence of unusual blessing. Their intercession soon bore fruit.

Ginsburg reported answers to prayer. For seven years, there was an upsurge.[20] 'The wandering Jew'—as he liked to describe himself—claimed in 1911 'over one thousand souls in one year.' The first three months of that year had been used to mobilize prayer and to rally the believers; the second quarter for planning and training; the third for the evangelistic services; and the final quarter for baptizing and instructing the converts. Ginsburg noted 850 converts baptized and 150 backsliders restored, besides some 500 received into fellowship after legal marriage.

The first Brazilian Baptist Convention was held in 1907, reporting 5000 members after twenty-five years' growth. The membership doubled within three years. It doubled again in the next decade.[21] It is fair to say that the Revival of 1905 added twenty-five years' growth in three years.

Within five years, from Manaus a thousand miles up the Amazon to Pôrto Alegre far to the south, there were 142 Baptist churches, the membership being ten thousand.[22] In 1911, 2169 persons were baptized as believers, thirty-five churches in the state of Bahia adding by baptism 851 people. On average, the Brazilian Baptists gave to foreign missions the same amount as Southern Baptists in the United States, and missionary efforts were sustained in Chile and Portugal. And in the same space of time, the Rio Baptist College and Seminary grew from five students to 300.

Solomon Ginsburg had helped pioneer a work in the town of Alto Jequitibá,[23] in mountainous eastern Minas Geraes. The congregation there called a young Presbyterian student from seminary, Matatias Gomes dos Santos. In 1902, the town possessed barely eighteen primitive houses, and the surrounding area was a hideout for fugitives from the law. But a church was organized with a hundred members, and in the times of revival it increased to 525 communicants in 1908. Presbyterian converts did not escape persecution, for in 1909, a mob led by the local priest and deputy sheriff destroyed a church across the mountains in Espíritu Santo. But Samuel Barbosa assumed leadership there in 1909, and added 632 people on profession of faith within four years. He itinerated on foot and on horseback through forests and mountains, burned by the sun and drenched by the rain. In 1913, he died of typhoid at the age of 32, lamenting that he had done so little for the Gospel.

As a result of a challenge given by a seminary professor in times of revival, Anibal Nora, a young pastor, entered the valley of the Rio Doce, and in ten years from 1908 onwards reported six churches, thirty preaching points and 1371 communicant members.[24] His work during the times of revival resulted in the foundation of two future synods.[25] To the work of dos Santos, Barbosa and Nora was added that of Cicero Siquiera and Synval Moraes. A third of the number of communicants in the Presbyterian Church of Brazil were residing in that area when the present writer participated in another great movement of revival in the churches and college community of that valley.[26]

In the capital city, Rio de Janeiro, the Presbyterians experienced much prosperity.[27] The outstanding leader was Alvaro Reis, who found a congregation of four hundred in 1897. He was both an evangelist and polemicist, and as many as fifteen hundred crowded to hear him. In twenty years, Reis received fifteen hundred adults on profession of faith. He recruited a dozen men for the ministry.

The awakening years found the Presbyterians of Brazil suffering from a three-year old division, attributed to dissension over Freemasonry and secular enterprise.[28] At the end of 1905, the two Presbyterian bodies together had 14,000 members and were larger than the Episcopal, Methodist and Baptist denominations combined. The Igreja Independente trebled its membership in a quarter century; so also did the larger body, indigenized shortly after the separation.[29]

The general statistics suggested that the Methodists and Congregationalists and other bodies shared in the benefits of the First Brazilian Awakening, as Edwards called it,[30] a conclusion borne out by denominational records.

Indirectly, these Awakenings of the 1905 period had an enormous effect upon the evangelization of Brazil, although the narration belongs to the Pentecostal aftermath of the worldwide Revival. The Pentecostal movement of 1906 in Chicago thrust forth two very different teams of pioneers. One, Swedish-American,[31] led to the establishment of the Brazilian Assemblies of God; whereas the other, Italian-American,[32] culminated in the founding of the Christian Congregation. The Pentecostals in Brazil within fifty years numbered more than a million and a half members, though they suffered various splits.

Gunnar Vingren and Daniel Berg, moved in the Chicago stirrings which followed the 1905 Awakening and the 1906 Pentecostal Revival, were told in a word of prophecy to serve God in Pará.[33] To discover the location of Pará, they needed to consult an atlas. In 1910, they arrived in Belém, Para, without support, hence they worked hard to sustain themselves. They built up a congregation and a movement throughout Brazil which passed the million mark in total membership in the 1960s.[34]

In 1910 also, Louis Francescon arrived in São Paulo, and reached out to the multitudes of Italian immigrants then pouring into Brazil.[35] He succeeded in establishing a more exclusively Italian-Brazilian Pentecostal fellowship which claimed a quarter of a million communicants in fifty years. It embodied the features of a classic people movement until the passage of the years Brazilianized its membership.

The sequel to the 1905 Awakening in the denominations in Brazil may be seen in church growth in the twenty years following 1910. The Baptist membership, which had almost doubled in the three years before that date, doubled again to twenty thousand in 1920; in the next decade, communicant members increased to thirty-seven thousand.[36] In the same twenty years, the Presbyterians trebled their membership, to 44,000 in 1930.[37] During the same period, the Assemblies of God grew from nil to 14,000, thus matching Presbyterian growth 1865-1905.[38] The total Evangelical membership in 1906 was 25,000 in a nation of twenty million; and twenty years later, it was 100,000 or so in a nation of more than thirty million.

8

SOUTHERN SOUTH AMERICA, 1905—

As in Portuguese-speaking Brazil, the prime factor in the evangelization of the Spanish-speaking republics was the work of Bible distribution. Persistently, the Bible Societies pressed their main objective, and their faithful colporteurs risked assault and death to make the Word of God known; and ever obdurately the opposition, from mitred bishop to tonsured monk, tried to destroy both literature and peddlers. T. B. Wood, experienced in Argentina and Chile as well as other republics, said it well:[1]

> The pioneering has been done all over the continent, mainly by the American Bible Society, whose work in the two Americas makes it the first and noblest of societies. . . In the future will come religious revivals sweeping the whole continent and changing the moral character of the people.

Far to the south, in Patagonia, a phenomenal awakening began in mid-winter 1905 among the Welsh colonists of the Argentine province of Chubut, bilingual, Welsh and Spanish. The news of the awakening in Wales reached them in letters written in their Cymric mother tongue.[2]

The fact that the fastest-growing Evangelical fellowship in Argentina was possessed by a general disinclination to count heads has made it very difficult to assess the impact of the Revival of 1905 upon the tiny churches of Argentina. In 1903, the Christian Brethren bought a lot in Buenos Aires and pitched a tent where William Payne proclaimed the Gospel.[3] This assembly on Brazil Street became the first of many permanent Brethren Assemblies in the nation. About the same time, Carlos Torre borrowed a building used by the English-speaking community as a church, and started Spanish-medium services therein.

Payne appealed to Plymouth Brethren people at home to send out missionaries equipped to deal with the educated and intelligent people of Buenos Aires.[4] In the enthusiasm engendered by the 1905 Revival in Britain, many younger men were moved to offer their services for God.

According to Arno Enns,[5] the first decade of the century saw a phenomenal increase in Plymouth Brethren activity. In 1900, there were congregations in Buenos Aires, Córdoba, Quilmes, Rosario and Tucuman; in 1910, there were local assemblies throughout the provinces of Buenos Aires and Santa Fe, and offshoots as far west as Mendoza and as far north as Joujuy and Salta, twenty-four in all.

Not only had William Payne become one of thirty-eight Brethren missionaries in the Argentine, but Carlos Torre was one of just as many self-employed evangelists. Many Brethren were employees of the British-built and operated railway network, and they took advantage of their opportunity to witness far and wide and to establish Brethren assemblies in the provinces, without any missionary assistance.

In their evangelism, the Brethren used wooden-sided and canvas-roofed tents, pitched in places where the greatest concentrations of population were found, in Buenos Aires and the larger provincial cities. Payne affirmed: [6]

> This has proved to be one of the best means of getting the people to hear the Gospel that has been tried in Buenos Aires. At the end of five months' meetings, the interest has in no way abated, and our difficulty at most of the meetings is to provide seats for those who wish to sit and listen to the Gospel. At least 400 persons hear the message of salvation at each meeting.

Some trouble was caused by younger men who came to oppose and disrupt, but the police gave every assistance in maintaining order. The hecklers made it almost impossible to hold after-meetings, hence follow-up was done the very next day by visiting inquirers in their homes. Many of the converts were rootless Italian immigrants.

It was during the revival decade that the Southern Baptist missionaries entered Argentina.[7] Sidney Sowell and Baptist pioneers owed much to the work of Pablo Besson, a Swiss immigrant in the republic. They came from a constituency experiencing revival and they pitched into ardent evangelism immediately. In 1909, a Southern Baptist missionary wrote from Rosario: [8]

> We are having a real revival. A special prayer meeting was followed each day by those attending going to the homes and market places. As many as 300 attended each of the evening services. On the closing night there were 22 professions of faith ... never in Argentina ... have I seen such a manifestation of God's Spirit.

The Methodists had by far the largest Protestant following in Argentina in the first decade of the twentieth century.
They shared in the times of prosperity, but their growth
was not as spectacular as that of the Brethren before the
First World War, or that of the Pentecostals afterwards.
The Christian and Missionary Alliance built its first
church in Argentina during this period, but turned it over
to the Baptists[9] Missouri Lutherans entered the country
in 1905, but served the German-speaking immigrants and
their Spanish-speaking second generation.[10]
Across the Andes in Chile, the various denominations
experienced times of revival during the first two decades
of the twentieth century.   According to J.B.A. Kessler's
exhaustive studies, the Presbyterians, the Methodists, the
Baptists, and the Christian and Missionary Alliance all
showed a rapid growth in membership during the revival
years,[11] this quite apart from the phenomenal advance of
indigenous Pentecostalism during the period.
Methodist membership had more than doubled in size
between 1893 and 1897; it doubled again between 1897 and
1903.[12] An American Methodist mission-teacher, Willis C.
Hoover, with medical and theological training, had begun
to teach at a school in Iquique and soon became the pastor
of the local Methodist church (1894).[13] During his absence
on furlough, Alberto Vidaurre—who had left the employ of
the Presbyterians because of what he felt was discrimination
against nationals—became pastor.[14] On Hoover's return, he
was faced with a split, and Vidaurre took almost all of the
members with him to found a national church.   Hoover began
again with a score of members, but out of the conflict, he
developed a respect for national feelings.
In 1902, W.C. Hoover became pastor of the church in
Valparaiso.[15] A local revival began among the members, in
which—to Hoover's surprise—they raised their voices in
simultaneous, audible prayer.[16] About a hundred people then
joined the church, the whole conference increasing by 44%.
This movement preceded the worldwide awakening of 1905.
Valparaiso was considered 'one of the wickedest cities
on earth.'[17] It was wrecked by an earthquake in 1906, the
year of the San Francisco earthquake.   The local clergy
blamed it, and also a previous smallpox epidemic, upon the
Evangelicals, some of whom, losing their place of worship,
were meeting in homes for lay exhortation.   Thus far, the
movement was within established churches.

The Alliance missionaries reported times of revival in their work in Chile.[18] However, they suffered a setback when nearly all their Chilean pastors with three hundred of their membership separated to align themselves with the Baptist cause.[19] Contact was made with the Southern Baptist missionaries in Brazil and a Baptist Convention was begun. The Alliance rebuilt its strength.[20]

The Presbyterians at this time reported 'a turning to the Lord' in great numbers at their church in Valparaiso, almost a hundred confessing their faith in Christ for the first time, J. H. McLean adding 'without the semblance of frenzied emotion,'[21] doubtless a reference to the startling developments in other circles.

In 1907, Pandita Ramabai's American helper, Minnie Abrams, sent Mrs. Hoover (a former classmate in Chicago) some information[22] about the awakening at Mukti in India. The Hoovers and their Chilean associates shared the news and sought a new outpouring of the Spirit.[23] Hoover started corresponding with the early Pentecostal leaders overseas.

At a watchnight service, 31st December 1908, held in their nearly completed church building in Valparaiso, those present burst into simultaneous prayer and praise. Vigils of prayer became the rule.[24]

While Hoover was absent in Temuco, church members seeking blessing prayed and confessed far into the night. Upon Hoover's return, services of confession and prayer were continued until unusual manifestations began to occur, including tongues, visions, trances, laughter and crying. They were accompanied by the fruit of changed lives.[25] In the uproar, auto-suggestion and fraud were also recognized as a 'satanic counterfeit.' The movement spread to other congregations of the Methodists, and affected people of the other denominations.

Among the questionable activities were the antics of an English girl, Nellie Laidlaw, who had professed conversion from a life of drunkenness and debauchery. Nellie Laidlaw professed a gift of prophecy, not only making public predictions but walking among the congregation with closed eyes, singling out somebody, calling for repentance.[26] Even Hoover seemed deceived by these goings-on. The so-called prophetess attempted to repeat her performance in the Methodist church at Santiago, but was repulsed by the local American missionary, scenes of disorder ensuing. Police removed the girl from a subsequent meeting.[27]

Nellie Laidlaw's worth may be gauged by the fact that she later became a drug addict and died apparently far from grace.[28] But the effect of the disorder was so great that many Methodists left their congregations, protesting what they considered the high-handed actions of the missionaries. But Hoover had much closer rapport with his Chilean brethren than with fellow-missionaries who often seemed more interested in education than evangelism; and these colleagues regarded him as critical, over-confident and 'holier than thou.'[29] In due course, Hoover resigned from the Methodist ministry, but considered himself a Methodist until the day of his death. His following organized themselves into a national denomination,[30] la Iglesia Metodista Pentecostal de Chile.

Attendances at the meetings shot up, 800 in August, 900 in October, and Sunday School also increased.[31] Hoover was charged in court with intoxicating people with a beverage called 'the blood of the lamb.'[32] The case was dismissed. In the aftermath of the Revival, there were squabbles and disagreements, misunderstandings and lawsuits. It was not until years had passed that the Methodists recognized the legitimacy of the movement.

This Pentecostal division caused a definite but not a catastrophic loss in the Methodist membership in Chile, in the judgment of Kessler.[33] Methodist success in Chile still exceeded that in Peru, where no such division occurred.

After the division in Valparaiso Methodism, dissenting members scattered to their homes, as they had done after the earthquake.[34] Nearly a hundred meetings were held in more than a dozen homes, led by church officials and each visited in turn by Hoover. It was not until 1912 that they secured the use of a hall holding five hundred people.[35] A newspaper reporter visiting the meetings, appreciatively wrote of Hoover's excellent sermon but deplored the noise. Yet the noise of the meetings attracted burglars before they set out on their night's nefarious work, and many were truly converted.[36] The authorities sent Hoover a greeting card adorned with two dozen photographs of ex-delinquents who, they insisted, should be listed in Hoover's files, not those of the police. Success also attended the ministry of Manuel Umana in the large Pentecostal assembly in Santiago. Soon there were assemblies in a score of places in Chile.[37] The Pentecostals adopted open-air preaching as their method of winning the outsider,[38] fellowship meetings to integrate him.

The progress of Evangelical Christianity in Argentina and Chile contrasted strongly with the state of affairs in the other two republics of Hispanic America south of the tropic of Capricorn.

Paraguay remained a neglected country, although there was a successful work going on among the Lengua Indians served by the Anglican South American Mission whose able missionary, W. B. Grubb, had built a fellowship of about a hundred and fifty between 1906 and 1910.[39] Another pioneer, John Hay, appeared on the scene with a New Testament Missionary Union, adopting a method of self-supporting local leadership.[40]

In Uruguay, the Waldensians remained the largest of the Protestant Churches, having built their strength through immigration from the piedmont of Italy.[41] The Methodists in the country constituted the largest foreign mission, but the work was limited. The Southern Baptists entered the republic in 1911.[42]

It is obvious that the Evangelical denominations made greater progress in those countries in which an earlier pioneering had occurred, a higher standard of education prevailed, and a greater freedom existed. Yet it is highly significant that the greatest progress was made during the days when all of Evangelical Christendom was experiencing a time of revival. Not only did the spirit of prayer and of renewed dedication bring out pioneers for neglected fields but harvesters for the ripening ones. And a spirit of prayer possessed the indigenous Christians themselves, sometimes even more than the missionaries.

While there were splits and divisions, often due to trans-cultural tensions and national pride, every evangelical work seemed to enjoy a measure of prosperity. Growth was often greater among the rootless immigrants. Pentecostalism was planted in Brazil by Pentecostal pioneers from North America, but it seemed to be an indigenous movement in Chile. And while the Chilean movement was charismatic in the extreme, the Argentine movement spearheaded by the Christian Brethren seemed to be the opposite in nature, nevertheless equally presenting prayer and the preaching of the Word as its main means of evangelization.

9

STIRRINGS IN TROPICAL AMERICA, 1905—

In the other republics, the years of revival were marked by an influx of new workers from the sending countries, by steady evangelism and by occasional local revivals of the dynamic sort. The Evangelical constituency was tiny in tropical America, and even its doubling represented only a few hundred gained.

Comparable to the movements of revival reported from Brazil and Chile, there was little occurring in tropical America. Apparently, the period of pioneering had scarce begun and the freedom to preach was still too limited in a majority of the republics between Bolivia and Guatemala. More often one has read of difficult pioneering or trying persecution than of movings of the Spirit, apart from the conversion of an outstanding man now and again.

Archibald Reekie, pioneer of the Canadian Baptists, had won only six converts in seven years when he took his first furlough in 1905.[1] When he returned, it was not long before the mission emphasis switched from a school approach to direct evangelism.[2] The Bolivian Congress, on 6th August 1906, had passed a constitutional amendment permitting religious liberty. Not without influence in the matter was William Payne, Brethren missionary, who had not scrupled to challenge a persecuting Archbishop in Sucre before the Supreme Court, which case he won.[3] The witness of the Canadian Baptists helped accelerate the action.[4]

Maximilian Rohrsetzer, an Austrian colporteur of the British and Foreign Bible Society,[5] visited La Paz at this time and drew standing-room only crowds in his preaching. The Methodists began their first permanent work in Bolivia in 1906,[6] Francis Harrington opening an American Institute next year, an obligation to education, not evangelism.

In 1907,[7] George Allan formed Bolivian Indian Mission councils in Britain, Australia and his native New Zealand. He returned to Bolivia in 1909, devoting time and personnel to the rural Indians, most sadly neglected. Progress was slow indeed at first, and persecution was persistent.

In 1907, a remarkable missionary, John Ritchie, reached Lima in Peru.[8] Coming from his homeland in times of great revival, he was possessed of a desire to further fellowship with all other Evangelicals and to evangelize by word and printed page. He played a leading part in the foundation of Iglesia Evangélica Peruana, one of the leading fellowships of Peru.[9] He was ably assisted by two Peruvians, Juan Guerrero and Juan Virgilio, both converted during the decade of revival, and by an Ecuadorean, Alfonso Muñoz. All four were busy in evangelism.[10]

During the revival years, the evangelistic outreach of the Methodists had become the specialized activity of gifted missionaries and well-trained Peruvians.[11] The Methodists in Peru pushed their membership from two hundred in 1905 to a thousand in 1913.[12] It is not surprising to read that a revival had begun under the ministry of a Peruvian.[13]

At the end of the nineteenth century, a missionary had written of 'Enslaved Ecuador.'[14] Alongside the oppression of the priesthood, there was a widespread spirit of scepticism, materialism, and occultism. But the Liberals in power began to encourage the Evangelicals, inviting the Methodists under the direction of T. B. Wood to open up schools,[15] and offering protection to evangelistic meetings. The Gospel Missionary Union and Christian and Missionary Alliance alike pressed their opportunities.

The first use of the word 'revival' in newly-pioneered Ecuador occurred in 1909,[16] when Harry Compton reported the cheering news of a stirring among the few believers and the professed conversion of more than forty people who were added to the Methodist church. This provoked the anger of the priests, who incited a mob to attack the church which fortunately received the governor's protection.

Evangelical missionaries and colporteurs in Colombia, in a struggle for existence, were often subjected to beatings, jailings, expulsions, and the like. Seven societies entered Colombia in 1907,[17] but the fruit of their travail was long deferred. It was a difficult field for evangelization.

In 1911, the Presbyterians reopened a station in the city of Medellin, sending in two missionary families. The local church and classes took on new life. The archbishop issued a decree of excommunication against any who sent their children to the new boys' school. But evangelistic services attracted inquirers, and the missionaries were encouraged by such response amid the opposition and persecution.[18]

The Presbyterian and Brethren efforts in the republic of Venezuela were reinforced by the arrival of the Rev. and Mrs. T. J. Bach, of the Scandinavian Alliance Mission, who came directly in 1906 from revived Scandinavian churches in the United States, sharing with the Christiansens a work of pioneering. Bach was a Danish immigrant to the United States already converted in Copenhagen through the witness of a tract distributor.[19] It was some time before a local congregation was gathered in Maracaibo. Fredrik Franson, founder of the Mission, visited the pioneers just before his death in 1908. T. J. Bach later became general director of the society, later called The Evangelical Alliance Mission (T.E.A.M.), which developed the field in Venezuela.[20]

The isthmus of Panama was separated from Colombia by insurrection supported by the United States and set up as a republic in 1903. Methodists from Britain and the United States entered the country in 1905, partly to care for the many English-speaking West Indians employed in the construction of the Panama Canal.[21] By 1910, within the Canal Zone, there were two score churches, seven Roman Catholic, thirteen Episcopal, three Methodist, seven Baptist and the others undenominational.[22] Their influence spread throughout the Republic proper.

In 1912, there was an unusual awakening reported from San José, capital of Costa Rica. The evangelist whose work had produced profound effects was a Hebrew Christian, the Rev. A. B. de Roos, an evangelist of the Central American Mission, who was fluent in both Spanish and English.[23]

De Roos was effective also in Nicaragua, where the American Baptist Home Mission was active as well as the Central American Mission. The largest Evangelical body, however, was the English-speaking Moravian Church on the Mosquito Coast. The Central American Mission was busy also in Honduras and El Salvador, and the times of revival brought pioneers to Honduras from the California Friends.[24]

In Guatemala, in 1912, the first reports were made of a 'remarkable awakening' in the capital city, chiefly through the exhortation of A. B. de Roos of Managua. Presbyterians and the Central American Mission cooperated, and both received new life. About two hundred people were known to have publicly declared their faith in Christ.[25] Sixty of the converts were enrolled in a class seeking baptism and local church membership. A police official, converted along with fifteen of his family, opened his home for meetings.

The news of the Welsh Revival stirred up united prayer meetings among English-speaking residents of Mexico City, and in 1905 an awakening was reported among Americans, Canadians, British and bilingual people.[26]

A spirit of revival was still strong in Mexico City in the wake of the news of further awakenings around the world, so Mexican pastors of the capital agreed among themselves to cooperate in a series of meetings for revival and direct evangelism in 1907, using in turn each of four Evangelical auditoriums during four weeks.[27]

A unique feature of the campaign was a meeting for the parents of families, in which prayers were offered for the conversion of their young people. A subsequent meeting for young people was held, in which more than fifty young people prayed publicly with deep sincerity, some moved to tears, consecrating themselves to the service of the Lord. There were also several professed conversions.

During the succeeding weeks, the meetings were in turn directed by the Mexican pastors in whose churches they were held, and there was not a single meeting without some inquirer coming forward seeking salvation.[28] Evangelical strength in all of Mexico numbered only .004 of the total population, and churches were so small that such results were considered very encouraging.

The spiritual uplift, reported Vicente Mendoza, was immense, the faith of many wonderfully increased, their convictions strengthened and hopes renewed, while many who had become lax in living returned to their first love.

Not only was Vicente Mendoza busy in evangelism, but his Presbyterian counterpart, Arcadio Morales, was filling the Central Presbyterian Church in Mexico City, while a dozen of his associates ministered in suburban locations. The Baptists were also producing ardent evangelists.[29]

By 1910, all leading denominations in the United States were maintaining their missions in Mexico, with a comity of cooperation so cordial that missionaries avoided trespassing upon territory entered by others.[30]

Evangelicals had gained an entrance to Cuba and Puerto Rico at the beginning of the twentieth century and, as in the Philippines, local awakenings and a heartening response to evangelism and primary education were experienced.[31] A dozen missionary societies were at work in the island, a hundred churches serving three thousand members. And it was much the same in Puerto Rico.

The wave of revival had soon reached Jamaica and other evangelized West Indian Islands.[32] As in other parts, there was a great earthquake in the Caribbean island (in 1907) but reviving of spiritual life had begun long before that event.

Despite what the Methodists called 'fanatical revivalism in some places,'[33] the Wesleyans were reporting that the spiritual state of the societies had not been so satisfactory for years, and membership increased by fourteen hundred. In 1906, there was a gracious visitation of Divine power in Grateful Hill, with a thousand penitents responding. The Baptists and other denominations likewise responded.

A spontaneous revival occurred on the island of St. Kitt's in the Leeward Islands,[34] a movement which transformed individuals, changed homes, and raised the spiritual tone of the Church. Other Leeward Islands were also moved.

The revival also touched the Windward Islands, as far south as Barbados and Trinidad.[35] The manifestations of the movement were ardent prayer and intense conviction of sin, followed by not a few conversions.

There was a spontaneous revival also in the Bahamas, where the churches were quickened[36] by a spirit of prayer. In 1909, a Negro couple converted in Florida returned to the islands and there began the work of the Church of God, a Pentecostal enterprise from Tennessee.

Quite a colony of Portuguese had settled in Bermuda, to the west of Madeira and the Azores. In 1912, a stir was made among them by the ministry of a missionary from Brazil returned to the United States. Of the three thousand Portuguese in the islands, three hundred had declared for an Evangelical faith.[37] Kyle's meetings drew the crowds, night after night, and intense interest prevailed.

Throughout Latin America, the direct and indirect effects of the awakening of 1905 and subsequent evangelism were reflected in the growth of the Evangelical churches. In 1903, there were 1438 missionaries, 6000 national workers and 132,388 communicants in Latin America and the Caribbean; seven years later, there were 2112 missionaries, 6199 national workers, and 369,077 communicants, the latter representing an increase of 180 per cent.[38]

The gains of the revival period proved to be the prelude to a burgeoning Evangelical advance following World War I throughout Latin America, in which the main factors again were the 'sweeping revivals' and biblical evangelism which had been prophesied at the turn of the century.

10

THE DECLINE IN THE WEST

The want of a worldwide awakening in the Western world and the lack of nationwide revivals— with few exceptions— in nominally Protestant countries marked the thirty years between World War I (1914) and World War II (1945).

Undoubtedly, there were many secular factors to account for the absence of significant movements of revival—the disillusionment of war, the demoralization of the 'roaring twenties,' the distress of the economic depression, and the discouragement of international relations. But there had been great awakenings in the past in spite of or because of such secular difficulties. The lack of renewal must be first attributed to spiritual handicaps within the Churches which seriously prevented a turning to God in prayer for revival.

The historian of the Student Volunteer Movement cited ten reasons for the sorry decline of that great organization which reached its peak of usefulness in 1920, decayed into ineffectiveness by 1940,[1] and later unlamented died away. Among them were the preoccupation with race relations, economic injustice and imperialism supplanting the earlier concern for Bible study, evangelism, and service; the evangelistic imperative blurred by the rise of the 'social gospel'; evangelism (described as 'revivalism') and its assumptions giving way to uncertainty regarding the validity of the Christian faith, especially in its claims to exclusive supremacy. These factors had a more general application.

Another like judgment is derived from the history of the Y. M. C. A., which underwent vast changes in theological conviction, and— to all intents and purposes— abandoned its primary purpose in order to concentrate on its secondary reasons for being.[2] The Y. M. C. A. had operated from an evangelical position for the first half century of its existence; from the mid-1880s, according to a standard historian, a 'new theology' began to emerge, capturing the loyalty of a few leaders in the mid-1890s; but it was not until the 1920s that the whole movement shifted its loyalty to what was described as the modernist viewpoint.

The nineteenth century and the decade following found most Protestants largely united in two great loyalties: the authority of Scripture and the unity of the Body of Christ — both generally taken for granted.[3]

At the same time, Protestant forces were engaged in two great enterprises: evangelism and social action. True, those who emphasized the social implications of the Gospel had begun to advocate a 'new evangelism,' one which aimed at 'redeeming' societies rather than individuals. But a majority affirmed evangelism's priority without denying their social responsibility.

Just as the western world's population was dividing into two opposing camps which finally pitched into open warfare, so also was the Protestant establishment being polarized. Modernism rose to dominate denominational leadership and fundamentalism rose to challenge it.

Protestants had united on scriptural authority and unity: the modernist proved weak in the doctrine of the authority of Scripture but strong on the unity of the Body of Christ; the fundamentalist proved strong in the doctrine of the authority of Scripture but weak on the unity of the Body of Christ. The modernist was weak in the primary task of the Church, evangelism, the winning of men to personal faith in Christ, but strong in the social work of the Gospel, even making it the primary message of the Church; the fundamentalist was strong in conventional evangelism, but often weak in social action, more so when propounded by the modernist.

This tragic polarization divided almost every Protestant denomination ideologically. It split or alienated many inter-denominational organizations, reducing effective evangelism and undercutting prayer for revival of all the Churches. In the 1920s and the 1930s, in the English-speaking countries, most modernists agreed that the days of revival had given way to days of education; many fundamentalists affirmed that the days of revival had given way to apostasy.

A generation was growing up which did not know what to do in times of spiritual decline—to engage in intercession as did the churches in the late eighteenth century. Even among those most evangelistically inclined, the Finneyan notion that revival is nothing more than the right use of the appropriate means left the zealots seeking techniques and gimmicks rather than spiritual power. Too much energy was spent in polemics against the modernist establishment and not enough in prayer for an awakening.

Although the years between-Wars brought no evangelical a vakening to Britain, a movement arose which helped to k ep evangelism wholesome at a time when it deteriorated in the United States. Out of the campaigns in the wake of the Welsh Revival held by the Anglican laymen, Arthur and Frederick Wood, grew the National Young Life Campaign, which not only provided an interdenominational fellowship and activity for the converts, but also provided a sponsor for worthy evangelists, many of whom through N. Y. L. C. reached nationwide usefulness.[4] Older societies continued to provide regular sponsorship for evangelists, so that the British evangelist was less irresponsible and undisciplined than his American counterpart.

Towards the end of the 1920s and the beginnings of the 1930s, there was an evangelical stirring of sorts in Britain resulting in the emergence of British-trained evangelists who soon gained a worldwide usefulness — J. Sidlow Baxter, J. D. Blinco, Bryan S. Green, Roy Hession, J. Edwin Orr, Alan Redpath, T. B. Rees, James Stewart and Ian Thomas, all of them active for a generation, and all of them busy around the world.[5]

The outstanding evangelist of the between Wars period was the Australian-born Lionel B. Fletcher, who took up a Congregational pastorate in Cardiff in wartime, and soon became a missioner for the Free Churches of Britain. In Glasgow, Birmingham, Sheffield, and other cities, Fletcher conducted successful campaigns in 1922-23; then London and other cities before returning to New Zealand for a seven-year pastorate in Auckland during which he conducted a London Youth Evangelistic Campaign in 1930-31.[6]

In 1932, Lionel Fletcher became 'empire evangelist' for the Movement for World Evangelization and began his city-wide missioning in Leith, the port of Edinburgh. Then came a remarkably successful series in Belfast, with thousands of inquirers registered and an impression made on a young layman (the writer) which prompted Fletcher in later years to refer to him as 'a kind of Timothy of mine.' Fletcher's Edinburgh mission gained support from Church of Scotland, Free Church, Anglican, Baptist, Congregational, Methodist and Salvation Army leaders. Inquirers numbered more than a thousand also in Glasgow and Newcastle-on-Tyne before he took refuge from the unheated rooms of Britain in the sunny cities and towns of South Africa in 1934.[7] In 1936, he was missioning for the Free Church Council.

All the while, A. Lindsay Glegg, a London industrialist, preached throughout Britain in campaigns and conventions. Gipsy Rodney Smith also continued to exercise a ministry in Britain, but, unlike Fletcher, he was much in demand in evangelism in the United States.[8] As he passed the three-score-years and-ten in 1930, his ministry tended to become rather sentimental and the response of his hearers more vague. His messages were thoroughly evangelistic, and his cordiality won him the widest support.

Wilbur Chapman, Moody's friend and protege, died a few weeks after the end of World War I. His colleague, W. E. Biederwolf, became secretary of evangelism for the Federal Council of Churches while continuing in an uncompromising evangelistic ministry.[9]

Billy Sunday succeeded to the popular fame of Chapman, but not at all to his cultured ministry.[10] A converted baseball player, he had a ready-made audience and soon indulged in his flair for the spectacular in preaching. He thought nothing of smashing a chair on the platform to emphasize a point. In the polarization of the Churches by fundamentalism and modernism, he espoused a fundamentalist distaste for social reform, though he ardently crusaded against gambling, the liquor trade, and prostitution.[11]

Sunday claimed that he had preached to a hundred million people in the days before radio broadcasting. He preached during forty years in nearly three hundred campaigns, but his greatest meetings were held in the years before 1920, when he reached Philadelphia, Baltimore, Detroit, Boston, New York, Los Angeles, Washington, and Chicago.[12]

Sunday's method was to build a wooden tabernacle for his meetings, and—with considerable support from local churches—preach sensationally on attention-getting topics. His invitation to 'hit the sawdust trail' fell far short of the follow-up methods of the second half of the century. In ten years, his huge thankofferings added up to a million dollars —one heard his closest associate concede that he indulged 'an acquisitive instinct.'[13] However, in Sunday's twenty most successful campaigns in the United States there were some 593,004 professions of faith, and even his critics admitted that there were cooperating pastors who reported additions to their congregations through his tabernacle evangelism. Sunday's influence waned during the 'roaring twenties'; he died in 1935.[14] At the time, mass evangelism suffered from a loss of esteem in the minds of many leaders.

During the great economic depression of the 1930s—to cite a twentieth century encyclopedia of religious knowledge:

> J. C. Massee, Walter MacDonald, Paul Rader, Charlie and Laurie Taylor, S. D. Gordon, Walter Kallenbach, John R. Rice, J. Edwin Orr and a host of lesser-known evangelists ministered to America's sobered soul. . .[15]

In the South, there were evangelists such as 'Bob' Jones, and Mordecai Ham—in whose ministry in 1934 Billy Graham professed conversion.[16] A converted Jew, Hyman Appelman, also conducted cooperative campaigns. It should be noted that the Orr campaigns were directed towards the reviving of the churches rather than direct evangelism, even though attendance reached 10,000 on occasion, with fair response.

It would be unfair to list the evangelists cited in Schaff-Herzog with a host of others who imitated Billy Sunday's faults and not his virtues. Billy Sunday used the temporary tabernacle as a means of working with the local ministers; his imitators found that they could use the same device to operate independently of the churches or against them.

Bishop J. F. Berry in 1916 issued a blast against the 'tabernacle evangelists' as a class, denouncing sustained attack on local ministers; exaltation of visiting evangelists; 'shake-my-hand' methods of dealing with inquirers; misinterpretation of statistics; vulgar display of largess; and high-pressured solicitation of offerings.[17]

A quarter of a century later, the writer published his observations on the subject:[18]

> Evangelism in the United States suffered a severe setback in recent years, chiefly due to financial scandals in the private lives of evangelists, extravagance in preaching, liberalism in the churches and a drift from God. . . Some hit upon the idea of carrying a large portable tabernacle, invading a city or town, preaching away in spite of the churches . . . generally the result was an independent tabernacle working more against the churches than with them . . . the gap between the churches and tabernacles widened . . .

Between the lukewarmness of many churches and the dubious work done by divisive evangelists, the outlook was dark indeed for evangelism. The professional evangelist had come into ill-repute and the sincere and dedicated man faced a necessity of living down the scandals of the others who besmirched a noble calling.

There were exceptions to the rule that awakenings were absent in the countries of the West. In each case, where there was revival, it occurred in a country emerging from or about to enter a period of national distress.

Conditions in Northern Ireland, granted parliamentary autonomy in 1921, were deplorable, due to an I.R.A. attempt to make the province ungovernable and the sectarian violence thus provoked. In 1926, a Faith Mission publication stated, in a judgment applicable fifty years later: [19]

> Four years ago, the North of Ireland was in a state of chaos. Fear and uncertainty filled the minds of the people. Politicians were at their wits' end. Murder and destruction, for the time being, seemed to be on the throne. No one could possibly describe the hopelessness of the situation, as things continued to travel from bad to worse.

At night, the sound of machine guns and bombings rent the evening curfew. Republican gunmen were on roof-tops sniping at police and passers-by. Protestants were being murdered in cold blood in Roman Catholic counties, and angry Protestants were driving out innocent Roman Catholic families. Such was the bitterness that faithful Christians began to intercede with God for a counter-action of the Holy Spirit. The answer to prayer came in an awakening.

In the midst of 'the troubles,' W. P. Nicholson appeared. Born in Bangor, a sailor before the mast for many years, most religious when drunk, he was converted at home in 1899 and entered the Bible Training Institute in Glasgow in 1901, serving in Lanarkshire for four years until in 1907 he joined Wilbur Chapman's team to serve in Melbourne in 1909. He was ordained a Presbyterian minister in Carlisle, Pennsylvania, in 1914, and later served on the staff of the Bible Institute of Los Angeles. [20]

Nicholson commenced evangelizing in Bangor in autumn 1920, and the attendance overflowed. [21] In May 1921, he had another successful series in Portadown, followed by Lurgan, Newtownards, Lisburn, leading to an outstanding mission in a Belfast working-class district, and then series after series in that capital city. On occasion, the shipyard men marched en masse from the Island to the meetings. [22] Those qualified to judge described the movement as a revival, for the religious life of Ulster was profoundly affected. [23] There were missions in Ballymena and Carrickfergus before the evangelist departed. [24] The results were lasting. [25]

There were debit items in the ledger. Crude indeed was
Nicholson's jocularity and vulgar was his language. He had
little tolerance for any who differed from him.[26] But there
were thousands of converts added to the Churches, and the
numbers of candidates for the ministry doubled for several
subsequent years. Presbyterian first communions increased
by 2500 in 1922-23, and membership of Christian Endeavour
doubled (by 5000) in a like period.[27]

The quality of the Norwegian resistance to the German
occupation provoked an almost universal admiration. Its
spiritual roots appeared to begin in a general awakening in
Norway, from 1934 until 1941. Frank Mangs, a Swedish
Finn, began a series of remarkable campaigns in Oslo and
other Norwegian towns in 1934, and both Free Church and
State Church congregations reaped a benefit. The Oxford
Group Movement, which adopted some of the techniques of
evangelical revival without its essential theology, received
a hearty welcome to Norway in 1935, the revived evangelicals
interpreting the message in evangelical Lutheran terms. A
nationwide awakening was effective for a number of years.[28]

In the Baltic States, there were successive revivals in
the seven years before their occupation by the Germans and
their annexation by the Russians. William Fetler, who had
been driven out of Petrograd, established Dom Evangelia
in Riga; the visits of Oswald J. Smith, J. Edwin Orr, and
James A. Stewart coincided with outpourings of the Spirit.[29]

James A. Stewart, a converted Scottish footballer, began
a remarkable work in the Hungarian capital in 1937. The
Magyars knew him as Stevarti Jacoby, and he enjoyed the
support of Lutheran and Reformed clergy as well as Free
Church leaders. His meetings were held in the cathedrals,
theatres, skating rinks, and churches, with huge crowds
attending.[30] Hundreds of formalist ministers professed conversion to God. So great was the movement that the Regent
of Hungary supported the meetings.

Stewart also operated successfully in other European
countries, launching a Euopean Evangelistic Crusade of
considerable proportions majoring in ministry to the Slavic
countries. This appeared to be the last great movement of
the Spirit before the night of Nazi domination descended.

The remarkable expansion of the Evangelical cause in
the Union of Soviet Socialistic Republics from 1919 till 1929
came to an end through the Stalinist terror of the 1930s. In
the most brutal fashion, religion was crushed.

For the first time in the history of world Evangelical Christianity, a full generation witnessed a dearth of great revivals in the sending countries while such awakenings were occurring among the younger Churches overseas, for there were sweeping movements in the 1920s and 'thirties in both Africa and Asia.

In the 1920s, an awakening began in the Congo, partly in the missions-related churches and partly in an indigenous movement led by Simon Kimbangu. In the 1930s, other deep revivals began, so that between 1925 and 1937, Protestant communicants increased from 9259 to nearly 200,000, the community from a hundred thousand or so to half a million.[31]

In Nigeria, a spirit of prayer produced the Awon Egbe Aladura or 'praying bands' which influenced the course of spiritual life for fifty years, both in missions-related and indigenous churches, including the Church of the Lord. In Ghana, the Ivory Coast, and other parts of West Africa, there were other awakenings.[32]

In the 1930s, the East African Revival movement began, first in Rwanda during famine conditions. By 1936, this spontaneous movement was sweeping Rwanda and Burundi and touching churches in Uganda, Kenya and Tanganyika— chiefly in the Anglican communion. The movement stressed a confession of sin to be maintained daily. Its leaders were many, two of the earliest being Dr. J. E. Church and his African colleague, Simeoni Nsibambi.[33]

There was an awakening in Malawi, where about 66,000 baptized Protestants in 1924 became 174,000 in 1936.[34] And in 1931, 35,000 communicants in the Cameroon welcomed 26,000 new converts in a short space of time.

In 1935, the Italians invaded Ethiopia and drove Haile Selassie from the throne.[35] Protestant missions were also driven out, and persecution set in for their tribal converts. In Wallamo, for example, the Sudan Interior Mission left only forty-eight believers, with portions of the Scriptures translated. When they returned, it was to find that only one church had multiplied into a hundred assemblies with fully 10,000 believers.

In South Africa, the visits of Lionel B. Fletcher added thousands to the European church membership, as did also the 1936 revival meetings of J. Edwin Orr.[36] About the same time, a Zulu, Nicholas Bhengu, professed conversion, and became a leader in a remarkable revival movement among the Bantu nations.[37]

In the 1930s, there were movements of revival in various parts of the Indian sub-continent, particularly in the South. In 1933, a young Sikh converted to evangelical faith, Bakht Singh, became a powerful evangelist and Bible teacher.[38] As a whole, however, nationalism absorbed people's attention. The 1920s and 'thirties were dark days for Christians in both Korea and Japan, suffering persecution under revived Japanese militarism.[39] The Christians in both countries were not without the evidence of spiritual power in those days, but none of the local revivals became nationwide.

It was otherwise in the vast area of China. By 1926, 'a sense of discouragement in the Church amounting almost to despair' was reported by missionaries overwhelmed by the turmoil throughout the country.[40] But in 1925, evacuated missionaries in Shanghai arranged a conference for the deepening of the spiritual life, and a movement of prayer began to spread. By the early 1930s, spiritual awakenings were reported, the central figures largely Chinese leaders.

Andrew Gih and other young Chinese evangelists formed the Bethel Bands which spearheaded revival and evangelism in all the provinces. Dr. John Sung, a band member, took off on his own tour of evangelism and achieved remarkable success not only in China but among the Chinese dispersion throughout Southeast Asia. In 1931, the major Bethel Band invaded the populous cities of Manchuria, resulting in a report of 'standing room only' in churches for years to come. There was a phenomenal movement of the Spirit in other parts of North China, especially the peninsular province of Shantung and the city of Peking. There were extraordinary meetings in Shanghai and throughout Central China, among churches of all denominations. Awakenings were reported in South China also, among the people of various dialects other than Kuoyu (Mandarin). Far to the West, from Kansu through Szechwan to Yunnan, local movements of revival were reported in the 'thirties.[41]

Evangelical Christianity was growing at the rate of about fourteen thousand members a year for a dozen years, and the missionaries were reporting men attending services in a proportion of three to every two women. The Bethel Band, for example, in which the writer served in 1938, in four years traversed 50,000 miles and held 3389 meetings in 133 cities with an attendance of 508,600 in aggregate and more than fifty thousand converts were won—significantly, 1863 local preaching bands were formed.[42]

11

THIRTY YEARS, POST-PANAMA

It has already been noticed that the World Missionary Conference held at Edinburgh in 1910 excluded the Latin American mission fields from the scope of its studies. The whole difficulty, according to William Richey Hogg, arose from an inadequate understanding of the actual situation in Latin America.[1] Those who disagreed with the exclusion of Latin America called a conference in New York in March of 1913, out of which came the Committee on Cooperation in Latin America, not so much concerned to convert Roman Catholics as to survey the needs of Latin America's many millions of unevangelized peoples, and to coordinate the efforts of Evangelicals to meet such needs.

In mid-February 1916, the Congress on Christian Work in Latin America met in Panama. Half of the three hundred delegates were Latin American leaders,[2] the remainder missionaries and church leaders from North America with a number of representatives from Europe, then engulfed in World War I. Roman Catholic leaders were invited to attend but declined to come. Anglicans and Lutherans participated officially, as did Northern, Southern and Canadian Baptist missionary boards or societies, plus Congregationalists, Disciples, Friends, Methodists, Moravians, Presbyterians, Reformed and United Brethren, together with interdenominational service organizations. Of course, the missionary groups which were to achieve the greatest results in the half century following were not even considered—the newly developing Pentecostal denominations.

The first business of the Congress was to survey the vast fields.[3] Valparaiso, with less than 200,000 population, reported more cases of drunkenness than London with its 5,000,000; Buenos Aires, a third the size of London, had less than a hundred churches of any kind, Roman Catholic or Protestant, Muslim or Jewish, with perhaps only one in a thousand attending. In Brazil, the educated people were ensnared by posivitism and the occult. Throughout Latin America, 98% of the 50,000 students professed agnosticism.

Among the educated classes in Cuba, unbelief became so widespread as to be practically universal. In Puerto Rico, as in Cuba, the masses of the common people were so far alienated as to live without religious practice.[4]

In Mexico, the majority of educated people considered themselves 'liberal,' with a general belief in God but not in any Church.[5] Three million Indians were utterly untouched by any Christian organization, Roman Catholic or otherwise. In Central America, infidelity and free thought were turning educated people away from the old system, and a majority of the people of Guatemala—sixty-five per cent pure Indian, twenty-five per cent mestizo—were essentially deficient in religion. Only the Moravians had evangelized the Indians of lower Central America, and that rather inadequately.

In Colombia, unbelief seemed universal among the upper classes, professional, commercial and the like, most men being unbelievers.[6] Roman Catholic activities among the Colombian Indians merely touched the fringe of the need. A revolution in Venezuela a generation before had ejected the clerical orders from the monasteries and convents as not affording any direct service to the people. The larger mass of the people attended services no more than three times a year, more or less as viewing a spectacle. The two hundred thousand Indians were objects of attempts by church and state to civilize them, largely failures.

A majority of the men in Ecuador avowed unbelief but conformed in the matter of baptism, marriage, absolution and masses for the repose of the dead, the coastal cities largely indifferent but the interior communities formally controlled by the Church.[7] The Indian tribes were sadly neglected. Unbelief was prevalent among the educated in Peru, university students and faculty being hostile to the Church. The Quechua Indians of Ecuador and Peru alike presented a condition of pitiful need.

Religion had been so imbedded in superstition in Bolivia that it rarely survived the spread of education, hence most Bolivian leaders and businessmen professed antagonism to the Church.[8] A majority of Bolivian Indians scarcely saw a priest more than once a year. The Araucanians of Chile were also in a state of misery, but the Anglicans operated some successful missions among them, as did the Bolivian Indian Mission among the tribes of Bolivia. In Paraguay, as in the Argentine also, great need afflicted the tribes of the Chaco. Brazil's Indians were almost untouched.

Within five years, another less official survey was made.
During the first two decades of the twentieth century Harry
Strachan, a Scot born in Canada, engaged in a ministry of
evangelism in tents and theatres, in the southern part of
the Province of Buenos Aires.[9] A missionary of the British
based Evangelical Union of South America, he resided in
the town of Tandil where he successfully organized younger
Argentine believers in team work.

A vision of extending such a work throughout the Latin
American republics began to obsess his heart and mind.
The field council and directors at home approved the plan,
but the outbreak of World War I prevented its implantation.
Harry Strachan continued his evangelism in the Argentine
until 1918, when he took his family to the United States for
a long-delayed furlough.[10]

So strong was the call to evangelization throughout Latin
America, that the Strachans tendered their resignations to
the E. U. S. A. board, receiving a cordial letter of regret
from G. Campbell Morgan, the chairman. They began in
simple faith; and, after making arrangements for the care
of their children, Harry and Susan Strachan together started
a personal survey of the Latin American republics.[11]

The 6th February 1920 found them in Guatemala, where
two thirds of the missionaries in Central America operated,
fifty workers in a population of two million.[12] From there,
they proceeded to El Salvador, a round of meetings and
conferences with missionaries. By dint of arduous travel,
they reached Tegucigalpa, capital of Honduras, consulting
with the Central American Mission and the Friends. Then
to Nicaragua, where the itinerary included Managua and
half a dozen lesser towns. In Costa Rica, they found the
only missionaries ready to leave because of ill health and
old age. Ten days were spent in Panama.

Harry Strachan estimated the population of the six tiny
Central American republics as six million.[13] In Guatemala,
there were but three Evangelical missionaries for each
100,000 people, and in the remainder only one for each
100,000. All missionaries contacted of the eight mission
organizations supported his plan and promised cooperation.

The Strachans found an utterly inadequate missionary
force coping with the need of evangelization in Venezuela,
with three million population.[14] They found Valencia, second
city, without a Gospel witness. They preached in Caracas,
the capital, and Maracaibo, the oil port, also.

Shipping out via Curacao, they reached San Juan, Puerto Rico in time to address a conference of 200 missionaries, two-thirds of the work force on the island and a reservoir to be tapped for the rest of tropical America.[15] Strachan also visited the major cities of Cuba, noting need and resources.

They found Colombia, next, a most neglected country. Commencing in Cartagena, they ministered in Barranquilla, Bogotá, Honda, Medellín, and Cali, concluding from their observations and experiences that in Colombia—the most fanatical of the republics—there were only twelve workers preaching Good News among six million people.[16]

It was late in October when the Strachans reached Quito in Ecuador.[17] They found twenty missionaries among two million people, yet their open air meetings and follow-up services showed that the people were responsive.

The missionaries in Peru were likewise cooperative in spirit regarding the plans for evangelistic campaigns in due time.[18] Strachan had visited Peru on previous occasions for evangelistic meetings, and knew the field.

The indomitable couple crossed from Puno across Lake Titicaca to Guaqui in Bolivia, thence to La Paz, where (on a previous visit) Strachan had held the first open air gospel service ever known there.[19] They visited Cochambamba and Oruro, finding the conditions socially and religiously very depressing—only a handful of missionaries and believers.

In Santiago de Chile, the Strachans held a conference with the body of missionaries, who promised cooperation in the plans for evangelization.[20] The missionary prospect in Chile, contrasted with the north, was encouraging.

Returning to Argentina seemed more like visiting home. The year's survey was completed, and, despite the time taken in hazardous travel, Strachan had preached to 250 congregations, in most of which there were professions of faith. Missionaries of two dozen boards shared fellowship and offered support.

Harry and Susan Strachan had spent a year in surveying all of Latin America. They had journeyed more than thirty thousand miles through Central America, the West Indies, Venezuela, Colombia, Ecuador, Peru, Bolivia, Chile, and Argentina, reporting that the scattered mission stations were but pin points of light, and that the membership of all the Evangelical denominations scarcely exceeded a hundred thousand.[21] They determined to engage in mass evangelism throughout the territories.

In July 1921, American friends formed a home council for the Latin American Evangelization Campaign, and the Southern Baptists set aside Juan C. Varetto, pastor of the largest church in Argentina, as Strachan's co-evangelist in the first series, the first of many able men thus associated. The Strachan family moved to San José, Costa Rica, there setting up headquarters for the Campaign to reach Hispanic America in mass evangelism. It was not long before Harry Strachan had 'preached to more people in Latin America than any other man.' [22]

Throughout the 1920s, therefore, reports are many of the evangelistic campaigns conducted by the able Scotsman and his associates, chiefly Latin Americans with successful experience in evangelism from the Caribbean to Cape Horn.

Harry Strachan was a veteran missionary, fluent in the Spanish of educated people in Latin America. Rarely were there outsiders lacking a knowledge of the language who undertook well-planned tours of evangelization.

In 1928, Dr. E. Stanley Jones—of Indian fame—made an evangelistic tour of South America.[23] Jones visited Rio de Janeiro and São Paulo in Brazil, Montevideo in Uruguay, Buenos Aires in Argentina, Santiago in Chile, and Lima in Peru. His ministry reached the more cultured classes and the results were few but choice.

Both the Latin American Evangelization Campaign and Million Testaments Campaign of Philadelphia cooperated in circulating a million New Testaments throughout the Latin American republics in 1929.[24] Everywhere, the distribution of the Scriptures began producing immediate results. The Strachans initiated a prayer campaign, a quarter million prayer cards being sent out to stimulate intercession for the production and distribution of the Testaments, for an outpouring of the Spirit on missionaries, pastors and other workers, and for the impact of the literature on the masses. Prayer and the propagation of Scripture were recognized as unfailing methods of producing revival and awakening, thus preparing the way for the proclamation of the Gospel, and the gathering of a greater harvest.[25]

By 1931, Harry Strachan and his Latin American teams had taken wings and were engaged in an evangelistic tour of the republics, using air travel for rapid transportation. It seemed as if the opportunities for evangelism in all of Latin America were multiplying, but there was still little to herald an awakening in the established Church.[26]

In mid-1926, it was reported that there were no more than 328 parish churches in all of Bolivia, 83 without a priest. Paraguay possessed only 84 priests in a population of a million, and half of them were in Asuncion, the capital. Huge areas of Colombia were almost without services. In Chile, many country districts were restricted to occasional missions. Even Buenos Aires, with two million citizens, possessed only thirty-five parish churches and eighty-one chapels, a figure to be compared with the number of Roman Catholic churches in Philadelphia with the same population, 285—not counting the more numerous Protestant places of worship. In all South America, population 60,000,000 in 1925, there were only 125,000 Evangelical church members. This was the situation ten years after the Congress held in Panama had declared the extent of the failure of the Roman Church to evangelize its own proclaimed preserve.[27]

The Evangelical Movement throughout all Latin America continued to encounter opposition and persecution, but it was not without friends in higher echelons of government. During the 1920s, several of the Presidents elected in the Latin American countries avowed their support of the work of Evangelical missions in their respective countries, the President of Chile declaring: 'I am a Christian. I believe in the doctrines of Christ.' He added that he drank from the pure fountain of the Scriptures, not the swamp of human accretions deposited down through the ages.[28]

But political developments posed a problem for ardent evangelists in country after country, revolution intervening. Kenneth G. Grubb, reviewing the centenary of the foundation of permanent Evangelical missions in Latin America, noted in 1936 that a pause in the development of evangelical work in a large part of Spanish-speaking America had transpired. The problem of church-and-state and the spread of anti-religion indicated that the State intended to apply a much closer restriction of the rights of religious and educational bodies in Mexico, Venezuela, Guatemala, Costa Rica and Ecuador, and perhaps other republics.[29] Mercifully, giant Brazil was spared most of the turmoil.

Meanwhile, in country after country, the new evangelists of Pentecostal persuasion were engaging in old-fashioned ways of witness with all the zeal of their experience and few of the inhibitions that hindered other Evangelicals— the day of mass evangelistic-healing campaigns had not yet arrived, nor the time of T. B. Wood's sweeping revivals.[30]

12

EVANGELICAL BRAZIL, 1916—1946

During the 1920s and 1930s, the evangelization of Brazil proceeded steadily.[1] Evangelical Christianity was still a minority movement, scarcely making an impact on society. But the Evangelical churches were bold in witness, and they gained a ready hearing.

Typical of what was happening in Brazil was a report from Florianopolis, in Santa Catarina State in the South of Brazil.[2] The Rev. Ashmun Salley visited the town of Tres Riachos and found ten people desiring believers' baptism as a result of the sale of two Bibles there twelve years before. Salley's meetings attracted such attention that a local priest reported it as a mass movement to the Evangelical faith. So many could not get within hearing of the message during a Sunday evening service that the missionary was compelled to hold another meeting directly afterwards.

Likewise in 1915, W. G. Borchers, in the interior of the State of São Paulo, was preaching to capacity crowds in obscure towns such as Piracununga and Santa Rita, scores making a profession of faith.[3] Attendances at Dourado rose from a hundred to five hundred, and thirty-three professed conversion publicly.

In 1916, J. M. Landers of the Brazil Mission of the Methodist Episcopal Church invited the Rev. Hippolyto de Campos to preach in Petrópolis, just north of the city of Rio de Janeiro. So great was the desire to hear the ex-priest that local clergy issued threats of excommunication, intimidating those who wanted to hear 'the apostate.' Some thirty inquirers nevertheless professed conversion.[4]

It was the same in the largest cities. First Presbyterian Church of Rio de Janeiro had been built in 1873 to seat six hundred people. In the jubilee year, a gallery was added to accommodate another three hundred. Alvaro Reis became pastor in 1897 and, in less than a score of years, the local membership had increased from 585 to 1395, besides those who organized five daughter churches and maintained a dozen developing congregations.[5]

When Gunnar Vingren and Daniel Berg arrived in Belém, their circumstances were so straitened that Berg engaged in manual work while Vingren studied Portuguese, passing on what he had learned to Berg in the evenings.[6] In Belém, their following grew into a very substantial congregation, and from there the work spread throughout the Northeast, along the coast to Recife and other cities, and inland to the towns of the great Sertão. The organization was simple, based upon the congregational autonomy practised by the Swedish Assemblies of God. By 1930, they reported 109 congregations and 13,511 members.[7]

At the same time that the Swedish-American pioneers of the Assemblies of God were church-planting in the North, the Italian-American, Louis Francescon, was busy in the working-class districts of São Paulo in the South.[8] There Francescon's preaching, in Italian, in the Bras district, led to the separation of a number of Italian Presbyterians from their local church, and resulted in the formation of the Christian Congregation, at first a wholly Italo-Brazilian Pentecostal denomination.

In early years, the Christian Congregation was small in membership, but soon it began to gather in the multitudes of Italian immigrants into its fold. Statistics were not kept before 1936, when the denomination incorporated, but the missiologist, W. R. Read, has estimated six thousand active members in 1920, thirty thousand in 1930, and sixty thousand in 1940.[9] Unlike the Assemblies of God, the Congregation tended to be isolationist. In the 1920s, its medium was Italian; in the 1930s, both Italian and Portuguese were used; and in the 1940s, Portuguese was dominant in the services.

As in the Assemblies of God, spontaneous, simultaneous audible prayer—which had occurred in the general revival throughout the Evangelical world in the 1900s—was usually heard.[10] Evangelism was constant in its practice and steady growth was the result.

The decade following the 1905 Revival was very fruitful. It was the same during the 1920s. Among the Methodists there began in 1924 a local awakening in Pórto Alegre, Rio Grande do Sul.[11] The leading evangelist was Derly Chavez, all of whose meetings were crowded out. Central Methodist Church had never been so crowded in all its history, and 118 candidates for church membership were enrolled, 108 in another congregation. In two months, fourteen hundred believers were accepted as probationers.

The most spectacular advance of the Presbyterian Church occurred in the Eastern Minas and Espíritu Santo districts, especially in the valley of the Rio Doce.[12] When Anibal Nora commenced his work in 1908, there were only two churches in Eastern Minas and one in Espíritu Santo. By 1927, there were thirty-three such churches and 5250 communicants, more than five hundred being added in 1927.[13]

A capable Brazilian Baptist, Casimiro de Oliveira, was appointed pastor of the First Baptist Church of the capital city of Minas Gerais in 1921, exercising in Belo Horizonte a beneficent influence for more than thirty years.[14] In 1924, David Appleby was sent to serve in Belo Horizonte, but died an untimely death, leaving a widow and a baby born on the night of his death. The baby boy became a professor of music, and Rosalee Appleby 'a leader of ability' near and far, with profound influence upon the more spiritual.[15]

Congregationalism in Brazil was of the more dynamic, evangelistic sort. Its leaders early adopted the practice of believers' baptism, thus emphasizing the necessity of a regenerate church membership. In 1913, Dr. Kalley's organization was incorporated into the Evangelical Union of South America, an interdenominational missionary society. With British support, the Society maintained several fields of missionary enterprise, and lent valuable support to the Brazilian Congregational churches.[16]

German Lutheranism in Brazil was concentrated chiefly in the three southern states.[17] The Synod of Rio Grande was serving nearly 150,000 German-Brazilians, and three other associated synods another 120,000, not counting the newer constituency of the Missouri Lutherans, begun before World War I.[18] The entrance of the Missouri Lutherans brought about a confessional conflict among the Germans, spewing 'words of hate' in a feud as bitter as only near relations could make it.[19] The Brazilian Lutherans constituted in the main a folk church, to which Brazilians of German blood all belonged. Impact upon Luso-Brazilians was much less than that of denominations of Anglo-American extraction, and a missionary burden was long a-lacking.

Towards the end of the 1920s, a revival of interest in religion was reported in Brazil,[20] and both Roman Catholic and Evangelical churches were being attended by increasing numbers; calls for more cooperation among denominational societies were heard, and steady progress was being made by all the Evangelical denominations.

In Brazil, the number of priests converted to the faith of the Evangelicals increased, and several became outstanding evangelists.[21] Hippolyto de Campos joined forces with the Methodists, and Victor Coelho de Almeida with the Presbyterians. The latter had studied seven years in Rome, and had served as Rector of the Theological Seminary of Rio de Janeiro. He became a professor in an evangelical seminary, but also worked as an evangelist, as did his fellow-convert, Hippolyto de Campos.

The population of Brazil at the beginning of the 1930s was stated as forty million, of whom thirty million were counted as Roman Catholics. There was only one priest for every five thousand inhabitants. A dozen dioceses had no training facilities for preparing the priesthood, and in a large diocese, only one priest had been ordained in 1926, while in another the only seminary was closed for the utter lack of students. Hence priests were recruited from Spain, Italy, Germany and Holland.[22] Of 307 priests in the great archdiocese of São Paulo, 216 were foreigners and only 91 Brazilian born. But Evangelical competition was causing the Roman Church to exert itself more actively. During October 1933, in the historic city of Salvador, the first Brazilian Eucharistic Congress was held, and was a fair success as measured by fervent faith.[23] Meanwhile, the multiplying Evangelical churches of Brazil found limitless and unprecedented opportunities for evangelism.

Among the more unusual ministries of the Evangelicals was that of Dr. Miguel Rizzo, pastor of the Presbyterian Church, Igreja Unida, in São Paulo,[24] which had 1350 adults enrolled. Rizzo embarked on a Mission to the Intelligentsia in the cities of Brazil. His method of operation was to hire a theatre for eight to ten lectures, twice weekly for a month. In one series, he counselled 528 inquirers, in another 324, many of them becoming Presbyterians.

The Presbyterians attracted the upper classes of Brazil, while the Baptists appealed to the lower middle echelons, and the Pentecostals to the proletariat. The Baptists built secondary colleges in Vitoria, Campos, São Paulo, Maceió, Belo Horizonte, Pôrto Alegre, and other cities and helped create an evangelical middle class.[25] The Baptists were strongest in the city and state of Rio de Janeiro, and had a number of outstanding pastors there, including F. F. Soren. Their second strongest base was São Paulo. Pentecostals were gaining steadily in the cities from Belém south.

In 1931, Harry Strachan, evangelist extraordinary to the twenty Spanish-speaking republics, conducted evangelistic meetings in the Rio São Francisco valley in northeastern Brazil.[26] In Juazeiro, the local theatre was filled, with the mayor, city council, professional people and the masses in attendance. No interpreter volunteered, so the Scotsman addressed the audience in Spanish—'it was an unqualified success.' It was prophetic that the pioneer Bible colporteur, F. C. Glass, told Harry Strachan in 1931 that 'the churches of Brazil are ripe for a revival . . . urgent and more important than trying to open up new fields.'[27]

In 1931, there were manifestations of spiritual revival in many parts of Brazil, moving Baptists, Congregationalists, Episcopalians, Methodists, Presbyterians and others, this revival, Brazil's second such movement, having immediate and long-term results.

Dr. George W. Ridout, a professor of theology at Asbury College in Kentucky, an evangelist of worldwide experience, came to Brazil from Argentina after two years of ministry around the world.[28] Occasional news of evangelistic success preceded him and ensured a welcome.

Ridout's first series of meetings were held in São Paulo, and the response to the preaching was spontaneous, without any 'altar call.' A prominent minister surrendered his diploma and asked his college to set regular examinations for subjects in which credit was falsely obtained. When the Methodist bishop, J. W. Tarboux, arrived, he concluded that the coming of the American was positively providential.[29]

So Ridout was prevailed upon to postpone his sailing for South Africa, and spent another month in Brazil. He went first to Campinas, where the cooperation of the professors of the Presbyterian Theological Seminary and the pastor of the oldest and largest Evangelical congregation in the city was assured.[30] Another 'marvelous outpouring' took place, leaving standing room only in the church thereafter, and a like blessing in the Methodist Church, whose minister, W. G. Borchers, was Ridout's interpreter throughout.[31]

There were similar movements in Ribeirão Preto and Piracicaba, both college towns,[32] in which there was deep conviction of sin among church members and a reaping of a harvest of souls among the young people. In Juiz de Fora, a college town in Minas Gerais, similar results followed, and a group of young theological students spent a night in prayer on a mountain nearby.[33]

Next followed two weeks of meetings in Rio de Janeiro, where Ridout's ministry began in Catete Methodist Church, the oldest congregation of the denomination in Brazil.[34] The accommodation being far too small, a move was made to a larger Congregational Church, which filled up immediately and overflowed until the pews, aisles, doors, side rooms and all available space was packed by two thousand people. Meetings continued till close to midnight, two hours of the preaching of the Word and an aftermeeting attended by all. Again, the attendance was wholly interdenominational, and the response was heartening. A Baptist interpeter took up the work of relaying Ridout's messages elsewhere.[35]

Each of the annual conferences of the Methodist Church of Brazil experienced an outpouring of the Holy Spirit upon the pastors and people attending.[36] At the Methodist Central Conference in the State of São Paulo, the experiences and scenes were indescribable, according to Bishop Tarboux. The rejoicing of the pastors and laymen went on after midnight into the next day. At the Conference in the South, at Alegrete, a reviving of the leaders occurred in conference sessions also; next week, the Methodist Church was overcrowded and more than seventy-five made public profession of faith. Bishop Tarboux himself was stirred, and began to preach on the enduement of the Holy Spirit, 'making it stronger, if possible, at every appointment.'[37]

A feature of the work of the Evangelical churches and missions in the 1930s was the success of evangelistic campaigns, a Baptist veteran declaring that 'there is a greater desire to hear the Word than I have ever known before.'[38] It seemed certain that an awakening accompanied the revival for in 1935, the Baptist Convention of Brazil reported that its membership in fifty years had increased from just two to fifty thousand. Baptist evangelism received a powerful impetus from the conversion of Dr. Rafael Gióia Martins, a Roman priest. In Salvador, for example, three hundred requested instruction in the faith following a campaign in a crowded auditorium in the historic city.[39]

Twenty years after these Ridout campaigns, President Walter Ermel of the São Paulo Faculty of Theology stated that he frequently heard impressive testimonies of those who had been helped by the ministry of revival. In the wake of Ridout's meetings, the words, 'Spirit of the Living God, fall afresh on me,' were sung in many churches. Ridout returned in 1940 for conferences in Rio and São Paulo.[40]

13

THE SOUTHERN REPUBLICS, 1916-1946

The population of the Argentine Republic rose from eight million in 1916 to sixteen million in 1946. Ninety per cent of the population were of European blood, the remainder mestizos and a few Indians.[1] It was much the same in the nearby Republic of Uruguay, where the population of more than a million also doubled, ninety per cent of European stock. Paraguay, on the other hand, entered the twentieth century impoverished by war.[2] Its population increased from half a million to more than a million in the period, the great majority of the people of Guarani Indian descent. Chile's population during the years considered increased from three-and-a-half million to five-and-a-half million, not so much by immigration as Argentina's, but by a high birthrate,[3] the racial composition of its people suggesting an absorption of the Araucanian Indian stock into Iberian, with a few Indian remnants north and south.

In Argentina, less than 20% of the Roman Catholic folk attended mass on Sundays.[4] There were not enough priests to serve the needs of their faithful, one parish priest for every 3750 parishioners, though many of the priests were absorbed in other than parish duties.[5] Much the same ratio prevailed in Uruguay,[6] though a revival of interest was noted. In Paraguay, there was one priest for every five thousand Roman Catholics. When American Redemptorists took over a parish of 30,000 in Asuncion, only sixteen came to the first mass, but within fifteen years (in 1959) the American priests had enlisted 20% of the total.[7] In Chile, the ratio was one priest for every 2666 parishioners, which was better than any other Latin American country.[8] In 1945, however, not a single Chilean was ordained in five dioceses with a population of a million Roman Catholics. A survey showed that just over three per cent of Chilean men and nine per cent of Chilean women attended Sunday mass.[9] A majority of the priests in the country were foreigners. On such grounds alone, there was a case made for evangelism by the Evangelical societies.

Statistics of the pre-War period had shown an increase in the memberships of the Evangelical churches of every denomination, following the worldwide awakening of 1905. Although no republic was directly involved in World War I, social and spiritual progress was not improved, and the slowing down of Evangelical effort occurred, with certain exceptions. Several new societies entered the field.

In Argentina, the Methodists had the advantage of long experience of presenting the Good News of Christ to the citizens of the country, having entered in 1843. In the wake of the 1905 Revival, their communicant membership reached 3817, with a related community of 11,829.[10] Between 1911 and 1916, there was a purging of inactive members which reduced communicant membership to three thousand or so at the time of the Panama Congress in 1916.[11] Ten years later, communicants numbered four thousand, prompting Webster Browning to affirm that, in numbers and influence, the Methodist Church ranked first among the distinctly evangelical organizations of the region.[12] In 1945, active membership was stated as five thousand, with a community in excess of ten thousand. It can be seen that Argentine Methodists were growing at the rate of a little better than three per cent, above the population rate of increase.

The evangelistic initiative seemed to have passed to the Christian Brethren, designated in Argentina 'los Hermanos Libres.' At the time of the Panama Congress, there were some forty local assemblies and others were being formed in rapid succession.[13] The Brethren continued to use street meetings and tent campaigns with increasing success. In the late 1920s, when the Methodist membership (4000) was ranked first in the country, Brethren counted six thousand in fellowship. Attendances at open-air meetings often rose to seven hundred.[14] Argentine leadership came more and more to the fore, to supplement the ardent missionaries' direction begotten in Britain in the decade of revival.

In the 1920s, therefore, the tent campaigns increased in number and drawing power. The veteran, William Payne, participated in a tent campaign in 1923 in the metropolis of Buenos Aires, in which 200,000 of the city's two million inhabitants heard the Good News.[15] There were hundreds of inquirers added to assembly life, 'the response and general effect of the effort ... nothing less than phenomenal.' The annual conferences in each of the assemblies waxed strong; young people were being thoroughly indoctrinated.[16]

During the 1930s, Brethren evangelism maintained its drive. Tent campaigns were extended to a full month, with aggregate attendance mounting to ten thousand. The opposition of the priesthood was provoked, especially after the Eucharistic Congress in Buenos Aires in 1934.[17] Brethren youth arranged an annual conference in Córdoba, starting with five hundred in 1930, reaching the two thousand figure at the end of World War II. In the 1940s, war years, the dynamic British missionary leadership was transferred to a very capable body of Argentine Christians well-trained in Brethren assemblies. Two thousand believers in 1916 had become fourteen thousand in 1946,[18] a 20% per annum gain. The converts of this dynamic evangelism continued in the apostolic doctrine and fellowship, and in breaking of bread, and in prayers, building up the body of believers.

Very similar success attended the evangelism of the Baptists, directed by able Southern Baptist missionaries. Fewer than nine hundred communicants in 1916 became more than seven thousand in 1946, an increase of more than 20% per annum.[19] J. C. Varetto, an Argentine preacher of great persuasiveness, engaged in tent campaigns that added many to the Baptist membership, even during the times of Peronista restriction.[20] As among the Brethren, a capable body of national leaders was generated. Churches thrived in Tucuman, in the northwest, and Santa Cruz in the far south, northeast in the Chaco and southwest in the Andes. Like the Brethren, the Baptists derived their early dynamic from revival in the sending country and extended their work by steady evangelism, caring for converts in teaching and fellowship, communion and prayer.

These same factors should have applied to the Christian and Missionary Alliance work in Argentina.[21] There were a couple of hundred Argentines in fellowship in 1916, but only five hundred or so in 1946; doctrinal dissension was one of the causes of limited growth. The Disciples of Christ grew from fifty to two hundred and fifty in the period. During the same time, the Mennonites grew from zero to more than six hundred.[22] The Assemblies of God grew very slowly from a handful to approximately three hundred in the thirty years, but other Pentecostal bodies achieved more, the Church of God (based in Tennessee) accelerating when J. H. Ingram was joined by an Italo-Argentine pastor, Marcos Mazzucco. Pentecostals numbered 15,000 in 1943.[23] The Seventh Day Adventists increased from 700 to 7000 in thirty years.

During the thirty years following the Panama Congress, the Lutheran Churches of Argentina grew steadily with German immigration and settlement. It is scarcely fair to compare such growth in folk churches with the pioneering and evangelization accomplished transculturally by other missions. There were more than seven thousand German-speaking communicants in the Missouri Synod in 1946, a considerable gain over the figure of a thousand in 1916[24] An equal number were members of the German Evangelical Church, La Plata Synod. But there was little to compare with the evangelism of the Brethren and Baptists in any of the Lutheran bodies, whose Spanish outreach began later.

Suffice to say, the Protestant cause in Argentina was growing slowly but steadily, from ten thousand members at the beginning of World War I to sixty thousand at the end of World War II, the related community from fifteen thousand to a hundred and fifty thousand.[25] Apart from the enrolling of ethnic Germans in the Lutheran Churches, the greater part of this growth was achieved by the dynamics of revival and the techniques of evangelism.

Conditions in Uruguay had been more discouraging than in Argentina.[26] The total Protestant membership rose in the 1930s to seven thousand, half of whom were Italians of Waldensian affiliation, who provided half of the community of twenty thousand also. In Paraguay, growth was slow. After three years, the Bolivian-Paraguayan War ended in 1935 in the defeat of Bolivia and the loss of most of the Chaco to Paraguay. Dr. G. P. Howard of Argentina, invited to lecture in Asuncion, came directly following cessation of hostilities.[27] A theatre and school auditorium were packed. President Eusebio Ayala listened to Howard's talks on radio and expressed warm appreciation.

West of the Andes, Evangelical Christianity thrived in comparison with slower growth in the Río Plata republics. The war years, 1914-1918, produced no startling develop-ments. In 1918, a united evangelistic campaign in Santiago won two hundred and fifty converts, while another in the port of Valparaiso brought forward more than four hundred, all adults.[28] At the same time, the Sunday Schools promoted a 'decision day,' and many young people responded, taking sustained classes of instruction. The Presbyterians and Methodists cooperated in interdenominational campaigns, as did the other groups, Alliance and Baptist, but the newer Pentecostal movement went on its own way.

By 1917,[29] the Pentecostal Methodists—growing more rapidly in the national capital than in Valparaiso—were able to establish themselves in a larger hall on a busy street, Jotabeche, in Santiago. They developed a work of promise in Concepcion also.

Willis Hoover, besides holding a pastorate in Valparaiso, used his influence as a Pentecostal editor to mobilize much prayer for a spiritual revival in the denomination, and in 1921 the expected movement began in Concepcion, again accompanied by unusual demonstrations, including dancing for joy.[30] The upsurge brought prosperity to the churches, increasing the rolls of membership; but Hoover's distrust of theological training helped deprive the exhortations of a needed doctrinal content. The American Assemblies of God declined to help develop the denomination because of their disapproval of sprinkling as baptism.[31]

Tensions developed between Hoover and Umana, who expressed Chilean nationalistic feelings against the gringo. A power struggle developed which threatened the unity of the churches.[32] Charges were laid against Hoover, more of indiscretions than of immorality.[33] Hoover admitted them, and retained the goodwill of his Valparaiso congregation; but the denomination was divided, the Methodist Pentecostal Church continuing under Manuel Umana's leadership, while Hoover's partisans established the Evangelical Pentecostal Church, and thirty other groups emerged.[34] Hoover died in 1936 while struggles for power were still going on. His greatest weakness was his reversal of Wesley's evaluation of the fruit of the Spirit as superior to possession of gifts.

While Chileans were demonstrating their nationalism, a New York insurance broker, William Strong, set out for Latin America in 1923, and arrived in Chile in time to find an unexpected opportunity to preach in regimental barracks. This led to the founding of a Soldiers' Gospel Mission.[35] In regiment after regiment, the middle-aged evangelist was given a welcome, officers testifying that his ministry had helped empty the guard-houses of military prisoners.

By 1927, twenty-eight regiments of the Chilean Army had been reached by the Soldiers' Gospel Mission, infantry, cavalry, artillery, engineers, marines and the like offered the Good News. In one series of meetings, more than a thousand men professed faith. By 1929, work was done in the Chilean Navy, and Strong was given written permission to preach in every jail and penitentiary in the country.[36]

In August 1928, Harry Strachan and his team preached in the republic of Chile in cooperation with the Evangelical churches, the Y. M. C. A., and the Salvation Army.[37] Talca, Chillan, Valdivia, Valparaiso, Santiago and Concepción in turn were visited. The Latin American evangelistic team tackled the town of Talca, using a theatre for the meetings, which were crowded out as thousands listened to the messages, many registering as inquirers.[38]

As usual, there were extremes of clerical opposition but the Evangelical churches and missions greatly benefitted. In each city, theatre meetings attracted professional folk as well as the masses. In Temuco, for example, the largest theatre in town, seating fifteen hundred, was first filled and then overcrowded, and there were four hundred inquirers registered and followed up.[39]

Such campaigns were held in Chile regularly, and the churches grew by evangelistic enterprise. There was little participation by the Chilean Pentecostals in such efforts, and none by the Seventh Day Adventists, between whom and the other Evangelicals there was little cordiality, Robert E. Speer declaring:[40]

> Seventh Day Adventists' . . . deliberate policy seems to be to go to the congregations which other mission-aries have gathered and proselyte them. These earnest people . . . are acting in accordance with their con-sciences, but they are doing a great deal of harm all over South America.

It would be a mistake to imagine that the Adventists in practice proselytized other Evangelicals only and neglected the evangelization of the utterly unindoctrinated. But the fact remains that they were regarded as sheep-stealers by the missionaries of other denominations.[41]

Dr. G. P. Howard was known as 'the evangelist to the unchurched intelligentsia of Latin America,' his field the Spanish-speaking republics just as Brazil was that of Dr. Miguel Rizzo. In Chile, in 1936, he reported on the unusual responsiveness of students, professors, members of service clubs and other thinking people to the Good News presented in their language. Theatres and halls were crowded. In a single year, Dr. Howard addressed 28,000 of the educated classes, mostly unchurched, thousands becoming interested and hundreds enrolling in Bible classes.[42]

14

TROPICAL SOUTH AMERICA, 1916-1946

Contrasted with Mexico, in a similar upheaval, the five republics of tropical South America produced the poorest record of Evangelical progress in Latin America. There were, nevertheless, reasons for hope and encouragement.

In the period, 1916-1946, the outstanding event in the history of Bolivia was the disastrous Bolivian-Paraguayan War of 1932-1935. It was fought by a well-trained army of soldiers, accustomed to the climate of the highlands, in a terrain whose heat and humidity and parasitic life was much more tolerable to the Paraguayans used to it.

The three million people living in Bolivia were more than half Indian, a third mestizo, and one-seventh European. In the Indian communities, the Catholicism of the people was half-Roman and half-pagan, their life of deprivation and misery interrupted by drunken fiestas. The Indian parish clergy were not much better than their parishioners, and priests and people were fanatically bigoted. There was one priest for 4500 people in the country, but only a third of the priesthood was engaged in parish ministry.[1] In thirty years, only forty-five priests were ordained in the See of La Paz, and, at the end of 1946, there were only 227 Bolivian-born priests serving three million or more people.[2]

The Methodists in Bolivia reported a membership of 78 believers in 1916, and in 1946 the figure passed 300.[3] The first ten years of this period produced no growth, nor did the war years from 1939 onwards; but the middle years were encouraging. The Baptists had 80 members in 1916, and the total in 1946 was approximately 500.[4] The Chaco War had a devastating effect upon the Baptists, but the ten years following showed some growth.[5] What became the Evangelical Christian Union, composed of churches founded by several faith missions, grew from almost zero in 1916 to approximately 300 in 1946.[6] Only Seventh Day Adventists showed remarkable growth, membership rising from 10 in 1916 to approximately 2500 in 1946.[7] This Peter Wagner has attributed to a folk movement among the Aymaras.

The Southern Baptists released Juan Varetto, pastor of the largest congregation in the Argentine, an able evangelist, to accompany Harry Strachan to Bolivia during the closing months of 1926.   About a thousand people—segregated on the main floor and galleries according to the law of the land for 'gente decente' (whites), cholos, and Indians—crowded a theatre in Oruro for the first meeting, at which Varetto spoke on 'Why Christ came into the World.'   In the Oruro meetings, there were only thirty inquirers.[8]

After modest meetings held in San Pedro during a fiesta marked as usual by drunken debauchery, the evangelists went to Cochabamba.[9]   The first meeting was held in a local theatre, but the night following its use was denied, so the evangelists continued in the church nearby.   The opposition provoked a certain sympathy on the part of liberals to the message.   Meetings were held in Quillacola, Potosí, and Sucre, thence to La Paz.[10] There was considerable success in the capital, but difficulty elsewhere.

Half of the ten million people living in Peru were Indian, a third mestizo, and a tenth European of Spanish descent. Augusto Leguia, as President, dominated the country until 1930, despite efforts of the Alianza Popular Revolucionaria Americana to shake him.   The founder of A.P.R.A., Victor Raúl Haya de la Torre, a student idealist, had been much influenced by John A. Mackay, principal of the Evangelical Colegio San Andrés in Lima.[11] A more liberal government ruled Peru during World War II and its aftermath.

In 1916, Roman Catholicism was the state religion, and the public exercise of any other worship was forbidden.   In 1920, liberty of conscience and religion was declared, but in 1933 a new constitution emphasized its protection of the Catholic Apostolic and Roman religion.[12] In 1923, Leguia arranged to dedicate Peru to the Sacred Heart of Jesus. A mammoth demonstration organized by Haya de la Torre and his allies caused the government to abandon its project. Haya de la Torre was arrested and deported.[13]

The ratio of Roman Catholic priests to parishioners was one to 5000, and a majority of the priests were foreigners, mainly from Spain.[14] Yet Peru was considered the most Catholic country in all Latin America.   As in Bolivia, the plight of the Indians was desperate, and around the civic magnificence of Lima were barrios where slum conditions were 'scarcely matched elsewhere on the planet for abject poverty and physical and moral degradation.'[15]

In 1916, the Methodists in Peru decided to drop the names of non-residents from their rolls, hence the figure dropped from a thousand to 600. Methodist missionaries increased their numbers (from 5 to 25) in the years after World War I, and membership rose to 1600 or so.[16] But the economic depression in the United States forced workers to return, and membership dropped to 800 by 1946.

Under the direction of John Ritchie and his Latin friends, Guerrero, Virgilio and Muñoz, the work of the Evangelical Union of South America grew steadily in Peru, so in 1922 a synod was held, and the designation Iglesia Evangélica Peruana was adopted.[17] This was followed by an outburst of evangelistic activity, as a result of which a new group was started every month for three years. Quarterly presbytery rallies took the place of the drunken fiestas in the lives of the Indians.[18] The Christian and Missionary Alliance began to cooperate in the Peruvian Evangelical Church,[19] but John Ritchie resigned from the work in 1929.

In 1919, missionaries of the Assemblies of God took up permanent residence in Peru and were assigned a district in keeping with Evangelical comity arrangements. After a few years, they disregarded the comity with other societies and established churches in Callao and Huancayo.[20]

In Huaráz, a town in the picturesque valley originally assigned to them, the Cragins and the Ericksons won a few converts, and arranged to baptize them in the river of the same name. The local priest told his congregation that the Virgin Mary would dry up the river if the Evangelicals were permitted to defile it.[21] The Indians attacked the party with stones, badly wounded Howard Cragin, and fractured Leif Erickson's skull, besides assaulting their womenfolk.[22] When the Huaráz came down in a disastrous flood and drowned hundreds of inhabitants, this was blamed on the Evangelicals for offending the Virgin.[23] Out of the disaster came several conversions to Evangelical faith.

The first occurrence of glossolalia in Peru was reported in 1928.[24] In 1929, Willis Hoover of Chile visited the Callao assembly,[25] and another 'outpouring of the Spirit' was noted. In the 1930s, difficulties developed between the nationals and the missionaries, as in other missions. Independent Pentecostal churches led by nationals were formed.[26] By 1946, there were more than 2000 Pentecostals in Peru, not necessarily in fellowship with each other, but advancing in numbers more rapidly than most other missions.[27]

Up until this time, the most remarkable development of Evangelical work had been seen in Seventh Day Adventist ministry around Puno, on Lake Titicaca, among Aymaras. On 3rd March 1913,[28] Valentín Ampuero, Bishop of Puno, accompanied by two hundred Indians, forcibly broke into the house of the missionary Frederick Stahl, then absent, wrecking the place and cruelly beating Manuel Camacho, an Adventist schoolteacher who, with five others, was jailed, but in August of that year the Peruvian Supreme Court in Lima upheld their acquittal. A revulsion of feeling towards the Adventists led to the modification of the Constitution.[29]

The Adventists extended their work to the Quechuas, on whom was visited savage persecution, resulting in the mass murder of as many as a dozen believers at a time. But less than a thousand church members of both tongues by 1946 had become six thousand, with a community of 29,000. Some credited the advance to education, which helped the Indians, but J. B. A. Kessler emphasized the preaching of 'free grace' by the Adventist pioneers, the Stahls.[30]

The Church of the Nazarene began to support a work of evangelism in Peru in 1917, and by 1919, there were thirty-seven Peruvians recognized as communicants.[31] The work grew slowly at first, beset by the usual problems of the missions in Peru. In 1945, missionaries and nationals participated in intercession for a spiritual outpouring.[32] In Oyotun, ninety people attended a conference for deepening the spiritual life, and the presence of God was felt. There were confessions of sin, reconciliations of enemies, and solution of difficulties. This 'outpouring of the Spirit' sent believers out to witness as the revival spread to the annual assembly in August of 1945, and membership rose to 800 by the year 1946.

Interdenominational evangelism in Peru was not lacking in Lima and Callao and other places accessible to visitors. In 1931, George Ridout, evangelist from Asbury College, held a successful series of meetings in Lima, and times of revival were reported among the Peruvian Evangelicals as members of various churches supported the effort.[33]

There were other visiting evangelists in the 1930s.[34] The ubiquitous Harry Strachan ministered in Lima and in other cities, again with the support of the various churches and with gratifying results. Strachan had begun to pray that the Lord would endue the rank and file with the Holy Spirit,[35] so he devoted more and more time in teaching and training.

In 1931, the Student Federation in Arequipa sponsored three conferences in the University, addressed by Harry Strachan, presided over by the Rector, and attended by the whole student body as well as many of the principal people of the city.[36] The remarkable feature of the Peruvian series this time was the friendly attitude of the authorities. Not only were theatres and public halls provided, but several opportunities were given to address meetings in schools, barracks and prisons. The concluding meetings of the 1931 campaign were conducted in the primitive settlements on the Amazon side of the cordilleras, after which Strachan left the river port of Iquitos for Brazil.

G. P. Howard exercised his specialized ministry among Peruvian intellectuals. Stanley Jones ministered briefly, but the educated classes, though interested, did not show as great an interest as farther south. One intellectual trophy was won in Cuzco, one morning in 1927, when a Bolivian priest of Italian extraction called on the Evangelical Union of South America workers.[37] Montano, a trained Dominican, was destined to become an evangelist of note in the English-speaking world as well as in Latin America.

The population of Ecuador was two-fifths Indian, and two-fifths mestizo, a tenth negro or mulatto, and a tenth of European blood.[38] Liberal administrations initiated reform, and fair progress was being made. In a typical year in the 1920s, records showed that of 70,397 births registered only 22,325 were noted as illegitimate, a figure less than half the legitimate total.[39] Literacy was improving also, for of 20,012 persons married, 8,246 were able to sign their names. Of a population of a million and a half in 1924, 92,500 were attending primary school, two thousand high school, while enrollment in university rose to 747.

Ecuador was almost wholly Roman Catholic. As usual, there were too few priests to serve their parishioners. In 1924, the total number of Evangelicals, exclusive of foreign residents was 75, but tolerance was increasing.[40]

In 1931, Harry Strachan stopped off in Ecuador on his way south, and almost immediately was invited to campaign. Strachan had found the whole city of Quito in the throes of great religious excitement, caused by the celebration of the twenty-fifth anniversary of the winking or blinking of the eyes of an image of the Virgin (La Dolorosa).[41] On the 20th April 1906, at 8 p.m., a devotee had noticed the eyes of the image being cast down in sorrow for the sins of the world.

Although this had occurred repeatedly, the twenty-fifth anniversary so stirred the hearts of the faithful that Harry Strachan found it wiser not to attempt to evangelize the people in the Ecuadorean capital. Instead, he commenced preaching in Guayaquil, where the few Evangelicals were willing to meet between 5 a.m. and 6 a.m. to pray for the salvation of friends and fellow-citizens. The evangelistic enterprise succeeded in reaching about 120,000 citizens in fourteen days.[42] As many as a thousand men, including city officials, doctors, and lawyers, as well as artisans, came to a men's meeting in Templo Bíblico. A hundred inquirers were registered in Guayaquil alone.

In Colombia, the population—which passed ten million by 1946—was 35% white, 60% mestizo, and the remainder negro and Indian.[43] From 1916 onwards, the Conservative domination of national life was loosening; in 1930 the party of the Liberals came to power, achieving some reforms; but, in 1946, the Conservatives took power again, ushering in a period of repression and violent disorder.

The Roman Catholic Church gained strength during the years under review. In 1919, a Marian Congress was held; in 1935, a Eucharistic Congress was organized, following the establishment of a Catholic Action group.[44] Missions were extended throughout the unevangelized Indian lands, successfully. Yet, in Colombia, there was only one priest for every 3500 parishioners.[45]

From 1916, Evangelicals strove to extend their foothold, and in late 1922, Harry Strachan arrived in Barranquilla. He had come alone, but his first meeting moved a well-known Colombian businessman to join him, Rafael Borelly, who later became a senator and mayor of Barranquilla.

Boycott forbade the renting of a theatre, so the meetings in Bogotá were held in the Presbyterian Church.[46] Seven hundred men, including professional people and artisans, and General Benjamín Herrera, the most influential man in the country, attended a lecture on social purity, giving a good start to the series, regarded by the missionaries as a triumph won by prayer. About a hundred professed faith.

In Girardot, a town of 25,000 with a reputation for open-mindedness, two thousand people gathered for the first of the Strachan-Borelly meetings. Like patrons of the theatre, they were smoking and talking; but, at a word from the chairman, they uncovered their heads and stumped their cigars, and gave all their attention to the evangelist.[47]

Meanwhile, Roberto Elphick Valenzuela of Chile joined the party. He was part-British, part-Chilean, a very able evangelist. He proceeded to Bogotá to help in follow-up. Alexander Allan joined Strachan in Libano. In San Lorenzo, Strachan was given forty minutes at a circus, but made such an impression that the crowd, almost to a man, left to follow him to another hall, much to the chagrin of the circus people.[48] In Honda, eight hundred men attended the opening meeting, and that night fifteen hundred packed the theatre. Harry Strachan and Roberto Elphick shared preaching and counsel, as well as training local workers.

Medellin was found to be hostile, thanks to opposition from the Archbishop, so the meetings were restricted to the Presbyterian hall, with a crowd of less than a hundred, and sparse results.[49]

Meetings in Barranquilla ended the Colombian campaign of 1922, Harry Strachan and Roberto Elphick commencing work in an open air theatre, risking opposition but finding only interest; five hundred people attended.[50] On subsequent evenings, many hearers attended meetings in a local church; a couple of hundred inquirers sought counsel. Strachan and Elphick were more convinced of the necessity of beginning in a neutral place to attract the interest of the outsiders.

In 1923, the Scandinavian Alliance and the Christian and Missionary Alliance entered Colombia, while in 1932 there arrived an independent Pentecostal missionary, Edward Wegner who established a church in Sogamoso transferred with a Bible Institute (founded 1943) to Assemblies of God.[51]

In December 1936, Harry and Susan Strachan made a survey of the department of Bolivar in Colombia, a result of which was the entrance of the Latin American Mission into Colombia, in a work of pioneering.[52]

Juan Vicente Gómez, president of Venezuela from 1909, dominated that republic until his death in 1935. He was abstemious in food and drink, but not in venery.[53] Imposing order, he improved the economy of the country and paid off the national debt with taxes on oil exports. Of the five million citizens reported in 1946, only a tiny fraction were pure-blooded Indians, a preponderance of European blood in the mestizo population being claimed.

During the Gómez years, the Roman Catholic Church made progress, being in fact (if not in law) a state Church. There was only one priest for every five thousand faithful, secular clergy being outnumbered by those in the orders.[54]

With a strength of about a thousand in 1916, Evangelicals increased to more than five thousand in 1946, Canadian Christian Brethren, the Scandinavian Alliance, and Seventh Day Adventists making the greatest gains.

In early 1923, the Presbyterians released Angel Archilla of Puerto Rico for campaigns with Harry Strachan in the republic of Venezuela.[55] A week was spent with Christians in Caracas, in spiritual preparation, after which they left for the Llanos with John Christiansen of the Scandinavian Alliance—a tour possible only in the dry season.

Meetings were held in many parts of the country, jointly in Sabaneta, Santa Rosa, Libertad and Nutrias, after which the Scotsman went to the Orinoco, while the Puerto Rican ministered in Palmarito, Guasdualito and Totumito in the State of Apure, Christiansen joining both men in campaigns in the State of Aragua.[56] Strachan fell ill with intermittent fever, and preached sitting in La Victoria. There was a gratifying response in these meetings, up to 400 attending a series in Carupano, where Archilla and Christiansen held two dozen meetings in two weeks. The converts were many, one result of the Venezuelan campaign being the sending of seven men to study for the ministry in Puerto Rico.

The Scandinavian Alliance Mission in Venezuela built its Maracaibo congregation into the largest evangelical church in that republic. Evangelicals of all denominations in six Venezuelan states met there in August 1927, enjoying a spirit of unity. Not only was there revival in the body of believers, but an awakening among outsiders, seventy-five such making public profession of faith.[57]

During the 1930s, the Pentecostals grew in number, a missionary zeal imported by Americans being matched in Venezuela by the enthusiasm of their converts. Little, if any, real comity existed in relation to other missions.

During 1939, Harry Strachan planned a lengthy campaign in Venezuela, teaming up again with John Christiansen of the Scandinavian Alliance.[58] He returned to the lonely places manned by missionaries, in the Llanos and in the territory of the Orinoco River Mission.

15

THE CARIBBEAN COUNTRIES, 1916-1946

During 1940, as associate pastor of the missions-minded Peoples Church in Toronto, the writer undertook a survey tour through the Caribbean countries.[1] Visits were made on other occasions to the Bahamas, the Leeward and Windward Islands, to Belize and the Guianas.

Cuba had its share of upheavals and turmoil in its first quarter century, but in 1925 Gerardo Machado dictated its government, till 1933. For thirty years, the United States regarded Cuba as its political ward, until the abrogation of the Platt Amendment in 1934. Shortly thereafter, Fulgencio Batista came to power, ruling the island through a series of puppet presidents until he himself assumed the office. He provided economic benefits, but muzzled press and people.

Of Cuba's population of 4,500,000 in 1940, a half were of European stock, a quarter were negro and the remainder of mixed blood.[2] Havana had a population of 600,000. The Roman Catholic Church was predominant, but provided only one priest for every 9000 faithful and, of five hundred or so, only eighty priests were of Cuban birth. Fewer than fifty thousand citizens of Havana attended mass weekly.[3]

In Cuba, the Evangelicals developed unusual activity in 1917 and 1918. Ezequiel Torres made far-reaching impact in a three months' evangelistic campaign in 1919,[4] adding to the commendable results being gained through schools maintained by Baptists, Methodists and Presbyterians.

While social action extended, aggressive evangelism increased in the 1920s, church attendance rising rapidly. In the 1920s, Pentecostals began to evangelize Cuba, though it was not until 1936 that the Assemblies of God were founded, first-fruits of a burgeoning movement. In 1928, a Cuban pastor, B. G. Lavastida,[5] started a Bible Institute at Los Pinos Nuevos, thus founding the West Indies Mission.

At the beginning of World War II, there were 40,000 or so communicant members in Evangelical churches in Cuba, and a constituency of 150,000.[6] About a quarter of these were Baptists, helped by Northern and Southern missions.

The population of Puerto Rico at the time was about two million, two-thirds of the population being European, the prevalent language Spanish, though English was well-known on account of its position as an American territory. Three quarters of the people were illiterate, a heritage of colonial neglect. The Roman Catholic Church claimed 94% of the population,[7] but there was only one priest for 6000 faithful. Protestants were 4%, their church attendance rated 80%.

In Puerto Rico, an interdenominational evangelistic campaign held in early 1917 created quite a stir.[8] In one town, all places of business were closed to enable customers and employees to attend a men's meeting. The secret of the success throughout the island was found in the preparatory prayer meetings held in all places concerned. In a smaller town, it was prophesied that there would be fifteen converts but more than a hundred responded. In all, there were more than six hundred professions of faith.

After twenty years in Puerto Rico, the Evangelicals had much cause for encouragement.[9] Thirteen thousand were members in Evangelical churches, twenty-two thousand in Sunday Schools. The first Puerto Rican church to attain self-support was the Baptist Church of Caguas.

During 1924, Harry Strachan engaged in an extensive and thorough evangelistic campaign throughout Puerto Rico, a number of younger preachers assisting him. A tent set up on the outskirts of San Juan attracted considerable attention and produced fifty inquirers for counsel, the sponsors being well pleased with the effort.[10]

At the time, a secular journalist in San Juan wrote of the 'Lutheran missionaries invading the Catholic countries of America,' making direct reference to Don Enrique Strachan as an emissary of 'the German rebel,' adding facetiously:[11]

> I am the first to admit the prodigious success of Senor Strachan. If he goes on giving his conferences to the same kind of crowds he had in the Municipal Theatre, I do not doubt that within six months we shall all be carrying our never failing Bible in our pocket.

In Puerto Rico, the Evangelicals maintained a vigorous evangelism as well as a cordial comity. In 1935, Puerto Rican churches engaged in a simultaneous Crusade of the Faith, culminating in Easter rallies.[12] Everywhere, local congregations were crowded out and Sunday Schools overflowing. Archilla reported the number of accessions in the united evangelistic campaign as approximately a thousand.

Pentecostalism reached Puerto Rico from Hawaii, where a number of Puerto Rican migrant workers were converted through the preaching of Pentecostal missionaries. In 1916, three of these converts began to preach in the open air at Ponce, on the south coast, and a dozen new converts were baptized on New Year's Day, 1917.[13] It was not until 1921 that the first American Pentecostal missionaries arrived. In 1926, the work was spreading rapidly, and by 1946 the membership stood at 9385, a remarkable growth.[14] Just as Harry Strachan had recognized the Spanish-speaking island as a reservoir of workers for the rest of Latin America, Pentecostals came to see that Puerto Rican Pentecostalism provided the dynamic for church planting in the Americas.

The Dominican Republic was occupied by United States Marines from 1916 until 1924. The constabulary left in power used its control of the government to dominate the country, its leader, Rafael Trujillo, coming to power in the year 1930. Of a population of about 1,500,000 in 1940, the majority were Spanish-Negro. The Roman Catholic Church supplied one priest for for every 8000 faithful,[15] and the rate of illiteracy was everywhere high.

In the Dominican Republic, the Methodist and Moravian missions confined their work to English-speaking negroes, the United Brethren and the Free Methodists reaching out to Spanish-speaking Dominicans, as did a Puerto Rican in San Pedro de Macoris, the vanguard of the Pentecostals. In 1921, in all, there were 750 English-speaking and 500 Spanish-speaking members of Protestant churches.[16]

In August 1924, Harry Strachan (and his team) arrived unannounced at Puerto Plata, on the north coast, and used the time to minister in a tent to crowds rising in number to a thousand, all before the opposition was well aware of his presence. Meetings followed in Santiago, Macoris, Sanchez La Vega and Moca, again with crowds up to a thousand. The Puerto Rican evangelists, including Archilla, assisted.[17]

Of the nearly three million Haitians—nearly all negroes, with a small though influential minority of mulattoes in the towns—the great majority were illiterate and very poor. The dominant denomination was the Roman Catholic, but voodooism was widely practised, with grossest superstition and rampant immorality, the laxest code of conduct in the civilized world. There was only one priest for every 5000 faithful,[18] and 'the faithful' were not noted for fidelity. The need was unsurpassed anywhere.

Haiti had been occupied by United States Marines from 1915 to 1934. In 1930, Stenio Vincent was elected president, ruling with discretion into the 1940s—when the writer was received at the Maison Blanc, the Rev. Reuben Marc aiding conversation. Vincent befriended the Evangelicals.[19]

The Haitian Baptists, supported by American Baptists, predominated in Evangelical witness, and operated twenty-four churches with 7000 members.[20] A tremendous spiritual awakening had moved their constituency, taking on the real proportions of a folk movement.[21]

In 1926, the Cuban-based West Indies Mission followed repatriated Haitians back to Haiti, and were assigned the southwestern peninsula, of which the principal town is Aux Cayes. A remarkable awakening began, as many as 10,000 professing conversion, 5000 baptized as members in 1940. This movement brought problems, chiefly that of supplying pastors to the hundred congregations.[22] The Unevangelized Fields Mission faced much the same situation in the northwestern peninsula, where rapid growth also occurred.

The Church of God (Tennessee-based) sent Pentecostal missionaries to Haiti, but encountered the opposition of the Haitian government at first, thereafter experiencing a rapid growth due to the awakening and folk movement that added a total of approximately a hundred thousand to the several Protestant denominations.[23]

Two itinerant evangelists, Fred Clark and George Bell, whose trail of blessing may be found widely in the world, engaged in evangelism in Jamaica in 1927. Extraordinary scenes were witnessed at Brown's Town. No awakening of such depth and magnitude had been witnessed in the district since 1907—in the wake of the Welsh Revival—when the church was open every night for a year. Clark and Bell's meetings were undergirded by prayer meetings which drew from a dozen to a hundred and attendances rose to fourteen hundred, of whom a quarter professed faith.[24]

The population of Jamaica in the 1940s reached a million and a quarter, with less than two per cent European, two per cent Asian, a quarter of the remainder of mixed blood and three quarters black; and the literacy rate was fairly high. But one of the problems of Christian life in Jamaica concerned sanctity of marriage, for 70% of all children all over the island were born out of wedlock.[25] This problem, due to the inhumanity of slavery, has persisted wherever the plantations used a work force of slaves.[26]

The Jamaica Baptist Union served more than two hundred churches, with 24,000 communicant members and a community ten times as large, Jamaican Anglicans having a similar sized constituency.[27] Church memberships in the British West Indies declined during the World Wars' period, except for the growth of the Pentecostals, who experienced revival in the '40s.[28] The writer visited Trinidad's 'shouting Baptists,' a lively group with century-old exuberance.[29]

Tens of thousands of Jamaicans settled down in Panama. The population of Panama in 1940 was about half-a-million, 50% being mestizo, with 80,000 Europeans, 70,000 negroes, 20,000 mulattoes, and 40,000 Indians.[30] One priest for every 7000 faithful was provided by predominant Roman Catholics.

Baptists and Methodists had entered Panama in the early 1900s, other societies following, but in 1928 the Pentecostal Foursquare Church sent to Panama its first missionaries, the Edwards, who won a remarkable ingathering.[31]

In 1940, two thirds of a million people inhabited Costa Rica, a tenth of them in the capital, San Jose.[32] European stock accounted for 95% of the population, which was 75% literate; political life was more stable than prevailed elsewhere in Central America.[33] The people were predominantly of Roman Catholic faith, if not practice; one priest, usually Costa Rican, was provided for every 4000 faithful.[34]

Harry Strachan invited Angel Archilla to join with him in a campaign in Costa Rica during the early months of 1927. Not one theatre owner in the liberal city of San José would rent his premises, for fear of boycott.[35] Instead, a lumber yard provided a tabernacle seating up to a thousand people.

Intensive newspaper promotion had been planned, but it became utterly unnecessary as the clerical opposition went 'into top gear,' with newspaper articles and thousands of leaflets denouncing 'the execrable heretic.'[36] Costa Ricans became curious about such heresy, and one distinguished official attending a meeting declared: 'If this is heresy, then I too am a heretic, for I believe every word said.'[37]

To everyone's surprise, a militant priest offered to debate Angel Archilla, but backed down when the offer was accepted, and backed down again from debate in the press. Threats were made against the preacher's life.[38] Instead of a thousand, twelve hundred packed the tabernacle and the street was filled with those unable to get in. A crowd of roughs and a band of seminary students provoked an uproar in the streets, and Archilla barely escaped with his life.

Mounted police cleared the streets for further meetings and protected the Bible Institute by day. In spite of the risk of assault, the crowds increased and there was 'a gracious outpouring of the Spirit[39] . . . that changed hearts and lives.' Leaders sought no redress, but Costa Rica's President took vigorous action against the attackers, seeking to prevent a fanatical priesthood from hurting the good name of the little republic; for a while, the Evangelicals were left unharmed. More than five hundred inquirers were registered, including whole families, and both missions extended their premises.

In 1929, Templo Bíblico in San José was dedicated, the fruit of persecution and evangelism, and two months later (in July) Hospital Bíblico was opened also. In 1940, there were two thousand communicants in Protestant churches in Costa Rica, some congregations thriving in San José.[40]

The Latin America Mission reported Edwin Orr's tour of the West Indies, Central America, and Mexico in 1940, Harry Strachan noting: [41]

> Mr. Orr spent four days in Costa Rica. It was the privilege of the Bible Institute to entertain him while in San José, and we were repaid by very rich blessing resulting from his ministry amongst us. The Central American Mission, the Methodist Mission, and the Templo Bíblico shared Mr. Orr's public ministry of the Word, but the students and missionary body at the Bible Institute were greatly favoured with special talks. There has been no such moving of the Holy Spirit amongst us for a very long time past. The new students especially have experienced a time of great blessing. We feel that Mr. Orr's visit was in answer to prayer for just such a movement of the Holy Spirit amongst us and we are deeply grateful.

Roberto Elphick had joined Harry Strachan in 1924 for an evangelistic campaign in Nicaragua. After a stormy time in Matagalpa, they set up a great tent in Managua, drawing up to a thousand people nightly.[42] About fifty people publicly professed faith, twenty-five joining each congregation. A score of younger people undertook an evangelistic tour of the villages surrounding the capital, and returned rejoicing.

Strachan and Elphick campaigned next in León, where priestly threats of excommunication restricted attendances in the big tent.[43] The evangelists passed on to seven other Nicaraguan cities, using tents or theatres for meetings. In all, hundreds of inquirers waited for counsel.

In 1928, Harry Strachan and Sergio Alfaro commenced a campaign of evangelization in Nicaragua.[44] It added to the growth of the Evangelical churches in the republic, besides encouraging younger Latin American evangelists to extend the work in city and town.

During 1933, Joaquín Vela was busy in evangelism in the towns of Nicaragua.[45] He was arrested and held for four or five days without explanation. Then he was released, still without explanation of any kind, and permitted to leave the country. Evangelists were subject to unpredictable treatment of the sort, but vastly preferred it to martyrdom. In 1934, it was reported from Nicaragua that the response in recent evangelistic campaigns had been remarkable.[46]

Nicaraguans numbered a million in 1940, a tenth in the capital city, Managua.[47] A sixth of the population were of European stock, the vast majority mestizo. The Roman Catholic Church was separate from the state, yet received preferential treatment. Anastasio Somoza came to power in 1937, and remained in power until 1946—and afterwards. He was friendly to Evangelical workers, who helped take up the slack, for there was only one priest for every 4800 of the population.[48]

The Central American Mission, the Baptists, and the Assemblies of God maintained the Evangelical witness in Spanish-speaking society. Progress was still being made in Managua in 1935, when a Baptist church among Spanish-speaking folk had built up a membership of 400, a Sunday School of 425, and evening attendance of 600;[49] while among mixed blood (Indian, mestizo and mulatto) people in the east, a Moravian church served a membership of 800 English-speaking people.

El Salvador, the most densely populated country of the Central American area, possessed about a-million-and-a-half people, one fifth Indian, the majority mestizo. Roman Catholic bishops provided one priest for every 8000 faithful in the population.[50] While occasional upheavals occurred, conditions were better than in republics nearby, and the literacy rate was higher.

By 1929, the Assemblies of God adjoined the established Central American Mission in the country, where Baptists also pioneered a work.[51] When the writer preached in San Salvador in 1940, there were only five thousand members in the Evangelical churches in the country, but their spirit was good and their evangelism optimistic.

The inhabitants of the Republic of Honduras numbered a million, only 35,000 living in Tegucigalpa, the capital.[52] The Hondurans suffered much from political instability, with a surfeit of revolutions and dictatorships. Roman Catholics met with various restrictions, and supplied only one priest for every 9000 people, mostly poor and illiterate.[53]

In 1940, when the writer preached for the congregations of the Central American Mission and the Friends (planted by the California Yearly Meeting),[54] there were some six thousand Evangelical communicants in the country.

In Guatemala, across the border from Honduras, were the Friends of California. Quaker missionaries arrived in 1906, and experienced local quickenings until 1916, when membership increased to five hundred.[55] In 1918, an unusual burden of prayer fell upon the missionaries at Chiquimula, followed by a phenomenal outbreak among the nationals, in which the prayer continued until midnight. It was reported that 'It is heaven's own evangel. The revival is not of any personality, except that of the Holy Spirit.' 'The Spirit of Pentecost is here,' said the Californian missionaries.[56]

There were peculiar manifestations in the movement. Murderers, thieves, adulterers, liars and idolaters openly confessed their sin. There were visions, trances, dreams and revelations, and things 'not lawful to reveal.'[57]

This striking revival spread only to other churches of the Friends, which grew considerably during the next few years—to 1800 in 1921 and 2600 in 1926.[58] The movement was renewed in evangelism between 1930 and 1935. In 1940, when the writer visited the country, the work was steady.

Revolution in the Central American republics was not so violent as in Mexico; but Estrada Cabrera, the dictator of Guatemala from 1898 till 1920, was followed by eight other presidents in turn—often after a coup—in twenty-six years. Five per cent only of the population was European, 65% being Indian, 25% mestizo, the remainder negro. There was one priest for every 30,000 parishioners![59] Most of the clergy were foreigners, the government expelling the archbishop in 1922, and accepting a successor only in 1928.

In November of 1921, Harry Strachan and Juan Varetto began an evangelistic campaign in Guatemala City.[60] Teatro Europeo filling up with more than two thousand people, the alarmed Archbishop denounced the evangelists by pastoral letter and raised attendance to more than three thousand a night. The opposition continued.

As part of a deliberate policy, the evangelists avoided all controversy, preaching only simple truths of the Gospel. A leading newspaper took the Archbishop to task for saying that the messages were directed against the Catholic faith. Strachan asked his packed out audience if anyone had heard in the discourses any attack on the Roman Catholic Church, and no one responded;   he then asked all who had not heard any such attack to stand, and the vast assembly stood.[61]

The secret weapon of the campaign was prayer—early morning prayer meetings and meetings in homes. A goodly number professed a personal faith; a cordial spirit was exhibited by a widening circle; and clerical opposition grew. By the time the party reached the town of Amatitlan, a mob was gathered to wreck the meeting, the evangelists were assaulted, but a military escort enabled them to escape; the mob wrecked the local dam and robbed the town of light! In Quezaltenango, meetings were conducted in the Teatro Municipal and Teatro Zarco, attendances averaging 500, of whom fifty professed faith, a majority persevering.[62]

Cameron Townsend in 1927 noted that, in Nahuala and Ixtahaucan, 'Where mobs formerly gathered to kill, sympathetic crowds listen hungrily to the Word of Life.'[63] In the years following, energetic campaign were held.[64]

The Latin American evangelist, Joaquín Vela, engaged in three months of evangelism in Guatemala in 1932, with revival in the churches and hundreds of converts among the Christo-pagan populace.[65]

The Presbyterians, and Baptists, and Central American Mission (Iglesia Evangélica) extended their work throughout Guatemala, progress being made in evangelism and training an indigenous ministry, and translating Scripture. In 1937, Assemblies of God missionaries settled in the country, the indigenous Pentecostals linking up with them, the nationals predominating in the leadership of such churches.[66]

16

REVOLT AND REVIVAL IN MEXICO

Mexico's strongman, Porfirio Díaz, had ruled the nation for a third of a century when his forced departure from high office led to decades of revolutionary turmoil. Madero was followed by Huerta and Carranza in quick succession, and in 1917 a new constitution was promulgated which not only nationalized the nation's resources but also all places of worship, the clergy being denied the right to teach in public schools, to vote or hold office, or to criticize fundamental law, constituted authority, or government in general.[1]

Of course, the Roman Catholic hierarchy openly opposed the religious articles of the insurgent constitution. Some clerics were arrested and deported or imprisoned; others slipped into hiding to avoid arrest and fines for opposition; and churches were closed in many places. Violence erupted here and there against both clergy and the churches.[2]

From 1920 to 1924, Alvaro Obregon was president with dictatorial power, using it to introduce a kind of rural folk school throughout the countryside. The Roman opposition waxed violent. To rally support, the hierarchy built a great cenotaph to Cristo Rey at Guanajuato in 1923, and in 1924 convened a Eucharistic Congress.[3] Elías Calles in 1925 came into headlong collision with the Church as he ordered enforcement of the articles. Pope, archbishops, bishops and clergy offered opposition, so Calles ordered deportation of foreign clergy and closure of many monasteries. The hierarchy then suspended priestly services everywhere, but the government decreed re-opening of the churches under lay supervision. Open rebellion followed, as bishops were expelled for supporting the use of violence while others hid for fear, and several priests and lay leaders were slain. Alas, the violence and even murder which the Mexican local clergy had inflicted upon the helpless Evangelical minority for years was being returned upon their heads, not by the Protestants,[4] but by leaders of the raging Mexican masses. Obregon, succeeding Calles, was assassinated in 1928 by a pro-Church gunman, and counter-violence intensified.[5]

What of the Evangelicals meanwhile? The Revolution was not anti-Evangelical at first, Carranza (for instance) showing an interest in their schools, but the Evangelicals suffered in the general turmoil. Nevertheless, they grew, total membership in 1916 being more than twenty thousand and in 1946 two hundred thousand.[6]

When revolution burst upon the country, Evangelicals took it as a sign that God was calling them to increased activity, but conditions worsened before they improved, for while in 1910 there had been three hundred missionaries in Mexico, by 1916 threats to life and property had reduced the number to thirty. Many buildings were destroyed, and believers scattered in all directions. Yet as early as 1917, the American Bible Society reported much success in Bible distribution,[7] now guaranteed a freedom of dissemination. By 1918, the churches told of great desire to hear the Word, and many congregations reached full autonomy.

The Mexican believers met the 1920s with a movement to prayer. Evangelicals of all denominations participated. By 1921, the Mexican Methodists reported a 40% increase in membership.[8] They organized more than two hundred weekly meetings for prayer, attended by half the members; In Mexico City alone, there were sixty prayer meetings.

Not only in the city, but in the country there was prayer. The southernmost state of the Mexican Union, Chiapas, was 92% illiterate in the 1920s, 80% of its inhabitants being pure blooded Indians, a majority of whom could not speak Spanish. San Cristóbal, at 8000 feet, with 14,000 people, was served by a score of churches and priests. This was the seat of Bartoloméo de las Casas,[9] and the religious life seemed much superior to that of nearby communities.

In 1910, there had been only six hundred Protestants in the state, half of them Germans and other foreigners. But in 1913, colporteurs from Guatemala distributed Scriptures and converts to Evangelicalism in other parts of Mexico returned to their birthplace. A spontaneous folk movement began, congregations springing up all over the state, more especially in the Soconusco area. They appealed for help, but no missionaries were able to visit them.[10]

When Don José Coffín, a Mexican pastor of gringo blood, came to investigate, he found a field ripe for the harvest. In a single month, he baptized more than four hundred adults. He settled down in Tapachula,[11] but the congregations here and there used elected elders to conduct their services.

There was a revival in Tampico, in the coastal state of Tamaulipas, where Associate Reformed Presbyterians had returned in 1919 to find their work almost totally destroyed. By prayer, preaching, testimony and Scripture distribution, they rekindled the flames,[12] reporting that 'a pentecost of great power' had swept the constituency.

Examples could be multiplied from all over the country. In 1925, there were local revivals in villages in the state of Oaxaca.[13] In one, a group of twenty-five met at 5.30 a.m. for prayer, kneeling on the hard dirt floor. By the end of the week, more than a hundred and fifty were attending the Evangelical services, and the church continued to grow.

The converted Jew, A. B. de Roos, organized a prayer fellowship to undergird efforts to reach the unevangelized multitudes of Mexico and Central America, especially the unreached Indian tribes.[14] Everywhere, a greater concern for the Indians was developing among Evangelicals.

By mid-1920s, Evangelical observers were proclaiming that Mexico was enjoying 'a great spiritual awakening,'[15] in part due to the fever of the times, but wholly undergirded by the widespread concert of prayer.

After World War I, the depletion of the American work force brought to the United States increasing numbers of Mexicans, until by 1930 nearly two million legal and illegal immigrants were found on American soil.[16] Fewer than one in eighty 'Chicanos' professed an evangelical faith, but as home missionaries developed interest in their religious and social needs, numbers turned to a more vital faith than they had known, and communicated it south of the border.

By the end of the decade, Samuel G. Inman, secretary of the Committee on Cooperation in Latin America, noted:[17]

> The recent celebration of the 1900th anniversary of Pentecost has brought some splendid spiritual results to Protestantism in Mexico. All of the churches had special retreats, sunrise meetings, and Bible studies for weeks before the day itself and a month after the celebration many of these meetings were continued as revival services. Large numbers were brought into church membership and ministers and members alike have had profound religious experiences.

Thus by the turn of the 1930s, Evangelical Christianity in Mexico claimed more than a hundred thousand members and adherents, and its influence was far greater than what its numerical strength suggested.[18]

The eye of the storm brought a temporary calm, for a truce of sorts prevailed in Portes Gil's administration, permitting priests to exercise their priestly functions and allowing spiritual instruction with the churches' walls. But Portes Gil pushed his land reforms and helped the cause of temperance, and offered aid to working men.[19]

Then the storm broke in renewed fury. From 1929 to 1932, Rubio and Rodriguez further repressed the clergy, only two hundred being allowed to minister in all of Mexico in 1933.[20] Then in 1934, Lazaro Cardenas came to power, carrying out the projects of the revolution, tightening up the interdiction of religious schools, and nationalizing every building used for religious purposes; the hierarchy seemed helpless in the face of such repression.

When, in the 1930s, the new outbreak of anti-clericalism aimed at eliminating the influence of the Roman Catholic Church from the life of the state intensified, all churches, including Evangelicals, suffered in the attack on religion, as speakers at the convention of the National Revolutionary Party shouted, 'Down with religion! Down with God!'[21] In 1935, as spiritual conflict was being waged in Mexico, the aggressive atheism broadcast daily over the radio was both blasphemous and deadly in its purpose.[22] Children in public schools were being taught to march to the tune of 'Uno, dos, no hay Dios' — 'one, two, there is no God.'

Prof. Gonzalo Báez Camargo, secretary of the National Council of Evangelical Churches of Mexico, noted several benefits to Evangelicalism in the organized agitation of the State against the Church.[23] Evangelical churches were beginning to experience a spiritual revival, quiet and steady, with much emphasis on united prayer, a meeting for prayer attended by all Evangelical pastors being held each week day at 6.30 a.m. in Mexico City. Under current restriction, greater unity and closer cooperation was manifested, and less time was spent in organizational business; laymen and women were more and more participating and young people were taking over more responsibility.

The movement to prayer spread all over the country. As turmoil continued, despite the opposition, congregations thrived in the awakening. For example, a Baptist church in Monterrey in 1935 was reporting revival and resurgence of vital evangelism, 'wonderful spiritual services, brimful attendance at every meeting.'[24] The prayer meeting and the evangelistic service were commonplace.

Captain Norman W. Taylor, an American Presbyterian, initiated a new venture in evangelizing Mexican soldiers in roadside camps.[25] In 1934, visits to four regiments resulted in the sale of Scriptures and the professed conversion of more than 800 officers and men; within two years, the work among Mexican military personnel had produced more than 1200 public professions of faith; after five years, Taylor had reached two-score regiments of the Mexican Army with the Word, and many hundreds had professed faith in Christ.

During the middle 1930s, Col. Rodolfo Curti professed conversion.[26] A protege of President Calles, he reorganized the police force in Mexico City, and was in charge of the Federal District division which took over the churches and placed them in the hands of committees of ten from each church. Converted through a dream, he became a member of Gante Methodist Church, witnessing to the upper ranks of the Mexican military while Norman Taylor worked among the enlisted men. After retirement, Colonel Curti became active in the Gideons of Mexico.

Norman Taylor's work among Mexican soldiers went on for more than a dozen years.[27] He visited barracks and outposts from north to south and from Baja California to the Yucatan peninsula. Often, commanding generals requested a visit because it was obvious that converted soldiers were better men in every way. To avoid opposition from Roman Catholic clergy, Taylor worked without publicity. In 1944, when he tried to present every soldier with a New Testament bearing a dedicatory note from the Chief of Staff, the Roman Catholic press denounced the work. President Cardenas requested the sponsors to stop the distribution, then told the press that no Protestant work was being done among Mexican troops. For many years to come, soldiers were found who still carried and read their New Testaments.

For nearly a year, the group of Evangelical pastors and missionaries in Mexico City met each morning at 6.30 a.m. for intercession.[28] They were wrestling with principalities and powers and refused to be discouraged. They prayed for revival and for restraint of revolutionary wrath.

Suddenly the tide turned.[29] The most radical members of the Mexican cabinet were dismissed, and a steady shifting of the wind followed. The Bible Society concluded its best year to date in 1937. The Y.M.C.A. reported a most fruitful twelve months, and pastors, missionaries, colporteurs and workers of every kind rejoiced in increased opportunity.

The door to preaching had been closed in the Federal Prison. After much prayer, a case was presented to the District authorities and orders were issued which allowed the workers to return, hundreds in the prison professing faith in Christ.[30] Bible classes were organized in four fire stations in the District. A government inspector began to witness to the 'down-and-outs' in the worst section of the city; without knowledge of the Salvation Army, Sr. Guzman trained a team of Christian soldiers and worked so well that the Salvation Army adopted them officially.[31]

The intercession of many months had as its main object a spiritual revival in Mexico.[32] Its intercessors were fully convinced that the wind of such a revival had begun to blow. Reports of revival increased in number— Chiapas, Oaxaca, Tamaulipas, Yucatán, Tabasco, Vera Cruz, Tampico, and the Federal District. From fifty thousand in 1936, the total number enrolled in Mexican Evangelical churches advanced to a quarter of a million by 1946. In the membership were many functionaries for, every six months for ten years, all mayors, municipal secretaries, school teachers, railway agents, and the like, had received literature by mail, postpaid, dispatched at great sacrifice of time and money by an ardent team of postal evangelists.[33]

Dr. Walter Montano, converted priest from Peru, began a visit to Mexico in 1938 with a cordial welcome from its chief of state, President Cardenas.[34] Prof. Báez Camargo prepared a month's evangelistic meetings. Montano held a week of meetings in a former Franciscan monastery leased by the Government to the Presbyterian Church in Mexico, and the thousand attending soon became fifteen hundred. A hundred penitents came forward for counsel during the final meeting in Mexico City.

United meetings were also held in Puebla, and large numbers were won to Christ. In Vera Cruz, the church was filled, as was later the platform space also with inquirers. Importuned for another meeting, Montano jokingly suggested 4.30 next morning, and was taken at his word. The hall in Orizaba was overcrowded with fourteen hundred people and the street outside was full; this was followed by a 5 a.m. meeting with six hundred early risers. In Mexico City, two thousand young people gathered for a rally. Successful work was done in Guadalajara, Aguas Calientes, San Luis Potosí, Saltillo, Torreón, Juárez and Nogales, and in the Mexican barrios in cities of the United States.[36]

The Pentecostals were beginning to develop as a force. The first Pentecostal missionary had arrived in Mexico in 1915: Cesareo Burciaga,[37] converted in Houston in Texas, founded the first Pentecostal assembly in Ciudad Musquiz. In 1921, a Pentecostal assembly was begun in Mexico City, the Assemblies of God in Mexico registered in the 1930s. A period of rapid growth followed in the 'thirties and 'forties, promising much for the future.

In 1940, Manuel Camacho succeeded to the presidency. He declared himself 'a believer,' and allowed restrictions, though not repealed, to fall away. In 1945, the Roman Catholic Church acclaimed its reestablished freedom—by stationing a jeweled crown upon the head of the statue of the dark Virgin of Guadelupe, so long an object of superstitious reverence.[38] Despite the Roman Catholic renewal, there was only one priest for every 4500 faithful.[39]

In mid-1940, the Irish evangelist, J. Edwin Orr, held a campaign in Mexico City, commencing in Central Baptist Church, and continuing in other denominational temples. In a single meeting in the Gante Templo Methodista, Vicente Mendoza pastor, there were 105 penitents counselled, and two months later,[40] 94 new members were received upon profession of faith, while 22 couples who had lived without recognition by church or state were married officially. It may be assumed that such results were typical of Mexico in the wake of the Awakening.

17

POST WORLD WAR II AWAKENING

The end of hostilities and return of fighting men from the battlefields of Europe, Asia, Africa, and the islands of the seas preceded another evangelical awakening affecting many, but by no means all of the countries of Evangelical Christendom.

China, which had experienced a nation-wide movement between 1927 and 1939, was suddenly closed to missionary effort by the Communist takeover of the country, and the witness of the national churches was first restricted and then practically obliterated by Communist repression.[1]

There was very little revival in 'tired old Europe'— some of whose countries were desolated by the ravages of war, others exhausted by the struggle for survival and the loss of empire, and others cramped by the unfriendliness of post-war dictatorships. One exception was the startling revival in the Hebrides of Scotland, phenomenal in effects but limited to the Gaelic-speaking islands community.[2]

But a resurgence of evangelical activity took place in Japan during General MacArthur's occupation.[3] And in 1947 a remarkable revival began in the Communist capital of North Korea, spreading to the south just before Communist armies invaded South Korea.[4] In Taiwan and Hong Kong, an acceleration of evangelization occurred.[5]

Freedom brought a blood-letting to people of the Indian sub-continent, but varied were the movements of revival and evangelism in the 1950s, usually national in origin and scope but often triggered by acceptable overseas visitors.[6]

In Africa, the missionaries returned to Ethiopia to find that less than fifty Wallamo believers under persecution had become ten thousand.[7] The 1950s brought expansion to the East African Revival movement, which not only survived the Mau Mau terror, but grew rapidly in Uganda, Kenya and Tanganyika,[8] overflowing into the Congo and the Sudan, so much so that the East African communicant membership and community of adherents doubled to 300,000 and 600,000, capturing the leadership of the Anglican communion.

There were revival-awakenings in the Congo, followed by a blood-letting in the 'sixties in which the churches gave evidence of the reality of their profession.[9] Farther south, there were advances in Zambia and a resurgence of vital evangelism in South Africa, especially in the ministry of Nicholas Bhengu.

In West Africa, indigenous revival movements were reported from Nigeria and Ghana, followed by evangelization of the masses.[10] The 1960s saw an expansion of evangelism in West Africa.

In Madagascar, yet another evangelical awakening began in 1946, under Rakotozandry.[11] Vast people movements began in primitive New Guinea, east and west.[12] The influx of many former soldiers returned to the Philippines as missionaries accelerated the work of evangelism there.[13] In Indonesia, the continuing struggle for freedom delayed the outbreak of widespread movements of revival and awakening until the 1960s, when they attracted world attention.[14]

Strange to relate, missionary experts—particularly in the historic denominations—allowed themselves to predict that the Christian faith was entering on a period of serious recession.[15] It proved to be otherwise, the post-war period becoming, in the words of Prof. Ralph Winter, 'the twenty-five unbelievable years' of advance, not everywhere, but in the most unlikely places.[16]

At the turn of the twentieth century, T. B. Wood had predicted the coming of 'great sweeping revivals' to Latin America.[17] Now, after fifty years, this prophecy was about to be fulfilled in a way that few had dreamed of— and much of the impetus came from the 1949 Revival in California.[18]

As early as 1941, a Missouri Lutheran ordained pastor, Armin Richard Gesswein, moved to Los Angeles to begin a ministry of encouraging pastors to pray for genuine revival —which he had seen in Norway in 1937.[19] At Eastertime in 1949, this ministry had become so successful that when the conference was addressed by Harold Ockenga and Edwin Orr, there were three hundred ministers and their wives continuing in penitence and prayer after midnight.[20]

There followed a series of revivals in Christian colleges throughout North America, capturing the attention of the secular press by their intensity.[21] An extraordinary revival movement occurred at a Christian conference for college students at Forest Home in California's San Bernardino Mountains, addressed by Billy Graham and Edwin Orr.[22]

Not only the students but the speakers were moved in the late-summer awakening, for it was here that Billy Graham received an immediate call to his worldwide ministry and entered upon a quarter-century of successful evangelism.[23]

Out of that revival came the ministry of William Bright, who shortly afterwards founded Campus Crusade for Christ which supplemented the ministry of Intervarsity Christian Fellowship, itself experiencing a resurgence of power.[24] At the same time was founded World Vision, with its outreach of evangelism and social service.

Throughout the United States and Canada, there was a reviving and an awakening in those times,[25] designated by Prof. Martin E. Marty as the revival of 'the Eisenhower years.' As early as 1950, David du Plessis reported to the organ of the world Pentecostal movement: [26]

> There is a revival in North America . . . It can be truthfully said that there is not a single Christian movement that is not experiencing a greater and more spontaneous interest in their work than has been known during the first half of this century.

This of course was written by Du Plessis long before he commenced his 'charismatic' witness in the churches of the historic denominations. An Intervarsity editorial added: [27]

> One must go back to the late nineteenth century to find any mass evangelistic appeal comparable to the continually expanding ministry of Billy Graham. Yet in addition to this meteorite there are many others— Hicks, Rosell, Vaus, Orr, Shuler, to name just a few— who have probably surpassed any records except Billy Sunday's between the two World Wars.

The outstanding development of the mid-century revival was the emergence of Billy Graham as a world evangelist in the tradition of Whitefield, Finney and Moody. His great campaigns of evangelization broke all records in reaching a vast number of human beings with the Good News of Christ preached in ever so simple terms.

There were other developments. The movement of the 1950s raised up a host of evangelists who practised a ministry of healing as well as of evangelism.[28] Their work was supported by the steadily growing Pentecostal churches and by many in the other denominations. Unfortunately, these evangelists were seldom subject to the necessary discipline of denominational or interdenominational approval.

Some of these independent evangelists maintained a high standard of ethical conduct, and retained the respect of the Christian public at large—in the case of Oral Roberts even generating much greater goodwill; but others were involved in scandals so serious that the public, the evangelical constituency, and the Pentecostal denominations themselves regarded them as scoundrels.[29]

From the ranks of the evangelists of the general revival of 1949 onwards came several who made an impact upon Latin America; from the ranks of the healing-evangelists came several who rode in upon a second wave and preached sensationally to even vaster crowds in the Republics. Cuba proved to be an exception, chronologically.

Meanwhile the first wave of revival—more conventional and less sensational—was being quietly generated. In 1950, Kenneth Strachan, a worthy son of the great evangelist of Latin America in the 'twenties and 'thirties, announced that he and his associates were more convinced than ever that a movement of revival and evangelism was the answer to the need and the opportunity in Latin America. Correspondence with the writer showed that the mid-century awakening to the north had provoked the rising expectations of revival.[30]

Carlos Hahn, in Brazil a well-known professor with an evangelistic missionary experience in several continents, noted in a British periodical of the early 'fifties that, for a long time, evangelism in the Latin American countries had been very slow work carried on in the face of the opposition of a reactionary Romanism, indifferent intellectualism, and superstitious spiritism. To his way of thinking, a change began in 1951. Many missionaries and some national leaders had been praying for a new thing to happen in Latin America —revival. In 1951, the seeds sown in many places, stated Hahn, received a sprinkling of water:[30]

> Edwin Orr, the Irish evangelist, regarded as eccentric by some but as theocentric by others, suddenly left the movement of revival in California, and started a tour of the South American republics, trusting God for his day-to-day supplies as well as travel expenses. To all and sundry, he announced a message from God —to prepare for a revival in Latin America. With significant strategy, he visited the Spanish Language School for Missionaries in San Jose, Costa Rica, and the Portuguese Language School for Missionaries in Campinas in Brazil.

Kenneth Strachan and his associates in 1951 reported the visit of an old friend to San José, one more aware of 'leading' than 'strategy': [31]

> First stop on the current Latin American itinerary of Dr. J. Edwin Orr, Irish-American evangelist, was San Jose, Costa Rica, in late July. Dr. Orr stayed a week in the city, holding at least three meetings a day, and brought a foretaste of revival to the missionaries and language students there. Although Dr. Orr was entertained by the Latin American Mission, all evangelical groups in the city cooperated in the meetings, and missionaries came from as far as the Atlantic coast.

Carlos Hahn,[32] writing with the benefit of perspective of events in 1952 but none of Evangelism in Depth, observed:

> ... In San José, there was an extraordinary revival among the young missionaries soon to scatter all over the Spanish-speaking republics. So impressed by this movement was the Rev. Kenneth Strachan of the Latin American Mission in Costa Rica that he left his responsibilities as director and made a tour with Dr. Orr around the continent, one man concentrating upon one country, the other upon another. Out of Mr. Strachan's tour grew the great evangelistic campaigns of the Latin American Team in Trinidad, Venezuela, Colombia and the Central American countries in extraordinary blessing in 1952. Out of Dr. Orr's tour grew the current Revival movement in Brazil.

A godly woman, of German-Brazilian stock, married to a brilliant lawyer, attended the Ridout meetings, her older daughter being cared for at home by her husband while she brought her infant daughter with her. When an invitation was given, she went forward, much to the surprise of Dr. Ridout, who recognized her as a devoted Christian. If it was not for salvation or assurance, he asked, what was the object of her seeking? Dona Else de Magalhães Lima said simply, 'I long for the reviving of Brazil. But what can I do, only a home maker? Here, take my baby, and pray that God may use her for the reviving of Brazil!' For a score of years, Dona Else became noted for her prayers for revival. Her younger daughter, named Silvia, recalled nothing of the incident—but that is another story, belonging to the nationwide movement of the 1950s.

18

REAVIVAMENTO EVANGÉLICO BRASILEIRO

The whole of this chapter, for obvious reasons of equity, is presented in the already published words of Dr. Rodolfo Anders, secretary general of the Evangelical Confederation of Brazil, and of other observers as specified, with only occasional changes of tense and interweaving of words to make sense and rhythm in a multigraphic narrative.

In the 1930 Census, 69,527 Brazilians described themselves as Evangelicals; in 1950, 1,657,524; and within two years, the Evangelical constituency passed the 2,000,000 mark.[1] Communicant church membership exceeded half a million, as did the number attending Sunday School, so that the number of Brazilian practising Evangelicals exceeded one million, compared with five million practising Roman Catholics. For twenty years, Evangelicals had increased twelve times as fast as the population.

There were already more Brazilian Evangelical pastors and evangelists than Brazilian Roman Catholic priests, supplemented by thousands of foreign R.C. missionaries. Brazilian Baptists (for an example) had more than 120,000 members in 1953, with 120 Baptist churches in metropolitan Rio de Janeiro alone and churches in Rio and São Paulo seating 5000. Reformed and Presbyterian Churches also had more than 120,000 members, Igreja Unida in São Paulo having two thousand members.[2] There were Lutheran congregations with a thousand families. Anglicans, Brethren, Congregationalists, Methodists and Salvationists had flourishing causes. About 1950, according to the missiologist, Dr. W. R. Read, there were 132,000 in the Italo-Brazilian Christian Congregation (Pentecostal), and approximately 200,000 members in the Assemblies of God in Brazil.[3]

All this resulted from ninety years of steady evangelization within the country, faithful missionaries and national pastors planting small churches here and there. But, for the first time in Brazilian history, 1952 brought a general spiritual revival affecting the churches everywhere, and better things seemed to be in prospect.[4]

Rodolfo Anders was not alone in thus assessing the state of the Evangelical enterprise. The Bible Societies, British and American, reported that while the economic situation in Brazil continued to deteriorate during 1952, and the cost of living rose steadily, 'it was a year of triumph' ... 'for it marked the largest distribution of Scriptures in the century old history of Bible distribution in Brazil'— 1,510,712 in 1951; 1,628,058 in 1952; 1,373,220 in 1953; 1,546,201 in 1954.[5] The Brazilian Bible Society explained 1952 further:

While most of the growth of the evangelical movement could be attributed to the day-by-day witness of its members, special efforts also drew the attention of the people. In a nationwide evangelistic crusade that crossed denominational lines and drew the interest of the multitudes, a special evangelistic team went from center to center calling for repentance and dedication to Christ. Time and time again, the largest auditoriums could not seat the thousands who came to hear the gospel, and hundreds upon hundreds came forward accepting Christ as their Saviour. Some there were who compared this movement with the great nation-wide revivals which laid the foundation for the Protestant growth in the United States, and there was a strong feeling that 1952 had been a crucial hour of victory in the winning of Brazil to Christ. So wrote the senior missionary.[6]

The international and world missionary reviews also— representing ecumenical and evangelical constituencies— cited the evangelistic campaigns which stimulated churches of all denominations, the movements after the campaigns often more fruitful than the campaigns themselves.[7]

In 1951, an unknown evangelist visited Brazil, an unusual combination of zeal and scholarship.[8] His was a prophetic message, telling the churches to prepare for Revival, a phenomenon Brazilians had read about without experiencing. Response was immediate. In São Paulo, for example, eighty churches commenced weekly prayer meetings for Revival.

The Centenary Commission of the Presbyterian Churches of Brazil—and of the United States—sensing the impending start of a real movement beyond its previous experience, hurriedly cabled Dr. Orr to return to instruct the Brazilian ministers in evangelistic methods.[9] With a truly catholic spirituality, they left the Evangelist free to work with Evangelicals of all persuasions, turning over the direction of local campaigns to committees of pastors designated the Reavivamento Espiritual Brasileiro.

Because of his ignorance of the language, it was thought that Dr. Orr's ministry would be restricted to meetings for pastors and seminaries.[10] This was changed, for in his first public meeting in São Paulo, more than a hundred in a congregation of three hundred publicly professed conversion. In the thus extended ministry of reviving the churches and evangelizing the masses, God raised up a young lady, Dona Sylvia Lima, to become Dr. Orr's interpreter, the most brilliant in the. experience of the Evangelical Confederation.

Brazil is much larger than the United States, possessing then a population exceeding fifty-three million. Within 1952, Dr. Orr visited all twenty states and all four territories of Brazil, outdistancing any missionary or national evangelist on record.[11] He traveled forty thousand kilometers (about twenty-five thousand miles) chiefly by plane.

Dr. Walter Ermel, of the São Paulo Faculty of Theology, reported to the religious press that the presidents of three seminaries there announced spiritual awakenings among their students, the most striking movement being in the Methodist Seminary, where there were tears, reconciliations and much prayer.[12] There was a similar response in the meetings for ministers.

Campaigns were also conducted in the interior of the State.[13] All the churches in Baurú cooperated in the revival movement, during which a hundred and fifty professed faith in one week of the campaign with Orr and his colleague, the Rev. William Dunlap of California, the main speaker.

In Campinas, in spite of obstacles, there were many blessings, with one of the largest churches in the city filled to overflowing for a 6 a.m. prayer meeting and attendances of two thousand people each night at the Municipal Theatre to hear the Rev. Antônio Elias, Prof. Elmir dos Santos, Dr. Gióia Martins and Dr. Edwin Orr preach the Gospel to the greatest gatherings of Evangelicals in seventy-five years of witness in Campinas.[14]

In Sorocaba there was a similar response, Dunlap and Orr preaching to standing-room-only crowded churches, concluding with a rally in the Municipal Theatre.[15] There were many conversions in these provincial towns.

During the closing weeks of May, Orr and his colleagues (Dunlap, a Presbyterian, Carl Hahn, a Methodist, and Don Phillips, a Baptist) preached simultaneously in the largest Baptist, Methodist, Presbyterian and Independent churches in São Paulo, in which city a thousand professed faith.[16]

In Belo Horizonte, Mrs. Rosalee Mills Appleby wielded a state-wide and nation-wide ministry through inspirational and devotional writing. In her own home, she maintained a thriving preaching point besides doing personal evangelism as a member of a local Baptist church.[17] Dona Rosalee— like Dona Else Lima—was known throughout Brazil as a woman of prayer, and both women carried a burden for revival in the Brazilian churches.

Prof. Alberto Mazoni Andrade of the University of Minas Gerais reported the movement in Belo Horizonte, the State capital.[18] All Orr's meetings were attended by packed out congregations, final meetings being held at the Auditorium of the Secretariat of Welfare and Health, all two thousand seats occupied. His address in the Municipal Park attracted thousands. The number of decisions was extraordinary in a city where people by temperament shied away from public demonstrations. Among hundreds of inquirers were self-described Roman Catholics, spiritists, and agnostics.

A retreat for missionaries, pastors and evangelists at Patrocínio brought a thorough awakening which invaded all the fields of the Mission.[19] In Gammon Institute in Lavras, where early morning prayer meetings and evening mass meetings were directed by Dr. José Borges dos Santos, 120 students professed conversion.

The Presbyterian leader, Dr. Synval Moraes, reported that in the mining city of Governador Valadares the evening meetings became so large that they had to be held in the open air in a sports field, believers bringing their own chairs. Aggregate attendance exceeded ten thousand in six weeknights, and 6 a.m. prayer meetings grew until they too were held in the open air. Not only were sinners converted and believers transformed, but a serious breach between churches was healed.[20] Conversions continued after Orr's departure eastward.

More than a thousand people heard Orr's opening address in Presidente Soares in the College Auditorium; there were 209 conversions in the first two days.[21] By the third night, attendances exceeded the town's population as busloads and truckloads of people augmented meetings until the street was blocked, people sitting on roofs of buses and balconies of houses opposite. The climax occurred on Thursday night when the street was filled with three thousand kneeling people who then filled every church in town until a late hour when they came back to the auditorium for praise till midnight.

Dr. Carlos J. Hahn, afterward a professor at Campinas, who had been released from his work of directing the Inter-American Missionary Society in Brazil in order to travel in preparation ahead of the Reavivamento team, reported that late in July the Orr party made a wide sweep, west, north, east, and south, ten thousand miles around Brazil's perimeters.[22]

William Dunlap, John Savage, and Edwin Orr preached in the inland state of Goias, the first named in Goiânia and Uberlândia, while the others tackled Anápolis, where the auditorium of the Central Christian Church was filled each morning at 6.30 a.m. and the Spirit of God operated in the hearts of the people because of fervent prayer.[23] Dr. James Fanstone of the Evangelical Hospital secured an auditorium where about a fifth of those attending professed conversion, generally nominal Roman Catholics.[24] The Baptists, led by James Musgrave, extended their evangelism for a year, and the Presbyterians rejoiced that their congregation in Anápolis was literally 'bustin' out all over' ! [25]

In Campo Grande in the remote state of Mato Grosso, revival meetings were held in the large Baptist Church, which welcomed a hundred converts, while the Presbyterian Church of seventy members received thirty-two professing faith in Christ, twenty-nine restorations or reaffirmations, fourteen volunteering for Christian service.[26] In the same state, the campaign in Cuiabá, South America's geographic center, proved very difficult at first, but the concluding meetings were fraught with power.[27] In retrospect, the local Presbyterians reported that 132 of those professing faith had been truly converted. The Presbyterian membership in the Mato Grosso increased very considerably.[28]

Crossing the remotest jungles of Mato Grosso and upper Amazônia, the Orr team preached in Manaus, a thousand miles up the Amazon. All the Evangelical churches united in meetings which moved to the great Teatro Amazonas—an opera house built in rubber-boom days—and filled it, a goodly number of people professing repentance.[29]

William Dunlap had visited the city of Belém at the wide mouth of the Amazon, but found the churches apathetic in spirit. After Hahn's visit, when Orr arrived, not only the Baptist pastors and missionaries but the Pentecostal folk cooperated with the other denominations.[30] Orr preached in the historic Assembly of God. His meetings began in the First Baptist Church but soon moved to Teatro da Paz.

The meetings in Fortaleza, capital of the State of Ceará, began in the First Baptist Church, but as crowds of three thousand gathered in the open air, the venue shifted from the Presbyterian Church to the Assembly of God, with two thousand attending.[31] It became necessary to hire Teatro Alencar, and three thousand attended nightly. Again, though the ministry was aimed at believers, there were many who professed faith for the first time.

Evangelicals in Recife, especially the Presbyterians, had been divided by a fundamentalist-modernist uproar.[32] A local Presbyterian minister had announced publicly that he would resist Orr's work—it was whispered that Orr was a Jesuit in disguise. On Saturday afternoon, no arrangements had been made for meetings, but on Sunday the evangelist spoke in eight different temples, concluding in an Assembly of God at 11 p.m. The opposing minister changed his mind and opened his church, and soon it was filled nightly with two thousand people, while the evangelist also ministered in another church each evening. So great was the revival in churches and seminary that Orr was prevailed upon to return in November. Dr. Munguba Sobrinho cabled Rio:[33]

> Dr. Orr has concluded his second great campaign in
> Recife in Capunga Church and in the American Baptist
> College with attendances of 2000 and many decisions.

A Congregationalist girl made notes of all the messages, and returned to her native city, João Pessoa, where she transmitted the teaching in the Congregational Church and in classes, and a spiritual revival began.[34]

Orr could not resist a change of plans to visit Campina Grande in the State of Paraíba, where the Congregational Church was maintaining a 5 a.m. prayer meeting with 200 on weekdays and 500 on Sundays. Missing a night's sleep, he preached four times on a day-off there, sleeping between meetings. The prayer increased the local revival.[35]

The meetings in Salvador, capital of Bahia, began with a huge rally in the main Praça, Italian Franciscan priests ringing the bells of nine historic churches to drown out the preaching.[36] None of the churches could accommodate the crowds, hence the auditorium of the Normal College was presented by the State Governor. Baptists (all seven of the churches), Presbyterians, Independents, Methodists, and Pentecostals cooperated. The 6 a.m. prayer meetings were crowded, and 'there was real revival in Salvador.'[37]

There were fifteen Evangelical churches in Vitória in the State of Espírito Santo, in which state the Evangelicals numbered nearly ten per cent of the population. Meetings began in the Presbyterian Church, so full that people stood inside and out, in doorways and outside windows.[38] Workers met in a Methodist Church. Then First and Central Baptist Churches with larger auditoriums were filled, and meetings moved to Teatro Glória where the crowds so increased that it was said that neither political rallies nor spectacles of art had drawn such multitudes.

In Cachoeiro do Itapemirim, the campaign was supported by the four Baptist churches, the Presbyterian, Methodist and Assembly of God churches, besides a score of pastors. The meetings were held in the Big Tent of the Bartoli Circus with hundreds of extra chairs added.[39] Daily meetings were held for pastors; the 6 a.m. prayer meeting filled the local churches. The degree of interdenominational cooperation surpassed anything ever known in the State, and again many decisions were made, adding significantly to membership in the churches.

The most fruitful campaign in the series seemed to be one held in Niterói, across the bay from Rio de Janeiro, the home of Dona Else Lima, the woman of prayer, and of David Glass, Anglo-Brazilian son of a famous pioneer. A beginning was made in the Municipal Theatre, overcrowded from the first night. As the crowds increased, the janitor called the police to seek help in expelling the hundreds of people overtaxing the capacity of the place. The chief of police inquired the nature of the gathering and, when told that they were Evangelicals, replied: 'Don't worry. These people are orderly. Nothing will happen.'[40]

Another five hundred, unable to gain admittance, were directed to the Fluminense Evangelical Church where they waited till 9.30 p.m. for Orr and Antônio Elias to address them. David Glass reported that never in the history of Niterói had such meetings been held, nor had the various denominations ever been so united in spirit.

Orr was dumbfounded when, arriving in Rio de Janeiro, he found that nothing had been done during five months set aside for preparation.[41] Lauro Bretones deemed it due to irresponsible procrastination and incredible pride of place. The meetings began in the Presbyterian Cathedral, moved to Meier Baptist Church and Colégio Bennett, and began to increase in attendance and impact.

There followed campaigns in Londrina and Curitiba in the State of Paraná. In Curitiba, the capital, the Anglican, Baptist, Congregationalist, Lutheran, Methodist, Mennonite, Pentecostal, Presbyterian and Salvationist congregations cooperated. 'The churches had been praying for revival,' reported a Scottish missionary, 'and last week the Divine breath came from heaven.'[42] The largest church was filled, and hundreds had to stand. Not only was there revival, but the movement among outsiders was profound and real, for on the first night there were fifty seekers for salvation, on the last night more than sixty. Again the secret lay in the 6.30 a.m. prayer meetings. John Savage followed up.

In Pôrto Alegre, Rio Grande do Sul, although six months notice had been given, there was neither committee, nor publicity, nor a place of meeting designated, and there was no spiritual preparation of believers.[43] Derly Chaves, state deputy and a Methodist minister, threw himself into the breach and a start was made in Central Methodist Church, from which the meetings grew.

Throughout these campaigns, the interpreter for Edwin Orr was Sylvia Lima, whose gift amazed not only the local pastors but governors of states in attendance. Her usual interpretation was exquisite in effectiveness.[44] Although far from robust, she endured the hardships of travel in difficult places. Pôrto Alegre was the last campaign of the series, and there she met a Methodist engineer, Samuel Torres, married him, and made her home in the southern city.

William Dunlap conducted many campaigns in Brazil— twenty as compared with Orr's thirty. Carlos Hahn, the missionary forerunner, became a professor in Campinas Theological Seminary. Don Phillips, another colleague in the movement, served many years in Brazil's Youth for Christ movement. The Brazilian evangelists active in the movement were too numerous to chronicle.[45]

According to Rodolfo Anders, as informed as anyone in Brazil, there were several striking features in this Revival. Unusual crowds attended prayer meetings in the churches at 6 in the morning, in the Orr campaigns and elsewhere. The Orr campaigns set the pattern for more direct biblical preaching in the Brazilian churches, instruction in righteousness and direct evangelism.[46] Many Brazilians, after sharing in some campaign, went forth to preach in a new power with success as great or greater than their teachers from overseas.

The conversions and the other visible results following often exceeded those during the campaigns, even though the latter numbered perhaps ten thousand.[47] In a metropolitan congregation, where the pastor had overworked and was ill following united campaign meetings, more than a hundred joined the church. In an interior city, the churches gained more additions in a month than in the previous decade.

The revival movement was free from all sensationalism. There often were tears, but no emotionalism, confessions but no scandals, rejoicings but no extravagances, meetings protracted for hours but always in decency and order, and no unfavorable reaction from people attending the meetings reached the offices of the Confederation.[48]

Wonderful reconciliations occurred among leaders, the mending of wide denominational breaches, never a division attributable to the campaigns. And never had any movement commanded so much cooperation: Baptists—95% of those able; Congregationalists, Methodists and Presbyterians— 100%; Anglicans and Brethren, Lutherans and Reformed, wherever encountered; and Pentecostals once contacted.[49]

Two new songs—"Sonda-me, ó Deus" and "Jesus Me Ama," the first written by Orr and the second popularized in all his meetings—swept the churches. The Portuguese translation of Dr. Orr's "Full Surrender" published by the Confederation enjoyed a phenomenal sale,[50] the first 5000 exhausted in two months. The secular press gave unusual coverage to the movement; the religious press was full of it.

It was reported to the Southern Baptist Convention that a 'genuine spirit of revival' existed among the Baptist churches in Brazil in 1952. Strange to relate, among a minority of Baptists arose the only significant opposition. A few older Baptist missionaries held the view that Baptists should not cooperate with other Protestant churches, and they resented Orr's success.[51] The controversy became more serious when the conspirators accused Orr of fomenting divisions among the Baptists, forcing confessions of sins, raising up the spirit of the Brazilians against the missionaries, planning to organize colleges or seminaries with schismatic intent—all of which was palpably false. The matter was not settled until 1953, when a champion in the person of a university professor universally well-regarded rose in the Brazilian Baptist Convention to give messengers of the churches the actual facts—demonstrating that there was a general acceptance by Baptist churches throughout Brazil.

Orr adopted a simple attitude to Brazil's Pentecostals. He preached on decisive dedication and the filling of the Holy Spirit, and won sympathy in Pentecostal circles as in Wesleyan. He considered Brazilian Pentecostals as true Evangelicals, allowing difference on points of interpretation. In general, the objections by others to cooperation with the Pentecostals concerned the noise they made in meetings; and Orr reminded the Baptists and Methodists that they too had been noisy in American frontier days. The moderate Pentecostals generally cooperated in the campaigns.[52]

The Orr team campaigns marked a coming of age in Brazilian evangelism, for 100% of the financial support was offered freely by Brazilians towards travel and keep, not a penny subscribed from outside the country in this respect.[53]

The Princeton scholar, P. E. Pierson, wrote of the 1952 movement: 'Despite those who soon drifted away, permanent results were seen in rising seminary enrollment and church growth. . . The total number of seminarians in Campinas and Recife rose from approximately 70 in 1950 to 150 in 1959.' W. R. Read's graph indicated that 1952 was the year of the greatest gains for Presbyterians in half a century.[54]

Read's graph of comparative growth of the Protestant Churches showed a great acceleration in the early 1950s. Assembly of God membership rose from 200,000 in 1951 to 500,000 in 1960. Baptists, despite several secessions, grew from 120,000 to 200,000 in the same period.[55]

Dr. Benjamin Moraes, vice-president of the Presbyterian World Alliance, stated in 1958 that 'an evangelistic mind has remained all over the Brazilian Church since 1952. . . the remarkable work of grace . . .'[56]

What was most significant was that, under Brazilian law, the electorate was composed of six million voters, duly qualified by literacy and education, and by 1953 nearly two million of them were Evangelicals.[57]

What about the Roman Catholic Church? Sometimes a Brazilian parish priest or an American missionary came to the services, and showed friendly feeling, but European missionary priests displayed hostility.[58] The hierarchy in Brazil was alarmed by the success of the Reavivamento Brasileiro, for, at the National Conference of the Brazilian Roman Episcopate held in Belém a few months later (1953), a predominant issue was the rapid growth of the evangelical movement.[59] Bishop Agnello Bossil warned that 'the largest Catholic country' could become Protestant all too soon.[60]

19

HISPANIC SOUTH AMERICA, 1950—

One result of the journey made by Kenneth Strachan and Edwin Orr in 1951 was that at least a score of committees in the major cities of Hispanic South America requested interdenominational, city-wide campaigns, it being evident —as Strachan noted in a letter to Orr—that a much larger campaign ministry than hitherto anticipated lay ahead for years to come.[1] The evangelistic experience of the team campaigns of the 1950s, together with the occurrence of phenomenal revival in certain countries, helped produce Evangelism-in-Depth in the 1960s.[2]

Thus the Latin American Mission team opened the year 1952 with a series of 'continental evangelistic campaigns,' moving from the Antilles to tackle Venezuela, Ecuador, Peru, and Bolivia, continuing into 1953, with other efforts closer to their home base in Central America. Campaigns were concentrated on the larger cities with the cooperation of the local Evangelical missions and churches which were responsible for the follow-up work.[3] In some ways, these Latin American team campaigns were similar to those of the founder of the Mission, Harry Strachan, a generation earlier; but the evangelistic mantle of Harry Strachan had not fallen upon Kenneth, who was glad to use evangelists of various Hispano-American national origins, though his own Spanish was equally fluent. Kenneth Strachan became the director and strategist of a developing movement, even its missiological theorist, all this in spite of the fact that his very years were numbered:[4]

> Kenneth Strachan was not an evangelist himself but during the 1950s he coordinated a series of great evangelistic campaigns conducted by Latin American evangelists and featuring gifted men like chalk artist Phil Saint, well-known operatic singer Anton Marco, and concert pianist Richard Foulkes—men whom God used to bring large crowds under the sound of the gospel in bull rings and theatres of cities like Lima, Guayaquil, Buenos Aires, Santiago and Caracas.[5]

Late in 1952, three members of the Reavivamento team in Brazil visited Argentina, Orr, Dunlap and Sylvia Lima meeting with leaders of various Evangelical denominations, recounting happenings in the vast Republic and passing on a vision of revival. There was much hope expressed that the team could exercise a similar ministry in Argentina—and Kenneth Strachan also for several years added overtures to share in a Hispanic America project of evangelism[6]—but nothing came of the invitations, Orr continuing to Africa and India, saying that another instrument would be raised up in the Argentine.

The events that followed in Argentina make one of the strangest stories ever told in the history of evangelism. In 1952, an evangelist—Theodore Hicks, a novice—saw a vision of South America as a vast field of yellow grain, ready for the harvest. A year or so later, in Red Bluff in northern California, the Macedonian call was singularly confirmed in a word of prophecy from a pastor's wife.[7]

Meanwhile, several Pentecostal and Alliance pastors in Buenos Aires were preparing for a healing and evangelistic campaign in 1954.[8] The evangelist invited, T. L. Osborn, with a recollection of a setback in Paraguay and a prospect of better times in Indonesia, was unable to come. Tommy Hicks, as he was known, set out in faith for the southern continent, praying with friends at the Los Angeles airport— for fifty thousand conversions.

Hicks had minor meetings here and there, concluding in a series in Temuco in Chile. He was so utterly uninformed that he asked the Argentine stewardess on the flight across the Andes if a name that kept recurring in his mind meant anything to her, the name Perón![9] He was surprised when she told him that Mr. Perón was the President of Argentina, no less. Hicks determined to see him.

Juan Perón possessed a magnetic personality, and the majority of Argentine people had followed him as he used Argentina's postwar gold reserves built up by demand for agricultural products to industrialize the country. At first, Perón enjoyed the support of the Roman Catholic Church, to which he made significant concessions for its support; but, as his grip on the masses grew stronger, he became impatient. He displayed his irritation by passing through Congress legislation to legalize brothels and divorce, and he even threatened to amend the Constitution to deprive the Church of its position as a state church.

The missionaries and pastors in Buenos Aires agreed to sponsor Hicks in a campaign, but were alarmed when he insisted upon seeing President Perón about the use of a stadium for the meetings.[10] Hicks was able to see the head of the Ministry of Religion, but had little hope of seeing the President until—it was reported—he prayed for the healing of a presidential guard;[11] whereupon the amazed recipient of healing took Hicks directly to see Juan Perón in person.

The President received Hicks cordially and granted him use of the Atlanta Stadium. And so the meetings began with six thousand or so on 14th April 1954.[12] It was said that the President had encountered friction in his dealings with the Roman hierarchy; it was said, and denied, that he himself had been healed.[13] Whatever it was, the meetings began and T. L. Osborn in passing gave the opening word. From then on, the order of service was simplicity itself, singing and preaching and praying—'There is power ... power!'

The campaign, in the words of researcher Arno Enns, was a typical Pentecostal evangelistic effort, with the usual strong emphasis upon Divine healing.[14] Hicks seemed to attribute the success of the meetings to miracles of healing beginning the first night and stressed the particular healing of a three-year old boy who walked with a brace on his leg. The radio and press proclaimed this incident far and wide, and attendance increased rapidly, until a hundred thousand were gathering in the stadium, necessitating a move to the larger Huracan Stadium.[15]

Of course, there was opposition. The largest Evangelical denomination, the Brethren, were ill-disposed to concede such a ministry of healing in the present dispensation. The press was friendly, neutral or hostile.[16] The hierarchy of the Roman Catholic Church professed alarm, but when the Roman Catholic Bishops protested to President Perón about letting Tommy Hicks conduct such great meetings, he said: 'Why should the mighty Church of Rome be afraid of one little Protestant who lacks the backing of a large church?' They retorted: 'But look at the multitudes who flock to hear him and to see the miracles.' Then said the President, 'I must conclude that he has the backing of Almighty God, and I can do nothing about that.'[17] With such opposition from the conservative Evangelicals and Roman Catholics, the liberal spokesmen of society expressed stronger censure on Hicks. The controversy added to the interest and attendance.

In the Hicks campaign, scarcely any money was spent in advertising.[18] The main topic of conversation in factories, offices, colleges, schools, plazas, trains and buses was the 'mago de Atlanta,' 'magician,' 'curandero,' 'witch-doctor' — many were the epithets — and along with him a discussion of miracles, healings, religious faith, and conversion. All of the newspapers were involved, the yellow press running articles several pages in length, sensationalist magazines exploiting the spectacular happenings. Undoubtedly, there were healings that no one could gainsay; but there were also stretchers and wheelchairs with far-gone terminal cases brought there by despairing relatives or scheming sceptics. Some died in the process, with accusations made against Hicks thereby.[19] A thick file of adverse reports and charges made by medical doctors and police officers was piled up.

Attendance at the Huracán Stadium rose from a hundred thousand to quarter of a million.[20] Some claimed even more. The aggregate attendances exceeded two million people — Hicks himself in the writer's hearing claimed six million hearers in sixty nights or so.[21] The impact was undeniable. The leading liberal periodical in the United States noted that Tommy Hicks had drawn bigger crowds, gathered more decision cards, captured more front-page press attention and provoked more controversy than Billy Graham in the Harringay Crusade in London the same year.[22]

And what were the results? Apart from the sensational healings, which sometimes were unrelated to a profession of evangelical faith, there were measurable results in the unprecedented sale of Bibles and Testaments, the Bible Society selling 22,000 Bibles and 26,000 New Testaments and flying in shipments from all over Latin America to meet the demand.[23] And the demand for the Scriptures kept on growing among both classes and masses.

What was the effect upon church growth in Argentina? The writer and others met with Tommy Hicks for breakfast in Los Angeles, and heard the evangelist claim that there were three million conversions, an estimate that found its way into the title of booklets published in 1956 by Hicks.[24] In seeking to substantiate the claim, Hicks said naively that the aggregate attendance was six million, and that half of the total raised their hands when the invitation to receive Christ as Saviour was given.[25] An associate more modestly claimed that a hundred thousand decision cards were taken by the multitudes pouring through the stadium gates.

The aggregate numerical gain by all of the Evangelical Churches seemed less than twenty thousand. But a gain of twenty thousand was unprecedented in Argentine history, 'a sovereign breakthrough by God,' just as were the Brethren campaigns in an earlier generation, in the opinion of the Baptist missiologist, Arno Enns.[26]

Many Argentine Evangelicals, whether well-disposed to Tommy Hicks's ministry or not, admitted that his meetings 'broke the back of the rigid Argentine resistance to the Evangelical witness,' according to the researches of Read, Monterroso and Johnson.[27] The impact was almost beyond belief, in the opinion of more liberal critics.

Tommy Hicks returned to Argentina in 1955, his second campaign sponsored by Pentecostal and Alliance Churches with support from Baptist, Brethren, Methodist, Mennonite and other enthusiasts. The Atlanta Stadium was hired, and early attendances passed the five thousand mark. But the police moved in and closed the enterprise after three night meetings, Hicks under house arrest while investigated on charges of practising medicine without a license![28]

The same year that Tommy Hicks was driven out of the country, Juan Perón was overthrown and forced into exile. Some there were who claimed that Perón had engineered the Hicks success to spite the Roman Bishops; others said that Perón himself had been converted, a charge that the dictator in exile laughingly denied to a friend of the writer at an airport in Panama.[29] It seems more likely that Perón was astounded by the response of the people to the healer to whom he gave permission to operate.

What was the effect upon the denominations? The early sponsors, both the Assemblies of God and the Christian and Missionary Alliance, received an immediate and enormous benefit.[30] Despite a lack of teaching and some fanaticism, a steady accession to the Pentecostal churches set in, the Assemblies of God multiplying tenfold in ten years.[31] The largest church of that affiliation before the campaign had seated 150; nine missionaries served a total of 174 adult members, and the outlook was discouraging. But five new churches were founded in 1955, and within a decade there were more than 150 assemblies in Argentina, with 5000 attending services and 8000 in church schools. Enrollment in the Bible School jumped from fifteen to forty-five. The Christian and Missionary Alliance built three new churches almost immediately, and continued to grow.[32]

The Christian Brethren (Hermanos Libres) continued to grow in spite of mixed feelings about the charismatic work of Tommy Hicks.[33] The Baptist churches, not involved at first in the Hicks campaign, also continued to increase.[34] In the Lutheran constituency, growth was less marked.

Methodist church membership in Argentina declined before and after the Hicks campaign.[35] The Church seemed occupied with other laudable concerns, and evangelism was given less attention. The Seventh Day Adventists, though uninvolved with Hicks, accelerated their rate of growth.

In 1955, shortly after the Hicks phenomenon in Buenos Aires,[36] a Latin America Mission team campaigned in the Argentine and Uruguay, winning 621 professions of faith in Buenos Aires, 217 in Rosario, 92 in Tandil—where Harry Strachan had served his missionary apprenticeship, 388 in Mar del Plata, and 237 in Montevideo. Without the appeal of miraculous healings, this was considered an encouraging response from the people of the Río Plata republics. Local evangelism greatly accelerated.

Late in 1957, the veteran pastor-evangelist,[37] Oswald J. Smith of Toronto, conducted a remarkable campaign in the city of Buenos Aires with the support of three hundred local churches. The meetings were held in Luna Park, attendances between ten and twenty thousand, comparing with a Catholic coincident mass rally of four thousand, Smith reaching an aggregate of 200,000, a thousand or more professing faith.

In Rosario, Argentina's second city, Oswald Smith conducted an evangelistic campaign in an auditorium seating more than five thousand.[38] There were more than three hundred professions of faith. The total attendance was 30,000 during the week.

The Evangelical success provoked the Bishops to action. The desperate condition of the Roman Catholic Church in Argentina was demonstrated in 1960, a year during which— to quote Archbishop Fulton J. Sheen— only six Argentine priests were ordained. After two years' planning, a Grand Mission of Buenos Aires was launched and financed by the Argentine Government.[39] Two thousand five hundred priests were imported for the mission; a statue of the Virgin of Lujan was placed in a Cathedral in Buenos Aires, and the salary of a full general of the army was granted it; but the public response was so poor, with so few people marching in the processions, that the Grand Mission was considered a desperate failure.

All of the Evangelical Churches of Uruguay evidenced some growth in the 1950s. The Waldensians, the largest of the denominations, celebrated their centennial in 1958 with four thousand communicants and a community three times as large, but these Italo-Uruguayans had made few efforts to evangelize the population round about.[40] Likewise the Mennonites concerned themselves with their community; whereas the Methodists excelled in social action. The total strength of Evangelicalism in Uruguay remained less than one per cent of the population, somewhat less than the net percentage in the Argentine.

Besides the Latin America team campaign in 1955, local evangelism increased, interdenominational work following. In 1957, Oswald J. Smith preached in Montevideo's largest auditorium, supported in unusual unity by seventy churches. Beginning with less than two thousand, he attracted sixteen thousand in all, of whom six hundred made profession of faith in the inquiry room.[41]

In the 1950s, unlike the encouraged denominations in the Argentine Republic, the Evangelical Churches in Paraguay suffered from pessimism.[42] Paraguay possessed very few Evangelical communicants, ten thousand or so, but its total population was the smallest on the continent, for Paraguay, a backwater in the stream of Latin American progress, had remained isolated from the flow of European immigration, its people still largely Guarani.[43]

From Brazil, John Savage moved to Chile[44] and observed the results of a more concentrated work in 1952, one with 'no human explanation . . . a time of the Lord's visitation.' One, Clifton Erickson, an Assembly of God evangelist with a healing ministry, preaching by interpretation, commenced a campaign in Valdivia with crowds in excess of 1250; but when he moved to Valparaiso, nightly attendances exceeded ten thousand.[45] The Roman Catholic authorities tried to stop the campaign by court action, increasing popular support.

By the time that Erickson reached Santiago, there was not an auditorium large enough to contain the crowds.[46] The great majority of the Protestant pastors gave support to the campaign, in which there was no extravagance to alienate the workers of the various denominations. Twelve thousand flocked first to a circus tent; then permission was granted to use the National Stadium; in spite of a transport strike, multitudes trekked out to the meetings, which soon over-flowed the thirty thousand seating capacity.

Santiago's Evangelicals numbered approximately fifteen thousand, which meant that twenty thousand or more were hearing the Gospel besides those who professed it. Finally a procession of sixty thousand through the city held up the traffic for hours, and the Stadium was utterly swamped by the attendance. The Stadium's managers refused to accept payment for facilities 'never put to a better use.'[47]

Besides many professed conversions, there were more than six thousand Bibles and New Testaments sold, and a tide of interest augmented attendance at Evangelical places of worship.[48] Such a demonstration of spiritual unity by the Evangelicals was unprecedented, the Evangelical Alliance claimed, while ecumenical observers announced 'a notable revival' in the churches which was spreading rapidly.[49]

The Latin America Mission team visited Chile in the wake of the 1952 Awakening in that country, and crowds up to eight thousand gathered to hear the preaching and listen to the singing of Anton Marco, a converted opera star in evangelistic service.[50]

All of the Evangelical denominations gained adherents through the 1952 Awakening.[51] The Baptists, for example, increased from five thousand to seventy-five hundred in membership in the 'fifties, much the same as the Seventh Day Adventists; the Methodists and Alliance causes grew more modestly; but the Pentecostal Churches trebled in membership in the decade from a hundred thousand to three hundred thousand, chiefly in the national denominations too many to track down.

On 21st November 1957, Oswald Smith began preaching in Santiago, five thousand gathering in an open stadium. A majority of those supporting the series seemed to be of indigenous Pentecostal persuasion, though denominational support was general. Smith was impressed by the depth of conviction manifested, the penitents seeking counsel in a workers' tent, where more than a thousand inquirers were instructed.[52] Attendances rose to fifteen thousand, with an aggregate of 75,000 in ten days.

Unlike the Christian Congregation, the indigenous Italo-Brazilian denomination which maintained its exclusiveness, the Pentecostal denominations of Chile easily cooperated in interdenominational evangelism while they themselves split often and readily to follow a popular caudillo.[53] Incessant was their street evangelism, bands of witness converging on Jotabeche when Strachan and Orr ministered there.

In Bolivia, the national revolution was inevitable because less than five per cent of landowners owned seventy per cent of all private agricultural property, and only half a million of Bolivia's three and a half million people had entered the market economy. The defeat in the Chaco caused a rise of nationalism that culminated in seizure of power in 1952.[54]

The Evangelical Churches in Bolivia gained much in the decade of revolution, members increasing in number from seven thousand in 1950 to twenty thousand ten years later. The largest Protestant denomination in the country was still that of the Seventh Day Adventists, who grew from three thousand to nine thousand in the 'fifties.[55]

The Bolivian Baptists began the decade with a setback. In 1949 a mob of drunken Indians, incited by a priest named Tumiri, attacked a truck carrying Baptists with a barrage of stones that killed eight of them, including the Canadian leader, Norman Dabbs, the president of the Bolivian Baptist Convention, Francisco Salazar, and the most able younger pastor in the denomination, Carlos Meneses.[56] Within a few years, the seven hundred Baptists increased to a thousand.

The Methodists had been in the spiritual doldrums in the late 1940s, but began to grow in the 1950s, matching the Baptists in strength.[57] The Andes Evangelical Mission and the Evangelical Union of South America united forces in the late 1950s, the Evangelical Christian Union churches growing in membership from five hundred to more than three thousand.[58] The Friends and the Nazarenes gained also.

In 1953, the Latin American Mission team conducted an evangelistic campaign in Cochabamba in Bolivia, the local attendance being reported as far greater than any previous evangelistic enterprise. Many churches benefitted.[59]

Early in 1952, there occurred a local revival in the Assembly of God Bible School in Cochabamba. In its initial stages, it caused prostrations among those who were convicted of sin and dancing for joy among those who professed deliverance.[60] This movement accelerated the outreach of the Pentecostals, conversions being reported especially in the ministry of Eduardo Rios in 1953.[61] Membership grew from two hundred to nearly nine hundred in two years, the Aymaras in La Paz responding. No landslide occurred.

The 'gente decente' or professional classes of Bolivia still seemed comparatively unreached by the Evangelical churches which thrived best among the workers and cholos. The aristocracy was liquidated in the revolution.[62]

In Peru also, the Seventh Day Adventist denomination maintained its position as the leading Protestant body, and the Aymara people movement around Lake Titicaca which accounted for most of the growth continued to expand.[63] The membership grew from more than twelve thousand to less than twenty thousand during the 1950s.

But the growth of the Iglesia Evangélica Peruana seemed hampered by John Ritchie's fear of a professional ministry, which encouraged itinerant preachers and discouraged a well-trained pastorate. In the 1950s, the churches of this denomination actually lost members.[64]

The cooperative work of the denominations was greatly helped by the direction of Dr. Herbert Money, a missionary from New Zealand, though several groups that entered the country disregarded comity arrangements.

As early as 1950, the Assemblies of God in Peru were claiming a spiritual awakening.[65] Interest increased in all their churches and, towards the end of the year, Clifton Erickson conducted a healing-evangelization campaign in Lima, attracting five thousand or more to the Coliseum. The work created interest and controversy, and Erickson who had entered as a tourist was expelled for performing services unrelated to his visa. But the Assemblies of God gained several thousand new members, and began to grow in various parts of the Peruvian Republic.[66]

Roberto Navarro, Eliseo Hernández, and Israel García were the evangelists of the 1953 campaigns of the Latin American Mission in Peru, the capable mission director, Dr. Herbert Money, reporting that it was the best campaign to date in Lima.[67] Arequipa was also visited. In the Bible Institute in Lima, a general revival broke out among the staff and students.

The field in Ecuador remained a difficult one, and the total number of Evangelicals of all denominations increased from only eighteen hundred to the four thousand mark in the decade of the 1950s.[68] In 1952, the Latin American team campaigned in Guayaquil. It was in 1956 that five American missionaries were killed by Auca tribesmen in the eastern jungles of Ecuador.[69] The tragedy focussed much prayer upon the equatorial Republic. The remarkable work of the hundred missionaries of the short-wave radio station in Quito, HCJB, also helped to attract interest to the country. But until the 1960s, there seemed to be a dearth of revival or awakening of the dynamic sort.

The end of World War II marked the beginning of civil war in the Republic of Colombia.[70] Between a hundred and a hundred and fifty thousand Colombians died in the ten years between the onset of 1948 and the end of 1957.

The National Police, actually an armed force of the Conservative dictatorship, began harassing the Liberals more and more in 1949.[71] In many parts of the country, a state of utter anarchy prevailed.

The violence—the period was known as La Violencia—spread over the whole of Colombia, not only with angry mobs attacking churches, schools and convents, but with systematic, cold-blooded murder of enemies.[72] Sometimes priests were attacked, and often Evangelical pastors were assaulted as part of the liberal constituency, whether they were active in politics or not. The atrocities and killings became more and more frequent, and a cruel persecution of the Evangelicals was instigated.

At first, Evangelicals found opportunity in the turmoil. In Sogamoso, the Roman Catholic Church was sealed and the priests were sent away. The Assemblies of God pitched a tent that attracted five hundred people nightly,[73] which gave some indication of the spirit of Colombian believers in the troublous times of 1950.

But soon the fury of the Right was turned on Evangelical people. In 1952, the General Assembly of the Evangelical Confederation of Colombia announced that two hundred local schools had been closed, forty-six church buildings burned or dynamited, thirty-four church buildings confiscated and seventy-five Evangelicals murdered.[74]

In Barranca Bermeja, in a leading Pentecostal assembly in Colombia, persecution continued to disrupt the services and harass the membership. A home-made bomb in the doorway of the church impelled believers to leave rapidly through the windows.[75] The guardians of the law exercised their duty of protection of citizens by assaulting the men, the missionary, Joseph Knapp, being thus assaulted, and his wife jailed. There were no charges sustained against the assailants, the persecutors being encouraged.

There was widespread beating and torturing of individual Evangelicals, insulting of Protestant pastors, priests interfering with Evangelical weddings and funerals, Protestant children being expelled from schools, and priest-directed mobs attacking the little churches of the Evangelicals—all of which has been amply documented.[76]

Aimee McQuilkin, daughter of the missionary educator, Dr. Robert McQuilkin of Columbia, South Carolina, served as a nurse in Colombia. On one occasion, as she directed a class of twenty-five believers in a private home, there approached a procession, led by a priest, which unleashed a barrage of 'Hail Marys' and coconut shells in the absence of rocks in a sandy soil.[77] The priest broke down the door and soundly slapped the American girl's face. In a reflex action the nurse raised her arm to protect her face, whereupon the priest rebuked her, saying that she was not acting like Christ, who advised turning the other cheek. Aimee McQuilkin removed her glasses and presented her face.

A year later, the same Father Heriberto Zapata, forced his way into a Protestant service in a private house, tore up the Bibles, and created a scene.[78] The police arrived but were unable to persuade the priest to retire until midnight. Shortly afterwards, the priest returned in civilian clothes, armed with a revolver. But the police intervened and made him desist from his harassment of the Evangelicals.

The attitude of Roman Catholic leaders to the persecution was simply one of disavowal, saying that unless the Church had actually ordered it, there was no persecution.[79] But the fact remained that those who attacked the Evangelicals almost without exception were conservative Churchmen, clergy or laity. The Evangelicals readily identified their persecutors as religious bigots and political reactionaries, and found no comfort in the thought that they were made to suffer as Communists, which they were not.

The disavowal of persecution was made overseas when friends of mission churches raised the issue in the press. In 1957, however, a leading newspaper of Colombia took a decided stand on the issue, admitting fierce persecution; it defended freedom of religion along with political liberty.[80]

Year by year, the violence against the Evangelicals was intensified, the minority suffering all-out persecution. In a two weeks' period, thirty churches were closed. A score of armed terrorists threatened to obliterate the Christian and Missionary Alliance church in La Plata, and the Mayor and the Governor in turn refused to provide protection of any kind. Examples could be multiplied. The Evangelicals in persecution gained their choicest members. In 1953, the Evangelical churches in the cities were crowded and there was a steady increase in membership.[81] Open evangelism being impossible, fearless laymen became lay evangelists.

By 1954, the Foursquare Pentecostal Church founded by Joseph Knapp in Barranca Bermeja—a town of only 35,000 population—six years previously, had become the largest Evangelical congregation in all Colombia. In mid-1955, a general convention was held in the big church, with fifteen hundred attending nightly and as many as a hundred converts in a meeting. Such success was regarded as impermissible. The Barranca Bermeja church, with its four hundred active communicants and an attendance of between a thousand and two thousand, was closed by the authorities as part of the official crack-down on Evangelicals.[82] Such persecution extended the Evangelical outreach.

By 1957, there were signs of a slackening off of violent persecution.[83] The Evangelicals were able to take stock and so discovered that they had grown in numbers—the Latin America Mission having 700 members and 2500 adherents, the Christian and Missionary Alliance 1714 and 824, the Presbyterians 1292 and 300, and the Baptists 1447 with a proportionate number of inquirers, the other denominations gaining likewise.[84] Ten thousand communicant members in 1950 became thirty-three thousand by the end of the decade. The violent attempt to destroy the Cause had failed, and conditions were likely to improve.

Late in 1959, the Puerto Rican Pentecostal evangelist, Eugenio Jiménez, was sponsored by the Assemblies of God and other Pentecostal churches in Bogotá, fifteen hundred attending on 28th October 1959; but Eugenio Jiménez being forbidden to preach, his brother Raimundo preached instead while Eugenio prayed for the sick. There were many who responded—six thousand inquirers—the other Evangelical churches sharing in the benefits.[85]

In post-mortem, what was the cause of the persecution? James E. Goff, noting that in a dozen years in Colombia more than a hundred Evangelicals were martyred, sixty-six churches destroyed, and a couple of hundred schools closed, attributed the persecution to six religious factors at work in the Violence:[86]

1, the clerical domination of Government from 1946-1958;
2, the determination of the Hierarchy to extirpate 'heresy';
3, the predominance of a medieval Spanish Catholicism;
4, the dangerous accusations made by the Roman priests;
5, the indoctrination of the National Police by the clergy;
6, the sustained 'hate-Protestants' campaign by the clergy.
Goff cited twenty-four ways the Evangelicals suffered.

Thousands of people had been uprooted in the violence, and family ties were broken.[87] The social structure of the Republic was shaken, and the population was wide open to evangelism in the peaceful years that followed, years of harvesting a crop sown in tears and fertilized with blood— soon to experience a heaven-sent benediction.

Venezuela was spared the kind of turmoil that afflicted Colombia, and its huge oil industry helped modernise the country.[88] The problems facing evangelisation in Venezuela were those of rapid urbanization and a rise of living 'costs.' The Evangelicals multiplied chiefly in the areas of rapid industrialization, thanks to a sustained evangelization that expanded with the opportunities.

The 1952 campaigns of the Latin American team in the cities of Venezuela were not as fruitful as elsewhere in tropical America, there being a hundred and twenty who professed faith in Maracaibo, and 260 in Caracas.[89] It was much the same in Guayaquil in Ecuador, where 210 people were enrolled as inquirers.   This represented about one-eighth of the 5500 total in the campaigns of 1952.

The largest denomination of Evangelicals in Venezuela in the 1950s was that of the Christian Brethren, who had experienced slow but steady growth for forty years, then suddenly accelerated in the mid-fifties from two thousand in active fellowship to nearly five thousand by 1960.[90] The Orinoco River Mission fellowship, half the size, increased in membership during the same years.

The Assemblies of God had entered Venezuela in 1910, but had not experienced significant growth.   In 1952, the Oklahoman evangelist, T. L. Osborn, campaigned in Punto Fijo and created great excitement among the people, the attendances reaching ten thousand nightly.[91] The effect was to stir up Pentecostals to aggressive efforts year by year.

In 1953, national ministers of the Assemblies of God engaged in intensive evangelism in Venezuela.[92] Healing, an attraction to the masses and a cause of alarm to the local establishment, was the drawing interest. In Ciudad Bolívar, five thousand attended, and hundreds were registered as inquirers, three thousand in San Fernando with like results reported. But, at the end of the year, the Assembly of God in Bolívar had no more than sixty members, which showed that assimiliation of professed converts was far from easy. In all Venezuela, however, the Assemblies of God grew in numbers in the 'fifties, and other Pentecostals thrived.

Although the 1950s were far surpassed in most places by Pentecostal growth in the 1960s, they were significant years. At the beginning of 1957, the Pentecostal movement in Latin America enumerated its gains in the seven years previous. There were no less than two hundred Assemblies of God in Peru; the Assembly of God in La Paz was the largest congregation in Bolivia; in Chile, the Pentecostal Methodist congregation of Santiago drew five thousand to its worship services; in Argentina, an Assembly of God in Buenos Aires integrated eight hundred of those reached by Tommy Hicks into a steady congregation.[93] What advantage did Pentecostal churches possess? In attracting the Latin American masses, it seemed to be the healing ministry.

While part and parcel of Pentecostal creed and practice, the healing and evangelism campaign posed many problems for non-charismatic Evangelical leaders and adherents in Latin America. On the credit side, the evangelist was sure to preach a simple gospel, sometimes crude or naive; and the people attended by the thousands to hear it, even though their attention was drawn by reports of spectacular healing. On the debit side, the divergent premises of the evangelist and his closest sponsors oftened conflicted with long-held convictions of other Evangelicals.[94] The growing tolerance of glossolalia was checked by the insistence of sponsoring groups that such a gift was indispensable, leading to blatant proselytism and the loss of members to the more insistent propagandists. On the other hand, the older Evangelical groups did not always oppose such teaching, but presenting it in moderate form encouraged a decisive dedication. The intransigent opponents simply lost out.

The fact remains that the Pentecostal missionaries and national leaders rode a wave of the future, for statistics of the 1960s indicated that in many countries the Pentecostal congregations were moving up to first place in numbers and in influence, remarkably so.[95]

20

THE CARIBBEAN IN THE 'FIFTIES

In 1950, James Nickolson of the Cuban Assemblies of God invited an Oklahoman, T. L. Osborn of Tulsa, to conduct two weeks of meetings in Santiago.[1] Osborn began his work with a thousand or so attending a rally, but soon there were fifteen thousand gathering. 'A mighty wave of revival' began sweeping over all of Cuba. Ten thousand gathered in Banes, a much smaller place on the north shore.[2] Great meetings were held outdoors everywhere, no church or theatre being able to accommodate the multitudes. In Holguin, a church of 2400 was born in less than three weeks of awakening, an offering of $9000 made by poor converts being sufficient for the purchase of a disused shoe factory as a sanctuary.[3]

As a result of three weeks of healing-evangelistic work in 1951 by Richard E. Jeffery of Phoenix with overflowing crowds in a baseball stadium in Havana, the Assembly of God there saw attendances increase from five hundred, so a new structure to accommodate a thousand was begun, the auditorium of Iglesia Evangélica Pentecostal being opened two years later, something 'several missionaries could not have accomplished in a lifetime.'[4]

There were attendances exceeding nine thousand in the town of Victoria de las Tunas, and there the Assembly of God was soon sponsoring a dozen congregations within forty kilometers of the mother church.[5] In Ciego de Avila, near Camaguey, similar growth was reported. The stirring was continued throughout 1952 and into 1953.[6]

In 1951, H. C. Ball insisted that[7] 'all the churches in Cuba' were enjoying the benefits of the Pentecostal revival, the Methodists alone having received a couple of thousand new members.[8] Indeed, every denomination showed a gain. By 1957, the Episcopalians in Cuba numbered 3712, the Presbyterians 3241, the Methodists 8145, and the Baptists 14,710—with two thousand more members in the west with Southern Baptist backing than in the east with Northern— and by the end of the decade, there were 264,927 declared Protestants, 3.89% of the Cuban population.[9]

During the first two years of the awakening, prophetic messages recurred with regularity—that the revival would flow like waters from an artesian well all over the island, and that trouble with the government would stop the great flow of living water.[10] In 1952, Fulgencio Batista set up his dictatorship and began to suppress the churches. Many of the Christians were stoned, some were killed, and others lost their homes because of lack of support for Batista.

The Latin America Mission team conducted campaigns of evangelization throughout Cuba in 1956, attracting large crowds—in spite of the political situation—in Placetas, Santiago, Havana, Santa Clara and Manzanilla.[11] There were many professions of faith.

The movement of revival seemed to have begun earlier in Cuba than in the rest of Latin America, which suggested prevenient grace, for towards the end of the 'fifties Fidel Castro succeeded in his revolt against Fulgencio Batista and established a Communist dictatorship on the island. It was most fortunate that Cuban Evangelicalism had become so indigenous, three-quarters of its ordained ministers and ninety per cent of its lay workers being national.[12]

As most of the missionaries at work in Cuba originated in the United States, tensions arising between Castro and the American government adversely affected their work, so they were withdrawn. The writer visited Cuba during the summer of 1962.[13]

As customary with Leninist dictatorships, the leaders of the revolutionary government assured the Evangelicals that they had nothing to fear. But some fled the country, while others submitting began to feel the pressure.

Meanwhile, advance continued in the Republic of Haiti, though there were fewer campaigns of healing-evangelism. Between 1952 and 1957, the total number of Evangelical communicants increased from 75,451 to 91,330, a twenty per cent increase, the Evangelical community from 259,523 to 313,279, also twenty per cent.[14] Baptists were the more numerous, with six hundred churches and 25,000 members, a community three times larger. The West Indies Mission field had likewise shown phenomenal growth, with a total community of 75,000, a third of them communicants. The Haiti Episcopalians were half as numerous, as were the Church of God, whose work had grown thus in less than a single generation. Other Protestant denominations were thriving, though Haiti remained desperately poor.

Two dedicated women missionaries of the Assemblies of God made an impact upon the Dominican Republic.[15] Adele Flower and Ida Sutherland in 1954 attracted great attention in their meetings in Bani, El Seybo and La Romana, more than three thousand being drawn to the messages of healing and salvation. This was a foretaste of the near future.

In 1955,[16] nearly all the Evangelical churches in Santo Domingo supported an evangelistic campaign directed by the Puerto Rican evangelist, David García, when healings attracted vast crowds of nominal Catholics.[17] Attendances were estimated as rising from thirty thousand to forty-five thousand, and a Princeton researcher declared that 'many evangelical church leaders regard it as the turning point of the evangelical cause in Dominican history.'[18] The Assembly of God extended the effort throughout 1955, growing steadily in the late 1950s.[19]

Puerto Rico continued to provide evangelistic talent for the work at large in Latin America. Between 1952 and 1957, Evangelical communicants increased from 44,279 to 48,136, a ten per cent gain, community from 137,185 to 147,441,[20] a seven per cent increase; but in view of the growth of the Assemblies of God, these figures must reflect a measure of slow-down in less dynamic denominations.

By 1957, there were 6092 Presbyterian church members in Puerto Rico, 6176 Baptists, 4931 United Evangelicals— Congregationalist-United Brethren, 4675 Methodists, 6283 Disciples, and 9895 Assembly of God.[21] There were several odd fringe groups, including one which considered the Mita goddess an incarnation of the Holy Spirit.

In Jamaica, the leading denomination for a hundred years —the Baptist Union—had lost its position.[22] After cresting in numbers in the wake of the Welsh Revival of 1905, the Baptists steadily declined from forty thousand to twenty-five thousand or so. The Methodists, who had not gained as many in the Welsh Revival period, also retained only what they had reported a hundred years before. The same was true of the Moravians and Presbyterians, and also of the Anglicans, whose statistics were difficult to assess, being based on infant baptism and adolescent confirmation.[23]

But the Assemblies of God and other Pentecostalists, as relative newcomers, were surging ahead with approximately forty thousand members, a figure not disputed by Donald A. McGavran, who studied Jamaican church growth at the end of the 1950s.[24]

The fundamentalist-modernist controversy, it was said, split off thousands from the older denominations.[25] Another factor cited by McGavran was the contented contact of the longer established denominations with the better classes in Jamaica, contrasted with the outreach of the Pentecostals to the patois-speaking masses. But the factor of dynamic cannot be disregarded, and the Assembly of God rank and file possessed dynamic a-plenty.

In 1953, Phil Saint—a Pennsylvanian evangelist with a talent for chalk drawing—campaigned in Jamaica, St. Lucía, and Grenada[26] for the Latin America Mission enterprise in the British West Indies, and three thousand professed faith.

Ministry in Jamaica was popular with tent evangelists of the United States who encountered uncongenial weather each winter farther north. These independents were ready for a call anytime during the season of snow. They apparently were a competitive crowd of workers. G. H. Montgomery, a Pentecostal Holiness editor afterwards associated with the Oral Roberts enterprise, scathingly challenged the objectivity of reports made by these enthusiasts, pointing out that in a two-year period such evangelists had claimed a total of three million converts in Jamaica alone,[27] almost twice the population of the island. Nevertheless, an impact was made, and Pentecostal statistics revealed its extent.

The Assemblies of God launched a revival campaign in Jamaica in 1956, attracting up to a thousand attendance, of whom two thousand professed faith and several hundred an experience in the Spirit.[28] The initiative for evangelism had seemingly passed from the historic denominations to the Pentecostals, though growth of a different kind was noted in the Seventh Day Adventist constituency.

In 1952, the Latin America Mission team was claiming a triumph in Trinidad, where they enlisted an experienced Atlanta pastor, Paul van Gorder, as evangelist.[29] In Port of Spain, between four thousand and fifty-five hundred people attended, jamming every available space. Meanwhile, the Afro-American evangelist, Efraim Alphonse, ministered in San Fernando on the southern side of the island. Decisions made in these campaigns numbered eleven hundred. In 1954 Phil Saint ministered in San Fernando while Jack Wyrtzen of New York campaigned in Port of Spain.[30] In 1956, a Latin America Mission team again drew forty-five hundred to a Port of Spain campaign, three thousand making profession of faith, a goodly number also registering in Barbados.[31]

Conventional interdenominational evangelism was given opportunity in Jamaica and other Caribbean islands when, in 1958, the Latin America Mission with Strachan directing coordinated the Billy Graham Team campaigns in the area. So Leighton Ford ministered in Jamaica,[32] Grady Wilson in Barbados, Joseph Blinco in Trinidad, and Israel García in Puerto Rico, each with assistance from Billy Graham, thus receiving a wider measure of denominational support than did the more controversial healing campaigners.

In Jamaica, Graham's first address was heard by thirty thousand people and twenty thousand were turned away. On the second night, there were twenty-five thousand hearers, of whom sixteen hundred made decision.[33] Sixty thousand in Barbados gathered to hear Graham's message—a quarter of the island's population—and nearly twelve hundred made decision. Black and East Indian Christians supported the Trinidad series, which drew more than thirty thousand and won more than two thousand for counsel.

Despite a warning by a Roman Catholic weekly that it was mortal sin to attend any of Billy Graham's meetings, there were many Puerto Rican Roman Catholics among the forty thousand who attended his rally there, and there was 'an overwhelming response.'[34]

Ford and Wilson campaigned in Panama in 1958, with assistance from Billy Graham whose arrival coincided with a newspaper strike and bus strike, 14,500 attending nevertheless and a goodly response being forthcoming.[35] All the Evangelical denominations accelerated in growth in the '50s but the most spectacular advances were made by the lay-preachers of the Foursquare Gospel,[36] Pentecostals whose work was spreading so rapidly in all parts of Panama that Protestants were often designated 'Salva-cuatros.' Leland Edwards ably directed the Foursquare efforts.

The Afro-American evangelist, Efraim Alphonse, led the evangelistic campaigns of the Latin America Mission on the Caribbean side of Central America, among the people who used English in British Honduras, Nicaragua, Costa Rica, and Panama in 1951. Meetings were held in Belize, Bluefields, Puerto Limon, and Panama, with heartening response.[37] Victor Monterroso directed the Latin America Mission campaign in Spanish-speaking Panama.

Meanwhile in 1952, in Costa Rica, the Tulsa-based but far-ranging healing evangelist, T. L. Osborn, conducted a campaign in San José and attracted international attention.

One night ten thousand people filled the stadium but next night they were locked out, the sponsoring pastors arrested and the evangelist deported.[38] Reports in the international news media were 'completely distorted and prejudiced,' wrote Kenneth Strachan in a note to Edwin Orr, for 'while there were certain objections, it is undeniable that he made a tremendous impact on the city.'[39] This campaign enjoyed support from Pentecostal churches and a measure of co-operation from other denominations, and the healing of the sick attracted Roman Catholics in the thousands.

In the decade of the 'fifties, the Latin America Mission, the Central American Mission,[40] the Methodists, and the Baptists counted a growth rate of one convert for every six members annually; the Pentecostals, in several groupings, shared in the evangelical advance, as did also the Seventh Day Adventist denomination. The Roman clergy were still in opposition, the Graham campaign of 1958 being boycotted by the Roman Catholic press, despite which ten thousand or so attended the rally concluding the campaign.[41]

The Latin America Mission team tackled Managua in Nicaragua in 1952, but suffered quite a setback when Israel García took ill and was unable to lead in the campaign.[42] The series achieved some good, for local evangelism continued, Nicaraguan evangelists tackling rural areas.

In Nicaragua, 'a notable spiritual awakening and a spirit of cooperation of other church groups' was announced in 1956 by Assemblies of God in the healing-evangelistic meetings of Roy Stewart, in which healings and conversions created much excitement.[43] That the Assemblies of God benefitted is seen in the dedication of a new auditorium seating fifteen hundred, a large place of worship for Managua.

The Moravian Church on the east coast continued to grow during the 1950s,[44] but this had little effect upon the rest of Nicaragua, for Moravian membership was Afro-American or Mosquito Indian, an English patois predominating.

In 1951, the Assemblies of God in El Salvador reported that their February conference was the greatest in spiritual power for twenty-one years. There were ten days of prayer and fasting in the Bible School.[45] A rising tide of prayer and expectation followed throughout 1952. In January 1953, the Tulsan evangelist, T. L. Osborn, campaigned in Santa Ana, the crowds growing until they filled two city blocks.[46] Five hundred inquirers were registered. Expectations continued for even greater results.

In the early months of 1956, Richard Jeffery of Phoenix conducted a healing-evangelistic campaign in El Salvador, reporting up to three thousand attending.[47] The lasting value of the work may be judged by the fact that six months later the Pentecostals baptized fifteen hundred converts in Lake Ilopango. The Assemblies of God grew steadily until they numbered two out of three in the Protestant population.[48]

The total membership of the Evangelical Churches in Honduras in 1950 was little over 5000; ten years later the membership had doubled.[49] Much of this growth was among the Pentecostals, whose missions stressed indigenous life and leadership; the same was true of the work of California Friends, another leading denomination which gained from a Latin American Mission campaign in Tegucigalpa in 1952 when the leading evangelist was Ernesto León, of Laredo, on the southern border of Texas.[50]

The 'fifties were fruitful years in the Guatemalan Church. In 1953, T. L. Osborn conducted a healing and evangelization campaign in Guatemala City that stirred up not a little grief in more conservative Presbyterian and Central American Mission circles in which it divided opinions.

With a Pentecostal sponsorship and public curiosity, it began in a large open lot without seating of any kind.[51] From eight to twenty-five thousand attended forty-eight open-air meetings and tens of thousands expressed interest.[52] Not all were gathered into membership, of course, but an Assembly of God trebled from three hundred to 964 in attendance, and denominational churches reaped a harvest in proportion to their cooperation. Three Assemblies of God were crowded, for eight hundred were baptized on 15th March following the February series, and another fifteen hundred baptized before twenty thousand witnesses.

Melvin L. Hodges, Pentecostal missionary expert,[53] was reporting in 1954 'blessings over a wide area,' adding 'it is clear to see that Guatemala is experiencing genuine revival.' Assemblies of God reported a thousand new members and eleven new churches, a total of 58 churches with 2639 adult baptized believers in that Pentecostal fellowship.[54]

The Presbyterian Church of Guatemala grew steadily in the 1950s and became autonomous in the 'sixties.[55] All of the Evangelical Churches grew in the 1950s, and out of the need for training the national leadership came Theological Education by Extension, adopted worldwide as suited to the need of training the indigenous leadership.[56]

The Puerto Rican evangelist, David García, requested the support of the Ministerial Alliance of Guatemala in his 1956 campaign in Guatemala City.[57] It was refused, due to Presbyterian uneasiness since the Osborn campaign and to Central American Mission opposition to efforts charismatic in character. But twenty-three churches cooperated and ten thousand people packed Olympic City. Again, Pentecostals benefitted most, though there were gains to other churches in the capital and country.

In 1958, Ramón Cabrera preached for four days to big crowds before the arrival of Billy Graham for a rally of an estimated eighty thousand, supported by all Evangelicals—it became impossible to invite inquirers forward.[58]

Evangelicals throughout Central America, while still a minority, thrived in the 1950s, the days of the worst kind of persecution being past. In the little Republics, during the 'fifties, the Assemblies of God were multiplying fast, fifty new churches founded in two years in El Salvador, and thirty in Guatemala,[59] while strength in Costa Rica doubled. Much of this growth was attributed to the impact of the great healing-evangelistic campaigns, but the zealous work of Pentecostal national pastors in follow-up was a much more significant factor.

Rogelio Archilla acted as interpreter for Billy Graham in all the Spanish-speaking countries of the Caribbean. The associate evangelists included Leighton Ford,[60] Joe Blinco, Grady Wilson, Israel García, Floratino Santana, and Ramon Cabrera. The Caribbean Crusade concluded in Mexico.

The 1960 Census of Mexico announced that 578,515 of its thirty-five million people were affiliated with the Protestant denominations.[61] Christian statisticians reported that there were 243,181 Evangelical communicants and a community of 879,227. More than half of all the Protestant members professed a Pentecostal faith, although there were 37,000 Presbyterians, 28,000 Methodists, and 17,000 Baptists.[62] A Roman Catholic authority conceded 645,145 adherents of forty denominations, 200,000 living in the Federal District, 100,000 in the State of Vera Cruz, 50,000 or more in each of the States of Chiapas, Tabasco, Puebla, Tamaulipas, Nuevo León, Coahuila, and Chihuahua, less than 25,000 in each of Yucatán, Campeche, Oaxaca, Guerrero, Michoacan, México, Hidalgo, and San Luis Potosí.[63] Following the time of trouble in the 1930s, all the Evangelical churches began to grow in the 'forties and accelerate in the 'fifties.

Among the faster-growing denominations in Mexico was the Apostolic Church of Faith in Christ Jesus, Pentecostal but baptizing only in the name of Jesus.[64] This Church had been indigenous since its beginnings in 1914. Assemblies of God were equal in numbers, with a dozen other associated Pentecostal bodies, and a hundred lesser groups with Pentecostal practices.[65]

At the end of 1949, the Pentecostals of Mexico claimed 800 churches and fifty thousand members, and membership was increasing in spite of difficulties, seven Pentecostals having been clubbed to death near Toluca.[66] The 1950s in the Mexican States were marked by the advent of healing and evangelization campaigns, sometimes spearheaded by an American evangelist using an interpreter but otherwise promoted by national pastors who lacked little in zeal and experience. The Pentecostals doubled in strength in the 1950s, and continued to outstrip other Evangelicals in the Mexican states.

The 1950s were years of opportunity for other churches. The people movements in Chiapas and Tabasco brought in thousands to the Presbyterian Church of Mexico.[67] During the 'fifties, the Methodist Church added ninety per cent to its membership, already augmented by the revival of the 'forties.[68] Southern Baptist work was helped by returning Mexican migrant harvesters from the United States. The year 1959 was a year of mass evangelism in Mexico for the Baptists associated with Southern Baptist missionaries, for there were 4400 professions of faith in Mexico, considered another record in that Republic.[69]

All the Evangelicals had been encouraged by the Billy Graham Campaign in 1958. Cecilio Arrastia of Cuba was to have conducted the first part of the series, but exigencies of travel hindered him, so Juan Isías and Kenneth Strachan took his place.[70] Graham's preaching was simple, Rogelio Archilla interpreting. As usual, hundreds crowded forward for counsel. The Roman Catholic authorities had forbidden the faithful to attend, and disturbances were threatened, but everything remained well under control. Graham preached to more than forty thousand.

Statistics of the aggregate attendances and professed conversions of the Billy Graham team in the Caribbean in 1958 detailed results from the associate evangelists' work in advance and the direct ministry of Graham himself in each country:[71]

dates	country	team		Graham	
January 5-22	Jamaica	99,100	2326	70,000	1565
January 12-26	Puerto Rico	44,000	1200	75,000	1300
January 19-30	Barbados	191,091	2047	48,940	1170
January 19-30	Guatemala	99,800	580	82,000	
February 2-13	Trinidad	34,400	392	33,500	2439
February 2- 9	Panama	32,680	368	27,000	1509
February 5- 9	Costa Rica	13,000	112	10,000	363
February 9-16	Mexico	21,000	606	44,000	2500

In Mexico, it seemed as if the days of persecution had given way to years of ever-expanding opportunity, and the Evangelicals moved from the 1950s into the 'sixties with a real spirit of confidence. Mexican Protestantism was being thoroughly indigenized,[72] and though the proportion of active members to the population was highest in the northern tier of States fronting the American Union, Mexican Protestant churches were thoroughly Mexican.

21

BRAZIL IN THE 'SIXTIES

The Baptist World Alliance held its meetings in 1960 in Rio de Janeiro, and made the most of presenting Dr. Billy Graham as evangelist in the great Maracaná Stadium, with more than two hundred thousand in attendance, and a total of ten thousand registering as inquirers.[1] (The writer wore a counselor's badge in that great gathering.) This rally, till then the largest gathering of Evangelical Christians in history, was supported by the Evangelical denominations of Brazil in association with the Baptists.

The following year, there was a remarkable overflow of blessing from that metropolitan rally to the far off city of Campina Grande in the hinterland of Northeast Brazil. The Revival of 1952 had been unusually effective in Campina Grande, especially in the Congregational Church.[2] In 1960, Gerson Barbosa, a layman of that church, attended the Rio rally addressed by Billy Graham, and returned to Campina Grande to share his renewed vision with Congregationalists, Presbyterians, Baptists and Pentecostalists.

An early morning prayer meeting was begun, as in 1952, between 5 and 6 a.m., with ever increasing attendance of all denominations.[3] Each home in the little city was visited by workers during three days of intense visitation. A retreat was held for pastors, missionaries and workers by Antônio Elias. During the first two weeks of the campaign, all the churches closed their doors and engaged in open-air meetings in the suburbs in the evenings, maintaining prayer meetings in the mornings and visitation in the afternoons. The last week of September was devoted to rallies in the Getulio Vargas Stadium, the crowds increasing from ten thousand to thirty thousand, despite steady rains. Three thousand professions of faith were made in the campaign, in which Antônio Elias was the main evangelist, assisted by a score of teams of preachers. A Paraíba preacher wrote enthusiastically, 'All Northeast Brazil, in fact, the whole nation, has heard of Campina Grande because of the tremendous revival taking place there.'[4]

In 1960, J. Edwin Orr and his colleague William Dunlap conducted meetings in Brasília,[5] chiefly in the shanty towns where the construction workers lived during the building of the new capital city. The visit was unannounced and the meetings unprepared, but soon the various churches were crowded. Many pastors and people were friends of 1952.

During the previous year, the Presbyterian Churches of Brazil celebrated their centennial, and in many places this took the form of evangelistic campaigns, often with the full support of other denominations.[6] Eudaldo da Silva Lima, a leader in the Bahia Revival of 1952, addressed large rallies in Recife, up to 2000 attending, and various Presbyterian churches in the area reported growth in membership. This seemed typical of Presbyterian evangelism during 1959.

In '52, the Presbyterians had spearheaded the movement for revival, in part because the more numerous Baptists hesitated over taking the leadership because of the influence of the minority of exclusivists, nicknamed 'casca-duras' by Edwin Orr who suffered at their hands.[7] The Baptists took up leadership in the 1960s, but throughout the 1950s, the Presbyterians had reaped a harvest from the revival of '52. Their leading evangelist, Antônio Elias, who had played a notable part in the movement, extended his ministry all over Brazil. So also did Alfredo Stein, likewise moved.

In the area of greatest impact in the movement of 1952, the Synod of Eastern Minas and Espírito Santo, the gains in church membership surpassed those of the rest of Brazil for many years.[8] That mainly rural synod contained a third of the total membership of the denomination, provided a like proportion of its candidates for the ministry, and won forty per cent of its professions of faith, though served by a sixth of its pastors.

Another focus of unusual success in the 1952 movement was Governador Valadares, in Eastern Minas. In May 1963, Antonio Elias conducted lively meetings in the Presbyterian Church, with three hundred professions of faith. About four months later, the churches together sponsored a Word of Life team, with Erodice de Queroz as evangelist, to hold meetings in a football stadium where attendances rose from eight thousand to twenty thousand.[9] Twenty-two Evangelical churches cooperated, and shared the counsel of nearly a thousand inquirers. Not only was successful evangelism reported, but the churches rejoiced in an outpouring of the Holy Spirit in the area.

Of course, there were many who professed interest at the time of the Revival and its subsequent campaigns, and afterwards drifted away. Nevertheless, permanent results were noted in church growth, for the membership rose to more than a hundred thousand by the end of the decade, and the number of ordinands studying for the ministry in Recife and Campinas doubled and more. A Princeton researcher, Dr. P. E. Pierson, noted that 'After the Orr visit, similar campaigns continued in all parts of the nation under the leadership of Brazilian pastors,'[10] with many candidates for church membership and many volunteers for the ministry of the Presbyterian churches.

In 1957, the Presbyterian-ordained evangelist, Oswald J. Smith, visited Brazil, beginning his meetings in Rio de Janeiro, where the various churches were filled to capacity. In São Paulo, Smith preached to crowded congregations each night and on Sundays addressed seven thousand people in the Pacaembu Stadium. In both great cities, there were 240 professions of faith and 340 volunteers for service.[11] In Curitiba, the largest auditorium was filled with 4000 people and densely packed with more than 5000 for the final night. Walter Kaschel ably interpreted.

In 1962, Billy Graham returned to Brazil and conducted a campaign in São Paulo, crowds of a hundred thousand or so flocking to a football stadium to hear the messages. As usual, there were many professions of faith, and the series received general denominational support besides attendance of many Roman Catholics, with the Cardinal's goodwill.[12]

The year 1959 was a great year for the Presbyterians in Brazil, commemorating their hundredth anniversary as a force for evangelism. After the celebrations, when the attitude of some Presbyterians was one of returning to a less energetic life style, there were many congregations that continued full-tilt in revival and evangelism, as the columns of a Presbyterian periodical show, scores of local evangelistic campaigns being reported annually.[13] But the Presbyterians suffered setbacks which scarcely affected the Pentecostalists or Baptists, who were less involved in social activism. Presbyterians who supported evangelism remained active therein; those who paid it lip-service soon dropped their interest, though there was general support of interdenominational campaigns, such as Graham and Smith. Baptists maintained support of interdenominational efforts, as declared in review of the 1952 Reavivamento.[14]

In 1952, there were approximately 125,000 members of churches affiliated with the Brazilian Baptist Convention. Five years later, the membership had increased to 155,000, and by the end of the decade had passed 185,000, Baptists of other affiliations rounding out the figure to 200,000. Rio de Janeiro state and city possessed eighty thousand active members, prompting Baptists to assert that Rio had thus become the Baptist capital of the world.[15] However, the São Paulo Convention added thirty per cent to membership in a year compared with four per cent in Rio de Janeiro, due to a steady flow of migrants to São Paulo as well as aggressive evangelism. Baptist evangelism increased in the 'sixties.

In 1965, the energetic evangelism of the Baptists culminated in a nationwide evangelistic Crusade. Brazil had its quota of dynamic leaders, F. F. Soren, an outstanding pastor known worldwide among the Baptists, David Gomes, a radio evangelist and teacher, and a hundred and one others of note. The pastor of a dynamic church in São Paulo, the Rev. Rubens Lopes, conceived the idea of a nationwide effort, and did not spare himself in persuading his denomination to undertake it![16] The Grande Campanho of the Brazilian Baptists followed the simultaneous evangelistic campaign strategy known in the southern United States.

It was truly a grass-roots enterprise. In Rondon, a newly settled town of a thousand inhabitants on the frontier of Paraná, an ambitious group of Baptists pitched a big-top tent and, assisted by other Evangelicals, attracted as many as four thousand to the preaching, most of them coming by trucks and jeeps over dirt tracks to attend; there were more than a thousand inquirers registered.[17] A church in Vitória, with 350 members, welcomed 201 converts. In Rio Grande do Sul, a German church in Santa Rosa rented a large warehouse, attendances averaging 2500, decisions numbering 368. These results were typical.

Of the hundred thousand who registered decision in 1965, an encouraging number satisfied the churches that their experience was real and were baptized, and in 1966 the Brazilian Baptist Convention recorded communicant gains of 22,363, bringing the total to 242,452; and other inquirers were added by baptism in the following year.[18]

Other Baptist bodies in Brazil gathered converts in the 1960s, and a charismatic group of churches which felt ill at ease in the Convention consolidated work in various parts of the Republic, including Belo Horizonte.

The impetus of the Grande Campanha of the Brazilian Baptists continued through the latter 1960s.[18] By 1968, the membership of the churches in states and territories had reached 313,569, the increase by baptisms that year being ten per cent. The state of Rio de Janeiro counted 74,083 Baptist members; Guanabara (the city of Rio de Janeiro) 46,816; the state of São Paulo 42,064; Pernambuco 24,623, Bahia 22,653; Minas Gerais 20,127; Paraná 11,491; others between two and ten thousand. The denomination was surely thriving, despite a controversy over charismatic worship.

The acceptance of the challenge of Rubens Lopes for a Crusade of the Americas by other national Baptist leaders brought a resurgence of evangelism into Brazil, perhaps more organized and less dynamic. In 1968, Wayne Dehoney addressed some ten thousand in Pacaembu Stadium in São Paulo, and Joseph Jackson preached to 80,000 in torrential rain at Maracanã. Three teams of American pastors held evangelistic meetings in eighteen states, addressed nearly a hundred thousand people, of whom sixteen hundred made a public profession.

In 1969, the year of proclamation, simultaneous series of evangelistic meetings—reported in English as 'revivals' —were conducted in the conventions of Espírito Santo, Guanabara, Mato Grosso, Minas Gerais, Sergipe, Roraima and Amazonas in April; Alto and Médio Tocantins, Espírito Santo, Mato Grosso, Minas Gerais, Goiás, Federal District, and Maranhão in May; Fluminense, Maranhão, Piauí, and the territories of Rondônia and Acre in June; Mato Grosso and Goiás in July; Maranhão, Pernambuco, and Fluminense in August; São Paulo, Sertaneja, Pernambuco, Rio Grande do Sul, Pará and Amapá in September; Paraná, Alagoas, Bahia, Santa Catarina, Pará, Amapá, and Rio Grande do Sul in October; Paraíba, Rio Grande do Norte, Paraná, and Ceará in November. More than eighty thousand professed faith in these campaigns, a much lesser number baptized. A hundred new churches were needed for the influx.

In São Luiz, Maranhão, Dona Dominges de Morais, an illiterate, personally won more than three hundred converts to Christ. Paulo Gunicks, a humble man working in the largest hospital in Brazil, Hospital das Clínicas, enlisted a like number. A thousand churches, average membership a hundred and fifty, each won forty converts in the effort. The Baptist outreach seemed to be surpassed only by that of the Pentecostals.

By far, the greatest growth in all Brazil occurred among the Pentecostal denominations in the 1950s and 1960s. A spirit of revival had been noticed by observers among the Pentecostal groups since the movement of 1952 had begun. Far to the south, for instance, a watchnight service held in Blumenau in Santa Catarina produced fervent prayer for revival among members of the Assembly of God. Before the end of that year, W. F. Garvin's meetings in various parts of Santa Catarina were resulting in outstanding conversions.[19] In early 1953, the Garvins conducted a three-months' campaign in Curitiba, São Paulo, Belo Horizonte, and Rio de Janeiro, with great success.

During 1952, the Assemblies of God maintained several large congregations in Brazil,[20] one with seven thousand members in Recife, one with four thousand in Belém and another with the same membership in Pôrto Alegre. These huge churches included many lesser places of worship.

On 1st May 1953, the new auditorium of the Madureira Assembly of God in Rio de Janeiro was dedicated, with five thousand crowded inside and two thousand outside the great building. Many attending were from outside the local membership of the mother church and daughter gatherings, for the attention of the population was aroused.[21]

During the Orr campaigns, the Assemblies of God had been welcomed into the cooperating churches' committees and shared in the 1952 Revival. Throughout 1953, their congregations continued in revival enthusiasm, and in 1954, revival all over Brazil was reported in this constituency.[22]

There was also a remarkable movement in another such Pentecostal group, the Foursquare.[23] Harold Williams made his home in São Paulo as early as 1946, but on his return from furlough in 1951 fasted and prayed for thirty days for revival, the year 1952 being a year of great encouragement. Williams and Boatwright extended their ministry of tent evangelism into 1953, stirring up much excitement and not a little opposition. Some Presbyterian leaders, for instance, wrote appreciatively of the results of the healing meetings —'tendas divinas,' they were called—noting that such were the crowds that the police were called.[24] Others, including the strongly evangelistic, regretted that the excitement was in contrast to the conviction of the interdenominational work experienced in 1952. The Foursquare evangelists enlisted their converts in membership in Igreja Quadrangular, the National Evangelization Crusade.[25]

The year 1954 was one of great Pentecostal activity in
the city of São Paulo, Foursquare Pentecostal missionaries
using a huge tent to extend their ministry of healing and
evangelism.[26] Other denominations were mildly interested
or strongly opposed. Attendances ran from seven hundred
to fifteen hundred in the afternoons and from one thousand
to two thousand in the evenings. Twenty thousand decisions
were claimed since the tent movement had begun, but not
all these inquirers were enrolled in membership. But the
Foursquare missioners had discovered a successful method
for presenting the message to Brazilian multitudes.

Before the end of 1955, after months of tent work in
São Paulo with the ministry of healing the great attraction,
eight hundred people were ready to form a congregation. In
1956, the Foursquare evangelists were operating a dozen
tents, and ten congregations had been formed.[27] In Rio de
Janeiro, Clifton Erickson was addressing thirty thousand
or so at Campo de São Cristóvão.[28]

Clifton Erickson moved north to Belém, four thousand
nightly attending his meetings which greatly interested the
curious.[29] There were twenty-five professed conversions
each evening, not a very high proportion of those attending
—one in 160, as compared with one in three at the beginning
of the 1952 general awakening.

In 1961, the jubilee of the beginning of Pentecostalism in
Brazil was celebrated. The Assemblies of God were then
led by nine thousand national workers, assisted by a couple
of hundred missionaries, and the membership had passed
two-thirds of a million.[30] The Foursquare evangelists were
operating five large tents in which 195,000 were reportedly
converted, a hundred thousand healed, three thousand being
baptized and two thousand 'filled with the Spirit'—all in 1961.
'Certainly this is the day of revival in Brazil,' they said.[31]

Five years later, the Brazilian Assemblies of God were
operating 5500 churches with a membership exceeding one
million.[32] What was the secret of their success? From the
first, the pioneer missionaries supported themselves and
identified with the people. The growing Assemblies early
practised tithing, and encouraged every member to take
some part in the activities of the congregation. Street
meetings involved the membership and reached the whole
community. Like the early Methodists, the Pentecostalists
rejoiced in conversion as a first step, but urged a convert
to 'seek the baptism' of the Spirit and holy living.

By 1960, the jubilee of the arrival of Louis Francescon in Brazil, the Christian Congregation denomination had r ached a membership of three hundred thousand, being st ongest in the states of São Paulo and Paraná, its Mother Church situated in the São Paulo suburb of Brás.[33] There being no paid leaders, the denomination has had no need to stress even tithing; and throughout its years of operation it has received no financial assistance from abroad. By the end of the 'sixties, membership had passed the half million mark. The denomination remained exclusive.

Besides the major Pentecostal denominations, a number of independent causes arose. A young northerner, Manoel de Melo, followed the flood of immigration to São Paulo, where for a while he assisted Harold Williams in the tent missions.[34] The Brazilian began preaching in the parks, and drew up to a hundred thousand and two hundred thousand at times.[35] De Melo broke away from the Foursquare leaders who had ordained him. Aldor Pettersson, a Swedish leader moved in the Bahia Revival of 1952, joined forces with him, but his ministry provoked covert criticism in Evangelical circles and overt persecution from Roman Catholics. In 1955, Manoel de Melo backed Governor Ademar de Barros in his bid for the presidency of Brazil, and the opportunist Governor presented him with a sizable piece of property on which to build a temple; but, after a beautiful auditorium was built, the Governor pressured by Roman Catholics did an about-face, and without warning bulldozed the building to rubble.[36] He failed in his bid for the presidency, but the evangelist failed to recover a cruzeiro. But the Brazil for Christ campaigns continued, Manoel de Melo determinedly building a church auditorium in São Paulo to seat a crowd of 25,000. Meanwhile, the movement was spread by fiery evangelism, and a hundred thousand believers had joined the Brazil for Christ congregations by the end of the 1960s, a quarter of a million claimed by the mid-1970s. Perhaps the most remarkable feature of the movement was the fact that each organized congregation on average maintained at least ten local meetings, incipient congregations.

William R. Read, researching the Brazilian Churches in the 1960s, estimated total membership in the Pentecostal denominations in excess of two million.[37] The Pentecostal people were far from being social activists in the political sense, but they exercised a ministry of social help and demonstrated a vast potential for social change.

The Charismatic Renewal movement began in the late 1950s. A Baptist pastor, Enéas Tognini, who became well-known as a charismatic leader throughout Brazil, traced the beginnings of the movement through three phases: first, the prayer and writing ministry of Dona Rosalee Appleby of Belo Horizonte, who distributed tracts and booklets with a wide circulation among all denominations; second, the far-reaching ministry of Edwin Orr, who visited churches of all denominations and preached the filling of the Holy Spirit openly, his book on commitment being widely published by the Evangelical Confederation of Brazil; and third, the work of José Rego de Nascimento among students of the Baptist Seminary in Rio de Janeiro, resulting in revival in 1958.[38]

Rosalee Appleby, whose prayers played such a part in the 1952 Awakening in Brazil, wrote of a continuing desire for spiritual blessing thereafter as 'an insatiable longing for a manifestation of God that lay on many hearts.' Though misunderstandings increased, there was 'a burning fire' shut up in her bones and she could not forbear.[39]

But there were differences between the teachings of the evangelist of the 1952 Awakening and some of the Renewal movement that followed within the decade.[40] Orr taught total commitment, followed by the filling of the Spirit, a term that he preferred to the more disputed 'baptism' which applied also to the baptism of incorporation into the body of Christ. Orr accepted the occurrence of all the gifts, contradicting those who insisted that certain gifts had ceased since the days of the apostles; but he did not hold that glossolalia was the essential evidence or even only the initial evidence of an enduement with power—in which matter, the Catholic Charismatics and some Pentecostals agreed with him. But Orr said publicly that an experience of the Spirit's power was far more important than the terminology about it. His message was often misrepresented but fortunately his book on the subject had a wide circulation in Brazil, and those who sought to blame his ministry for church splits agreed that they found no fault with his written word, while it was known that he opposed unnecessary secessions.

By 1960, what had begun chiefly in Baptist churches was spreading to congregations of other denominations.[41] There were Anglicans, Congregationalists, Lutherans, Methodists, Presbyterians and others involved. What is significant is that the movement of renewal did not reach them through classic Pentecostals, denominational or freelance.

Moderate leaders of the Renewal movement were ready to concede that the closing of certain denominational doors to the charismatic impulse was partly the fault of some of the leaders, who expected everyone to change overnight the form of worship, methods and customs of long-established congregations and to substitute unstructured, free-flowing meetings, with hand-clapping and ejaculatory worship.[42] The gifts were sometimes counterfeited and exposed as such, stressing the need of discernment and discipline. Carnal exhibitions were soon recognized,[43] and 'holier-than-thou' attitudes were deplored and discouraged.

The leaders of the Renewal avowed their desire to stay within the fellowship of their denominations, and they spent many hours in prayer for Divine intervention to avoid any splits.[44] But it must not be forgotten that the groups in Belo Horizonte faced opposition from an intransigent clique that had opposed a general revival in 1952 with unworthy means. Objections to the Renewal movement in Baptist circles in Brazil generally stressed two things, that the movement in fact represented a Pentecostal takeover—which was hard to sustain, even in the United States, and that it was alien to the Baptist tradition. To the charismatics, the tightly-organized worship services and time orientation seemed no longer adequate for unpredictable exercises. Their ways soon offended those who objected to their terminology. The Brazilian Baptist Convention finally resolved to separate the charismatic congregations,[45] and about forty formed the National Baptist Convention. There were already affiliated with the Örebro Mission, a Swedish fellowship charismatic for several generations, eight thousand Brazilian believers. Six Baptist churches in Pernambuco were expelled from the Brazilian Baptist Convention, the result of the renewal movement which spread from Campina Grande, but before long there were forty charismatic congregations in the state of Pernambuco alone.[46]

In 1964, the Renewal movement began promoting rallies to which people interested in the subject of the work of the Holy Spirit could come for study of the scriptures and for opportunity to hear testimonies of experience.[47] From these rallies, pastors and laymen individually influenced returned to their respective fields, sharing their renewal with others. This in turn led to movements in other denominations that were sometimes accepted and sometimes rejected by the denominational leaders.

Antônio Elias, already an evangelist of note in Brazil and significantly involved in the Revival of 1952 and in its aftermath, cooperated with the charismatic movement fully yet maintained his position within the Presbyterian Church, continuing his ministry in Niterói as a pastor and throughout Brazil as an evangelist and conference leader. When he encountered opposition to the idea of renewal within the Presbyterian Church, he mollified his questioners when he pointed out that Simonton, the pioneer Presbyterian, had expressed in his diary a desire for the Spirit's baptism.[48]

Acceptance was not always forthcoming. Both synod and presbytery in Paraná investigated the ministry of Jonathan Ferreira dos Santos, who had carried the renewal emphasis from Belo Horizonte in 1965, and they decided to prevent his Cianorte congregation from 'becoming Pentecostal.'[49] A division ensued, a majority of the presbytery joining the Christian Presbyterian Church, a seceding group, in 1970. A group of Presbyterian ministers in the state of Espírito Santo in similar circumstances seceded, as did others in central Brazil, in Goiás and the capital, Brasília.[50] In 1970, a rally attracted two thousand to the Presbyterian Bible Institute in Cianorte, a new city in Paraná.[51]

Gerson Barbosa, Campina Grande industrialist, claimed that his renewal in the Spirit dated from the huge rally in Rio de Janeiro in 1960, when Billy Graham preached in the Maracanã Stadium. He sold his factory in 1961 and began to preach, by radio and itineration.[52] He joined a team led by Antônio Elias, supported by the Billy Graham Association, serving for thirty months. At the Berlin Congress, he was profoundly influenced by Dr. Han Kyung-Chik on revival.

The influence of Renewal spread to a group in Campina Grande which had been meeting for early morning prayer ever since 1952. Enéas Tognini conducted meetings in the church, assisted by the new pastor, Raul de Souza Costa. As the movement continued, there were healings reported and there was occasional speaking in tongues, all of which caused tension with leaders unsympathetically disposed.[53]

The Congregational denomination in Brazil—unlike its counterparts elsewhere, a strongly Evangelical body—took action against its Campina Grande congregation and without a hearing expelled it from the denomination and sought to regain the property. From the expelled body and others of similar sympathies came the Alliance of Congregational Churches of Brazil.[54]

In Anápolis, renewed Baptists, Congregationalists, and Presbyterians, and two Churches of Christ, cooperated in a three weeks' campaign with the Assembly of God, the largest church in the area, and filled the largest arena, so winning many hundreds to faith in Christ.[55] The association of ministers was reactivated for cooperative enterprise.

In Paraná, Daniel Bonfim, a Methodist minister with a quarter of a century of service, experienced the glow of a renewal while praying in Londrina. His subsequent work was marked by tireless praying and preaching, amazing his own colleagues, including his bishop who found a hundred people receiving baptism in a single service. But division followed a controversy, and the denomination expelled the churches and members connected with the Renewal, seventy congregations forming the Wesleyan Methodist Church.[56]

Methodist churches in Brazil had participated heartily in the '52 Revival. Serving chiefly in the South, Methodists lagged behind the Baptists and Presbyterians in nationwide influence and numbers, less than forty thousand in 1952. In 1960,[57] communicants had increased to more than 48,000, who added more than 18,000 new members between 1960 and 1965, though communicant rolls increased by only 9369, some suggesting that numbers of Methodists were captured by Manoel de Melo's Brazil for Christ crusade.[58]

The Renewal penetrated even the Churches of Christ in Brazil,[59] but, although the sending churches in the United States and many missionaries were strongly opposed as a matter of tradition, there was no expulsion of churches — each congregation being utterly autonomous. Charismatic Churches of Christ returned to the early ecumenical ideals of the Restoration movement, but evangelically.

The Evangelical Church of the Lutheran Confession in Brazil claimed more than 200,000 adults in communicant membership in 1960, with approximately 350,000 children baptized.[60] The Lutheran Church of Brazil, affiliated with the Missouri Lutheran Synod, claimed a numerical strength about a third as large. William R. Read seemed to regard Lutheran growth in Southern Brazil as mainly biological, infants baptized and adolescents confirmed as the German-Brazilians maintained contact with the Church of their folk. There remained a legacy of bitter feeling between the older Synod and the younger Missouri-related fellowship. The charismatic movement began to infiltrate the Lutheran folk in the late 1960s, but it remained a tiny minority.

The 1950s had brought revival and awakening to Brazil, and the 1960s extended the movement by evangelism, both in city-wide campaigns and in incessant pastoral outreach. The 'sixties were years of great social tension in the vast country,[61] many Christians both Evangelical and Catholic feeling that a real danger of a Communist takeover existed. The counter-movement brought military control and strict discipline, but the change of government did not threaten the Evangelicals or the Roman Church in spiritual life, as a left-wing dictatorship might have done.

Brazilian Evangelicals developed the missionary vision. Including converts of the Brazilian awakening of the 'fifties, Brazilian missionaries made their way to Portugal, and to Portuguese territories in Africa, and to nearby Spanish-speaking republics.[62] Social concern, especially for the impoverished Northeast, began spreading,[63] though there was little inclination to identify with incipient revolution.

The Roman Catholic Church moved more quickly than the Hierarchies in other Latin American countries to seize the opportunities for propagation of its message and social concerns. The Second Vatican Council had a profound effect upon Brazilian Catholicism, shown in a much more ready willingness to approach the 'separated brethren' in matters of common concern, even in support of evangelism.[64]

Regrettably, other religions than Christian grew rapidly. Spiritism, both sophisticated and gross, became the second most numerous body in several Brazilian states, claiming as many as twenty per cent of the population in areas.[65] Odd cults also gained a following.

But the outlook in Brazil seemed excellent, with the Evangelical churches growing faster than anywhere else in the world, the five million adherents doubling in the decade and accelerating in the 1970s.

22

HISPANO-AMERICAN EVANGELIZATION, 1960—

The 1960s throughout Spanish-speaking Latin America were years of church growth and campaigns of continental evangelization, of movements highly structured and hardly structured at all, with outbreaks of revival in some places and with the rise of the charismatic movement in several of the historic Protestant denominations and (surprisingly) in the Roman Catholic Church, already influenced by its ripening interest in the Scriptures.

In generalized figures, there were approximately fifty thousand Evangelical Christians in Latin America in 1900; in the 1930s, the figure passed the one million mark; in the 1940s, the two million mark; in the 1950s, the five million mark; in the 1960s, the ten million mark; in the 1970s, the twenty million mark—citing Peter Wagner.[1]

Read, Monterroso, and Johnson, in their study of Latin American church growth,[2] discovered that the communicant church membership almost doubled in seven years, 1960-67, a 95% increase, ranging from 22% in Nicaragua to 179% in Ecuador, smaller countries with tiny Protestant causes, from 42% in Argentina to 107% in Mexico, larger countries where Evangelical strength 8xceeded quarter of a million.

In the style or form of mass evangelism, there were two highly structured enterprises operating during the 1960s, the Billy Graham Evangelistic Crusades, already under way in the Caribbean and Central America; and Evangelism-in-Depth, the product of the prayers and planning of Kenneth Strachan and his colleagues.[3] The less structured healing-evangelistic campaigns of the Pentecostal itinerants also continued, besides incessant local evangelistic efforts.

Billy Graham's interest in Latin America waxed during the five years between 1958 and 1962.[4] His North American plan of operation was transferred to the countries south of the border, duplicating the mobilization of prayer, the enlisting of a wide council of support, the appointment of a narrower committee of action, a project for training lay-counsellors, and wide publicity for team outreach.

Shortly before the presidential election of 1960, a life-long friend of Dr. Billy Graham flew over the Great Smoky Mountains for a visit.[5] The world evangelist sought advice about an article he had written supporting the candidacy of Vice President Richard Nixon against that of Senator John Kennedy. His friend urged him to withdraw it, pointing out that Queen Elizabeth had been faithfully served by a Roman Catholic admiral and Oliver Cromwell by a Roman Catholic secretary of state. The article was withdrawn.

A friendship developed between statesman and evangelist. When Kennedy learned that Graham was about to minister in South America, he jokingly suggested—in view of his visits to heads of state there—that he would be Graham's John the Baptist.[6] Doubtless, Kennedy's goodwill impressed many Latin Americans, but it had little effect on the Latin American Roman hierarchy, who had already made up their minds to oppose the evangelist. In New York City, in 1957, an official spokesman informed Roman Catholics that they were forbidden to attend Graham's services; it was readily conceded that he was a man of prayer, humble, dedicated and devout, but among the various reasons given for the spiritual boycott, the chief one was that he did not accept the Roman Catholic position of being the only true church.

Meanwhile, in 1961, Evangelicals in the Latin American countries were mobilized for a Graham Crusade in 1962, mainly in northern South America from mid-January to mid-February, in southern South America in mid-October and November.[7] Apart from the right-wing fundamentalists and the left-wing radicals, a majority of the Evangelicals including the Pentecostals prepared to cooperate.

In Caracas in January 1962, the British evangelist, Joe Blinco, conducted six meetings with an aggregate attendance of fourteen thousand, followed by Billy Graham who drew an estimated eighteen thousand, professions of faith in these team meetings numbering almost a thousand.[8] In Venezuela, the Jesuits announced that Graham was 'an ignorant farm boy unworthy of being given a hearing, an ex-door-to-door salesman'; but the crowds flocked to the meetings, and a dozen radio stations broadcast his message.

Grady Wilson preached for five nights in Maracaibo with aggregate attendances of thirteen thousand, followed by a meeting addressed by Billy Graham attracting four thousand of whom hundreds professed faith.[9] Political agitators tried to disrupt one of the meetings.

In Barranquilla, the Colombian port, Leighton Ford was the associate evangelist, and built up attendances to six thousand in the baseball stadium, but the Mayor on short notice forbade the use of the stadium to Billy Graham on account of the protests of Bishop Villa Gaviria, who not only threatened excommunication to Roman Catholics who attended the services,[10] but who insisted that Protestant preaching outside church property was illegal in Colombia. Graham's Barranquilla meeting was held on the grounds of the Colegio Americana, more than fourteen thousand in all attending, one in ten professing faith.[11]

There the redoubtable Rafael Borelly, associate of Harry Strachan and former mayor and senator, presented Billy Graham to Colombia's ex-president Eduardo Santos, owner of Bogotá's largest newspaper, who ordered his editors to cover the evangelistic campaign.[12] Hence a hurried meeting was arranged in Bogota, attended by three thousand pastors and lay workers; but President Alberto Lleras Camargo, tactfully and politely, avoided a meeting with the evangelist.

At month's end, meetings were held in Cali, in western Colombia.[13] The Gimnaso Cubierto seating twelve thousand was secured, but it became necessary outside the coliseum to provide fifteen hundred extra seats and sound equipment, more than eighteen thousand attending while eighteen hundred inquirers were counselled.

Carlos María de la Torre, Cardinal Archbishop of Quito, forbade Roman Catholics in Ecuador to attend the Graham meetings.[14] In a population of quarter of a million, a total of twelve thousand attended Graham's two meetings, including high officials, and nearly a thousand professed faith. This greatly enheartened the two thousand Evangelical believers in the Ecuadorean capital.

The Graham Crusade in Lima, citadel of conservative Catholicism as well as capital of Peru, produced an unusual unity of purpose among the four thousand church members of Evangelical congregations.[15] Young people in Lima had distributed three hundred thousand handbills and five thousand posters were affixed in public places. More than twelve thousand Peruvians attended each meeting on 11th and 12th February, despite the clerical opposition that prevented the press from mentioning the campaign. More than two thousand inquirers sought counsel, nearly a thousand during the last two nights. Again, the majority of Evangelicals cooperated heartily in the efforts.

Joe Blinco commenced the campaign in Santiago, Chile, on 10th February 1962. On 16th and 17th February, Billy Graham spoke to great crowds, attendances in the Parque Cousino Ellipse reaching thirty thousand. The majority of those supporting the crusade were Pentecostals, but other denominations cooperated cordially. More than in the other republics, the top echelons of society were reached, and Protestantism was given a new image by press, radio and television, though of course there were critical journalists ready to denounce the evangelist as a charlatan.[16]

How effective were the Graham Crusades of early 1962 ? In four northern South American countries and in Chile, the team had preached to quarter of a million people, inquirers numbering nearly ten thousand.[17] Attendances were often two or three times as large as the local Evangelical population.

The reaction of Roman Catholics ranged from cordiality to hostility, with some sullen and others puzzled by the up-surge of interest.[18] The improvements following the Second Vatican Council had not yet affected the hierarchy and so the clergy reacted against the campaigns, but without the violence that prevailed in the tropical countries in earlier generations. The wall of separation still remained.

In the southern spring of 1962, the Graham team returned. After enjoying the unsolicited support of Roman priests and unlimited coverage by the press in his Brazilian campaign, Billy Graham was disappointed to run into a virtual boycott of his meetings when he reached Asuncion, the Paraguayan capital.[19] Of a score invited to a press conference, only one showed up. Neither editorial, news report or news picture appeared in any city newspaper, though paid advertisement was permitted. President Alfredo Stroessner reprimanded the press for its affront to a distinguished visitor.

The British evangelist, Joe Blinco, commenced work as associate evangelist on 26th September 1962.[20] When Billy Graham arrived, the clergy planned a gigantic demonstration ostensibly in support of the Vatican Council, timed for just before Graham's final rally and only two blocks away; but an unusually severe storm with 100-mile an hour winds hit the city, cancelling all scheduled activities, but clearing to calm and starry skies for the final rally of the campaign, which attracted ten thousand people, an aggregate of forty thousand in the series, of whom eight hundred professed personal faith. The tiny churches of Paraguay continued to grow throughout the decade following.

Billy Graham and his team ministered in Uruguay only in the capital, Montevideo.[21] Apart from Protestants of the ultra right, the Evangelical denominations cooperated in the meetings. More than a thousand hearers professed to make decision for Christ. The Baptists and the Methodists both gained in membership in the years following the campaign.

Grady Wilson commenced the campaign in the Argentine city of Córdoba.[22] A well-known priest used a newspaper to warn the faithful to keep away from the Graham meetings, but both attendances and results were encouraging. And in Rosario also, Billy Graham's preaching was preceded by a week of evangelism conducted by a team associate, Roy Gustafson, again with encouraging attendances and results.

The Graham campaign in Buenos Aires began in Luna Park, with thirty thousand attending the opening rally and many thousands turned away.[23] Capacity crowds of twenty thousand filled the arena each night of the campaign, but fifty thousand gathered for the final rally in the San Lorenzo soccer stadium. No anti-American demonstration occurred in Buenos Aires, as in some other cities, even though the Cuban missile crisis exploded during that final week of the Graham campaign in Latin America.[24]

Attendances during the warm spring evenings in Luna Park in Buenos Aires exceeded the nightly average in the Madison Square Garden in New York City five years before. Nearly half of all television viewers were reported to have watched and heard the evangelist answering questions on a telecast beamed to most of the Argentine population as well as that of Uruguay.[25] Argentine Evangelicals were heartened by the mass media opportunities.

It is worthy of note that the word preached was relayed by interpreters into Spanish throughout the South American campaigns, for none of the associate evangelists preached in the language of the countries concerned. Paul Sorenson acted as Graham's interpreter throughout Spanish-speaking campaigns, and Walter Kaschel served well in the meetings in Pacaembu Stadium in São Paulo,[26] Ray Robles serving as campaign soloist in the Spanish-speaking republics.

As in northern South America, the reaction of Roman Catholics ranged from cordiality in Brazil to hostility in Paraguay. Billy Graham and the team preached to half a million, and another ten thousand inquirers sought counsel. This brought the attendances in the South American series up to three quarters of a million aggregate.[27]

When Kenneth Strachan itinerated with and interpreted for Edwin Orr around Latin America in the early 1950s, he was profoundly interested in the concept of revival as a manifestation of the outpouring of the Spirit upon believers. Several years running, following the 1952 Revival in Brazil, he wrote to his friend of a quarter of a century and asked him to return to Latin America for more sustained ministry. But Orr was following 'the pillar of cloud' in Africa and India. By the end of the 1950s, Strachan had become active in the Billy Graham projects of evangelism in Latin America.[28] It was then that Strachan sought to combine certain elements of revival ministry to the churches with those of direct evangelism to the masses, to mobilize the spiritual potential of believers and apply the successful techniques of experts in presenting the Gospel to the people.

Kenneth Strachan thus became a philosopher as well as an organizer of evangelism.[29] A comparison and a contrast between Evangelism-in-Breadth—as typified by the modern evangelistic crusade—and Evangelism-in-Depth—as tried and tested by Strachan and his dedicated associates—has widely propounded several striking points.

First, Evangelism-in-Breadth emphasized the role of the evangelist and his team; Evangelism-in-Depth emphasized the role of every Christian in witness. In-Breadth, second, used cosmopolitan specialists to train an elite of campaign counsellors; In-Depth used local leaders to train believers in general as soul-winners. Third, In-Breadth organizers concentrated on broadening the audience of the gifted evangelist; In-Depth organizers sought to multiply the number of lay evangelists. Fourth, In-Breadth appeals were to 'Come and hear the Gospel'; In-Depth behests were to 'Go and preach the Gospel'. In-Breadth Evangelism enlisted the church in support; Evangelism-in-Depth mobilized the church in witness.[30]

Prof. Peter Wagner, in his friendly critique of the impact of Evangelism-in-Depth in Bolivia, described the work as 'programmed revivalism.'[31] It is significant that it was not proposed that such Evangelism-in-Depth was 'programmed revival.' Scripture teaches that the reviving of believers is the work of God, Finney notwithstanding. History is lacking in instances of committees choosing instruments of revival, and the records of Evangelism-in-Depth evidenced instances of committees choosing occasional spokesmen and regretting the choice. Evangelism-in-Depth was not revival.

Evangelism-in-Depth began in Nicaragua with New Year watchnight services, uniting congregations wherever it was possible.[32] In March 1960, Kenneth Strachan joined a parade of Evangelical church members in the town of Rivas, and that night Rubén Lores preached to a great crowd in the town's plaza; and in five other places similar ventures in evangelization were begun. The training brought together believers of diverse traditions, and a measure of revival accompanied the unifying process.[33] Two thousand people took training as witnesses, and visited sixty-five thousand homes.[34] Five hundred prayer groups were formed, and in fourteen united campaigns 126,000 folk attended services. Some twenty-five hundred people professed faith. The work was not without opposition. The Roman Catholic parishes put on a Sacred Mission, using the services of a hundred visiting priests. In Masaya,[35] the faithful were warned that they would be branded as excommunicated for attending or facilitating the meetings of Protestantism, 'a social scar and a deadly plague.' One meeting was disrupted by passing protesters led by a Spanish priest, but this was reported in the national press as a cowardly attack on a mission priest.

Evaluating the Nicaraguan project, Evangelism-in-Depth planners moved to home ground in 1961 and promoted a six months' campaign in Costa Rica.[36] Preceded by rallies on Reformation Sunday, with fifteen hundred prayer cells and twenty-five hundred in training, outreach began in January with Fernando Vangioni arriving in April as evangelist in San José's Gimnasio Nacional.[37] The Bishops pressurized the Government into prohibiting the public parade, which distracted leaders from their main purpose for a while.

Evangelism-in-Depth in Guatemala involved more than thirty thousand Evangelical believers in training, and no less than 230,000 house calls were made. Kenneth Strachan had discovered the malady which was shortly to end his life, so it was mid-1962 before the prayer and training groups got under way.[38] There were six thousand prayer cells engaged in intercession. The climax of the national effort was in Guatemala City in the early months of 1963, when four to ten thousand people attended meetings addressed first by Bishop Eleazar Guerra, then by Fernando Vangioni. Thirty thousand people attended a final rally in the Olympic Stadium. In the Guatemalan enterprise, fifteen thousand people made public profession of faith,[39] the Central American Mission, with its outreach to Indians, gaining much in 1963.

In the Republic of Honduras, fifteen thousand believers met in more than twenty-five hundred prayer cells in 1964, and fully six thousand took training and visited seventy-five thousand homes. There were five thousand professions of faith in all. Fernando Vangioni preached to a thousand each night in Tegucigalpa. The churches of San Pedro Sula reported their memberships more than doubled as a result of the united campaign there, and more than a hundred new congregations were formed throughout Honduras.[40]

Toward the end of 1964, a Cuban exile named Adib Eden conducted an evangelistic campaign in Templo Bíblico in San José, Costa Rica, culminating in the Gimnasio Nacional with four thousand hearers and more than three hundred inquirers seeking counsel.[41]

In 1964 and '65, Evangelism-in-Depth involved more than five hundred Evangelical churches in Venezuela, about four thousand prayer cells, while more than seventeen thousand took training, in the course of which twenty-seven hundred people professed faith.[42] Evangelistic campaigns were held in twenty-eight cities in the months of September and October, then in Maracaibo and Caracas in November and December. Seventeen thousand inquirers in all sought counsel.

Kenneth Strachan spent the last twelve months of his life in California, lecturing as a visiting professor in the School of World Mission until infirmity overtook him; he died on 24th February 1965.[43] His influence continued on around the world, his insights widely appreciated.

In 1965, the seven hundred and fifty churches of Bolivia, representing less than two per cent of the population, embarked on Evangelism-in-Depth, a parade in La Paz on a Sunday morning in November enlisting fifteen thousand or so marching people—something that a Roman Catholic observer commended for its magnitude and lack of pomp. In La Paz, an Argentinian evangelist, Santiago Garabaya, held the attention of ten thousand hearers, of whom a thousand sought counsel.[44] More than four thousand prayer cells were organized, and eighteen thousand Bolivians participated in the visitation of homes. 'In this red-letter year,' reported Peter Wagner, 'the impact made upon the entire Protestant community was indelible.'[45] Nearly twenty thousand inquirers were registered, but by no means all were integrated into cooperating denominations,[46] perhaps six thousand in three years, non-cooperating Seventh Day Adventists receiving an equal number of additions in that time.

Evangelism-in-Depth was applied next to the Dominican Republic, 1965-66.[47] Regino Loyola preached in the city of Santo Domingo nightly to thirty-five hundred people. Eight thousand people gathered in Duarte Stadium, and up to two thousand inquirers sought counsel. Many more professed faith during the year of effort.

During mid-1964, J. Edwin Orr had visited Peru at the pressing invitation of an old friend, Dr. Herbert Money, and the Evangelical Churches of Peru, the lecturing directed towards preparing the Evangelicals for revival, meetings being held in Colegio San Andrés, Colegio María Alvarado, Colegio America, Instituto Bíblico, and in various churches in Lima. Illness in Arequipa brought the tour to an end.[48]

In 1967, Evangelism-in-Depth was promoted in Peru. No less than seventy-five thousand Peruvian Evangelicals were trained for witness, and twenty-four campaigns were held in various parts of the country.[49] There was Roman Catholic competition in a Christian Campaign which used the services of television stars and three hundred priests. On 7th May of that year, a hundred and twenty-five churches in Lima sent out fifteen hundred visiting couples.[50] In one of the desperate slums, the barriada of Comas, a dozen people professed faith in their own homes. On the other hand, in the inland Huancayo area, five hundred or more prayer cells operated and as many people professed faith therein, with an equal number making decision in the training classes— more than nine hundred becoming members in the churches which reached them. An Alliance congregation of thirty-five reported seventy conversions and a doubling of membership. A tiny church of fifteen members won four times as many in the visitation phase and another thirty in mass evangelism.

The campaign in Lima was held in the National Coliseum, Regino Loyola preaching to eight thousand people, those responding on three successive nights being 159, 115 and 138. Ten thousand Evangelicals paraded to the Plaza San Martín, despite efforts by the police to prohibit the parade, the Rev. Felix Calle being arrested and questioned.[51] In the Alliance church in Lima, fifty converts were baptized and received.

Also in 1967, Evangelism-in-Depth, somewhat of a disappointment in '60, was repeated in eastern English-speaking Nicaragua, George Taylor being the evangelist, with twelve hundred trained for witness and two hundred prayer groups in operation, revival reported in Bluefields churches, such renewal quickening the whole Moravian constituency.[52]

When Evangelism-in-Depth reached Colombia, believers in primitive village chapels as well as in prosperous city churches greeted the New Year with an all-night vigil. The attendance at prayer cells rose from six thousand three-fold.[53] Seventeen thousand trained callers went out from six hundred churches to visit a hundred thousand homes, and nearly five thousand people expressed desire for personal salvation on that day, 2nd June 1968.

By mid-1968, visitation by trained witnesses was in full swing in Colombia.[54] By year's end, Osvaldo Mottesi spoke to two thousand nightly in Circo Teatro in Cartagena; two thousand believers paraded in Barranca Bermeja, where Roberto Frias preached; Carmelo Terranova evangelized in Florencia, a town in restricted mission territory, four hundred attending and seventy-six professing faith; and in Buenaventura, a thousand listened nightly, including priests and nuns, to hear Pedro Gutiérrez, one hundred and thirty professing faith and as many or more attending the Baptist and Alliance churches for instruction; while in Cali, more than four hundred remained for counsel.

In Bogotá, the capital, a city-wide bus strike threatened the success of the evangelistic campaign, but the believers walked to their churches and spent the night in prayer, and a quarter of a million marched in the streets as an act of witness.[55] The campaign was well supported, but, good as it was, it did not compare with the audacious enterprise of an assembly of sixty in Florencia, whose numbers doubled, an outcome of the faith shown in hiring a theatre which seated four hundred. Campaigns were held in many other places, and the follow-up continued into 1969.

Preparations for Evangelism-in-Depth began in Ecuador in mid-1969, sixteen hundred prayer cells being operated. Campaigns were held in 1970, Fernando Vangioni preaching to great crowds in Guayaquil, inquirers helped being three thousand in number. The town of Cuenca, with a population of seventy-five thousand, produced three thousand inquirers, Hermano Pablo (Paul Finkenbinder) the evangelist.[56]

Evangelism-in-Depth carried on into the 1970s, when a total of seven thousand Evangelical churches cooperated in Mexico,[57] the method of evangelization having been tried and tested as one way of winning people to Christ, while moving the congregations spiritually. Unlike the Graham meetings, where interpretation was used, Evangelism-in-Depth teams excelled in their mastery of Spanish.

Luis Palau was born in Argentina in 1934, and came to a knowledge of personal salvation in Buenos Aires in 1946. He was deeply impressed by the work and dedication of the Child Evangelism Fellowship in Córdoba, in central north Argentina, where as a teen-ager he took a course of instruction in winning children to Christ. His first 'trophy of grace' was a member of his class of boys.[58]

Palau became ardent in Christian witness as a layman. Invited in 1960 to the United States by Overseas Crusades, he was in his mid-twenties when he studied at Multnomah School of the Bible in Portland,[59] where he met and married Patricia Scofield. In 1962, he served as an interpreter in a Graham Crusade in Fresno, California. Before long, Palau was conducting mass evangelistic campaigns throughout Latin America, ranging far and wide as did Harry Strachan forty years before, and attracting ever increasing crowds as did his friend, Billy Graham. His ministry was modeled on Graham's, so far as teamwork and the use of the media were concerned, but he developed his own style and gained the goodwill of national pastors and missionaries alike for sanity and thoroughness in his Overseas Crusades.

The Palau family moved first to San José, Costa Rica, where Patricia became proficient in Spanish. Later they moved to Mexico City, used as a base for larger and larger campaigns in Latin America. With the expansion of his work came the enlargement of his team of associates, bilingual and multi-talented.

In Colombia, in 1966, the Palau team participated in a four-day campaign in which the churches cooperated, the first such effort in Bogotá since the days of the Violence. For six weeks, it had rained steadily; but the young people met for prevailing prayer, and the rains ceased the day the meetings began.[60] Great rallies were held in Plaza Bolívar, and a parade was held, the first of its kind in Bogota's long history. The clouds gathered and the rains descended again after the final meeting and it rained for almost three weeks without letup. Those who professed faith in the campaign numbered 865: a year later, Bogotá's thirty cooperating churches were crowded to capacity. Campaigns in Cali and San Marcos, Girardot and Armenia attracted aggregates of about forty thousand in less than ten weeks, and seventeen hundred inquirers professed faith, bringing total attendance in Colombia to eighty thousand, professions of faith to 2700 or so.

In 1967, the Palau team visited Peru.[61] Among those who attended the meetings in the Coliseum in Arequipa were several Spanish Jesuits. Radio and television multiplied the number reached by the ministry, twelve thousand having attended in person, of whom more than six hundred became inquirers. The little companies of believers in Arequipa trebled in attendance. Huancayo also was the venue of a week's campaign, with eighteen thousand in attendance.

In 1968, Luis Palau preached again in Colombia, four thousand average attending during three days in Bogotá and three thousand five hundred average for four days in Cali, while a total of sixteen thousand met in Medellín.[62] In all three campaigns, there were fifteen hundred inquirers.

Also in 1968, a campaign was held in San Cristóbal in Venezuela,[63] during which Palau's life was threatened and a bodyguard was provided by the Governor. At one point, the audience fell to the floor or ran for cover, mistaking the cracking of light bulbs by the rain for gunfire. In fifteen days, the attendance in aggregate mounted to eight thousand and there were more than five hundred inquirers.

During the Baptist Crusade of the Americas in 1969, in Quito, the Ecuadorean capital, evening evangelistic rallies were held in a basketball coliseum and more than eighteen thousand attended meetings during an eight-day campaign, more than five hundred registered as inquirers.[64] So, five years later, in 1974, the Luis Palau team campaigned in Quito under indigenous Evangelical sponsorship, spending three weeks in the Coliseum where more than three thousand inquirers professed faith. The Bible Society sold out its stocks of ten thousand Bibles and seven thousand Spanish versions of the New Testament. The results were lasting. Months later, various churches in Quito reported upon the integration of the new converts into the congregations. An Assembly of God report noted most of those referred were attending Central Church faithfully, thirty men preparing for baptism; the South Church gained twenty-five new adherents, and was starting a new congregation in Machachi; a new church was beginning in the Chahuarquingo district with fifty new converts, while the Foursquare Church noted a score of new converts attending church faithfully, with a new congregation forming in Amaguana where fifty people were meeting at 5 a.m. before going to work. The Alliance Church opened a new congregation in El Placer district, and congregations old and new were catering to an influx.

During the first two weeks of October 1969, the Palau team participated in a Metropolitan Campaign in Mexico City.[65] Plans to rent a big-top circus tent seating more than six thousand fell through, so the campaign began in two of Mexico's downtown churches, situated back to back, each holding more than a thousand people. The times for gospel messages were staggered, as the Evangelist concluded his preaching in one church and began in the next. More than two thousand people professed faith, and so pleased were the cooperating churches that another series was planned for 1970. Meanwhile, a like number of inquirers sought for counsel in the campaign held in the Plaza de Toros in the city of Monterrey, where an aggregate of thirty thousand attended during nine days. Also in 1969, twenty-five local congregations cooperated in a campaign in Tampico, where television greatly added to the number of hearers.

In April 1970, Luis Palau and his associates returned to evangelize Mexico City, a hundred thousand citizens attending meetings in the Mexico Arena, averaging ten thousand a night. There were 6640 inquirers who made commitment to Christ after counsel. New life came to many churches.[66]

Sixty small and struggling congregations in Tijuana in Baja California cooperated in a campaign conducted in 1970 by Luis Palau, with Galo Vásquez engaging in a ministry of child evangelism.[67] Fourteen hundred inquirers professed a new-found faith, including a number of children.

In 1960, Netzahualcoytl was part of the dry bed of Lake Texcoco, high on the plateau of inner Mexico. By 1974, a million and a half Mexican migrants had settled in this new suburb of Mexico City, an impoverished community, hence the Palau team conducted a campaign of eight days to reach the displaced people, nearly fourteen hundred professing a personal faith.[68]

The Palau team tackled San Salvador, capital of the tiny Republic of El Salvador. During the ten day series in 1970, the results of a dozen one-hour television projects amazed the team and encouraged them to develop such a ministry, using a format of gospel singing, a fifteen-minute talk by Luis Palau, then a conversational evangelism as telephone lines were opened and questions from viewers flowed in. It was estimated that there were more than four hundred thousand viewers, one in ten of the population. A flood of letters and personal encounters followed, adding to the fifteen hundred inquirers who professed faith.[69]

In Honduras, the Palau team engaged in a campaign in San Pedro Sula late in 1970, and moved to Tegucigalpa, the capital, for a two-weeks campaign early in 1971. Meetings were held to reach high school and university youth, as well as the television audiences far and wide across the country. Palau helped the Central American Mission to celebrate its seventy-fifth anniversary in Honduras. Thirty churches in Tegucigalpa cooperated in the effort, which attracted a total of fifty-five thousand, 6500 jamming a baseball court on the occasion of a night for youth. Perhaps half a million people viewed the television presentations.[70] About eighty thousand aggregate attended the 1970-71 Honduran series, and three thousand inquirers received counsel— significant where only a tiny minority of Honduran folk went to church regularly, and formal marriage was distressingly rare; in the whole country, there were 237 Roman Catholic priests, a tenth of them native-born; Protestant churches were few.

Early in 1971, Palau conducted an evangelistic campaign in Guatemala City, using the Gimnasio Nacional to reach the masses. More than two thousand inquirers professed faith.[71] A simultaneous television campaign led to numerous telephone calls and such inquirers were followed up with Bible study materials. In 1970 and 1971 meetings, Palau ministered to an aggregate of a hundred and fifty thousand. In November 1972, evangelistic campaigns were held in the four western Guatemala cities, 20,000 attending rallies in Coatepeque, 27,000 in San Pedro and San Marcos, 18,000 in Huehuetenango and 50,000 in Quezaltenango. Associate evangelists from Mexico conducted 'pre-campaign' rallies in each city, and Edgardo Silvoso of Argentina trained fifty young folk as street evangelists. More than three thousand inquirers professed faith. A pastor visited sixty of those whose decision cards had been given him, invited them to a noonday meeting on Sunday for converts, and was happily embarrassed when three times as many showed up. Amando Osoro, pastor of the Central American Mission church in Huehuetenango, found sixty candidates for baptism and as many more in preparation for a public confession.

Six thousand Costa Ricans attended the opening rally of the Luis Palau Campaign in the Zapote Bullring on the outskirts of San José, in January 1972. Trained counsellors from Central American Mission, Latin American Mission, and other Evangelical Churches dealt with three thousand inquirers among the sixty thousand aggregate attending.[72]

Late in 1971, Luis Palau campaigned in Lima, capital of Peru, sponsored by eighty-five Evangelical churches in the Plaza de Acho Bullring. No less than 450 inquirers made a profession of faith during preparatory rallies and television presentations, and ten times as many sought counsel during the actual Crusade. In one of the notorious barriadas of the city, many parents reached by child evangelism professed conversion, so that a new congregation was formed therein. On New Year's Day 1972, fifteen thousand people filled the Bullring for the concluding meeting of the series.[73]

Despite uncertainties of weather and of peace, in March 1973 a Luis Palau Crusade was conducted in the Dominican Republic, where seventy-five thousand people in all came to the Duarte Baseball Park in Santo Domingo, more than 2500 responding to the invitation to profess faith publicly. Again, Edgardo Silvoso trained young people to be street evangelists, and teams continued to witness afterwards.[74]

Late in 1974, the Luis Palau team campaigned in three cities of Bolivia. In Santa Cruz, up to ten thousand attended meetings in the Bendeck Stadium, more than three thousand citizens registered as inquirers; in Oruro, the crowds of interested people gathered in the Teatro al Aire Libre, and fifteen hundred or so sought counsel; while in Cochabamba, the meetings in the Coliseo Coronilla began with about three thousand hearers and concluded with double that number— the best record of any series held to date.[75] As a result, the central Calle Bolívar Church of the Evangelical Christian Union reported morning and evening services packed out and fifty new converts welcomed into fellowship, the other participating churches engaging in 'conservation of results.'

In all, there were nine thousand professions of faith during the Bolivian campaigns,[76] which began with unanimous support in the first two cities and achieved the same in the third by the time it concluded.[77]

Managua, the capital of Nicaragua, was devastated by an earthquake in 1972. In 1975, the city became the unlikely site for an evangelistic campaign of an intercontinental sort, Continente '75, to reach all of Latin America by television and radio.[78] In November 1975, Luis Palau embarked on a Managua '75 Campaign, beginning with twenty thousand in attendance on the opening night, averaging five thousand in the nights between, and reaching twenty-two thousand on the closing night in a damaged stadium with limited bus service to the areas of relocated population.

Managua '75 proved to be the largest evangelistic campaign in the history of the Republic. Most of Managua's 125 Evangelical churches supported the effort, and six thousand people registered decision, a majority making a profession of faith.[79]

What was innovative about the Managua enterprise was the use of radio in a continent-wide network of stations as well as telecasts of a hundred television stations in a score of countries. It was estimated that a hundred million people were reached by the media, including the press. It was an eerie experience for associates, such as Edward Murphy, on the edge of the stadium crowd, to hear Palau's voice via satellite over Spain before it reached them from a hundred meters away.[80]

Opposition to the Palau Crusade in Managua came from an Anglican priest—formerly a fundamentalist Baptist—in the columns of a tabloid newspaper,[81] countered by Catholic writers in another journal, which noted the Archbishop's benevolent neutrality and urged the faithful to attend with assurance of receiving blessing. Catholic Charismatics in notable numbers attended enthusiastically.

By 1975, Luis Palau had become a Latin American international and continental evangelist of rare effectiveness. In the world field, no one surpassed him in the scope of his operations other than Billy Graham. The following year, but outside the purview of this volume, Palau and his team engaged in a campaign in Rosario, Argentina's second city, which developed an intensive follow-up plan that resulted in the successful planting of nearly thirty new house churches to conserve the results of evangelism. Six months after the campaign ended, more than half the three thousand converts were found in regular church attendance, a third baptized and a sixth receiving instruction therefor. Edgardo Silvoso reported that such baptisms in five months following this campaign more than trebled those ten months previously.

Luis Palau also succeeded Dr. Dick Hillis as president of Overseas Crusades,[82] a worldwide service organization, and extended his ministry to other continents, preaching as fluently in English as Spanish.

23

HISPANIC DENOMINATIONAL GROWTH

Roman Catholicism prior to the Second Vatican Council faced a sorry situation. Ignacio Vergara, a Roman priest, regretfully reckoned that 70% of the Chilean population were practising no religion whatsoever,[1] a reckoning rightfully extended to most Latin American nations. Despite a 90% rate of baptism, a lesser percentage took first communion, and a lesser percentage still contracted religious marriage, while less than 10% women and 4% men attended mass. The authorities in several countries had blamed the Evangelical churches for their plight, and had used fair methods and foul to crush the 'heretical interlopers.' But these attempts had failed utterly, and it seemed inevitable that a turn-about face would come in Roman Catholicism.

Meanwhile, the Evangelical movement made rapid progress everywhere.[2] Denominationally, the lowest rates of growth occurred among the historic denominations whose theology had been most affected by Christo-humanism at home, better rates of growth among avowedly Evangelical bodies, and phenomenal rates of growth among Pentecostal missions and churches.

In Argentina's population of twenty million, a quarter of a million at least[3] were members of Evangelical Churches. About a hundred thousand of these belonged to a variety of Pentecostal denominations, approximately forty per cent; ten per cent were in fellowship with the Christian Brethren; seven per cent were Seventh Day Adventists; and a similar number belonged to the Baptist denomination; four per cent of Protestants were claimed as Methodists; twelve per cent were Lutheran, but the bulk of the Lutheran members were gained by ethnic affiliation rather than evangelization; a great variety of minor ethnic groups and splinter churches comprised the remainder. Another researcher raised the total to 400,000 members; but the proportions remained much the same.[4] One thing is certain, the Hicks campaign in 1954 proved to be a significant mark in church growth for almost every Evangelical denomination.

While church growth came by evangelistic enterprise, in Argentine Evangelicalism[5] arose a movement of renewal. In the mid-sixties, an American missionary, Keith Bentson, was holding conferences for the deepening of the spiritual life, attracting members of Baptist, Brethren, Mennonite and other churches and encouraging them to express their praise to God openly. One evening, quite spontaneously and without prompting—Bentson was non-Pentecostal—a lady well-known in Brethren circles began speaking in tongues. Brethren especially being unacquainted with spiritual gifts —described by Darby as 'not for the church today,'—— Juan Carlos Ortiz of the Assemblies of God was called for, and guided the group into wider outreach, attracting a thousand to meetings while penetrating quite a number of Brethren, Baptist and Mennonite assemblies—though by no means all.

The autonomous structure of the Brethren denomination made it impossible to inhibit the spread of the movement of charismatic renewal. By 1970, it was supposed that a fifth of the assemblies' adherents were practising a charismatic form of worship.[6] Likewise, a number of Baptist churches became associated with the renewal movement, as did a number of the Mennonites. Some Pentecostal assemblies and leaders associated themselves more closely with their brethren in the historic denominations than others, and the Hidalgo Church with its pastor, Juan Carlos Ortíz, took a lead in promoting the work.[7] An acute analyst noticed that the renewal movement lacked evangelistic outreach, unlike the Brazilian revival of 1952.[8]

Events in Argentina generally affected Uruguay, where the growth of the churches seemed much slower. There the charismatic renewal had its recruits, but fewer in number. In the late 1960s, the largest Evangelical denomination in Uruguay was the Waldensian,[9] serving approximately five thousand communicants and a community two-and-a-half times as large. The Seventh Day Adventists counted about three thousand members, the Methodists two thousand, the Church of God two thousand, and fifteen hundred each in the Assembly of God and Swedish Pentecostalist denominations, making Pentecostals the most numerous Evangelical group; the Baptists counted less than fifteen hundred, Mennonites more than a thousand; hence the total of the Evangelical population scarcely exceeded twenty-five thousand, less than one per cent of the population, as compared with five per cent practising Roman Catholics.

The population of Paraguay was less than two million, of whom 95% were nominal Roman Catholics. The proportion of practising Roman Catholics seemed related to the total of Roman Catholic priests in the country, only double that of Protestant missionaries and pastors,[10] representing 1%. In the late 1960s, the Paraguayan Evangelicals numbered only fifteen thousand. A quarter of these were Mennonites, mostly ethnic Germans from various countries, but with a developing outreach to the mestizos and Indians. Ten per cent were Pentecostals, seven per cent Baptists. Ten per cent belonged to the interdenominational New Testament Missionary Union, no longer a fast-growing body. But the 1960s produced 10% church growth among all Evangelicals.

How different were conditions in Chile. With a population of seven-and-a-half millions, Chile numbered 85% as its nominal Roman Catholic population, its practising Roman Catholics as less than 10%—less than the number of the Evangelical community.[11] By the end of the 1960s, Chilean Evangelical church membership was approaching the half million mark, two thirds of these avowed Pentecostals with a quarter of a million in the two leading denominations.[12] In comparison, the other Protestant church fellowships in the country were small, fifteen thousand in the Adventist body and ten thousand in the Baptist.

Bolivia's population in 1960 numbered 3,316,000, and Roman Catholic reporters claimed their community as 102% of the total, considered over-optimistic.[13] The numbers of Evangelicals more than doubled in the first seven years of the 1960s, a third of them being Seventh Day Adventists, twice as numerous as the Evangelical Christian Union.[14]

Peru reported a population of ten-and-a-half million in 1960, of whom 90% were nominal Roman Catholics. Only sixty thousand were Evangelical communicants in 1967, of whom nearly half were Seventh Day Adventists.[15] However, the Protestant membership had doubled in seven years, and evangelistic campaigns were adding to church growth, as were folk movements in the Andes.

The population of Ecuador in 1960 was less than four-and-a-half million, of whom 90% were nominally Roman Catholic, served by a thousand priests. The Evangelical communicant membership trebled in seven years, and continued to rise, the Seventh Day Adventists the largest of the denominations, being rapidly overtaken by the Foursquare Pentecostals, followed by the Alliance churches.[16]

Colombia noted a population of nearly fourteen million in 1960,[17] over-optimistic Roman Catholic statisticians of the Vatican claiming a community equal to the population. The Evangelical community numbered only one per cent of the Colombian population, but the total of communicants almost trebled in seven years, in round figures to 75,000 by 1967. A third of the communicants were Pentecostal and showed a remarkable increase, three-fold and better in certain denominations. The Seventh Day Adventists noted a 60% growth, while other mission enterprises were growing at a rate many times that of biological increase.

The population of Venezuela in 1960 was estimated as six-and-a-half million, of whom 90% were nominal Roman Catholics. The Protestant community was less than 1%, of whom sixteen thousand were communicants. In seven years, the number of communicants trebled, twenty thousand of them adhering to Pentecostal denominations, though the largest single Protestant denomination was Brethren, with seven thousand in fellowship.[18]

Panama possessed a population of a million in 1960, of whom 80% were nominal Roman Catholics.[19] Nearly ten per cent were Protestant community, due to the immigration of West Indians, and communicant members numbered 27,000, a figure which increased by a third in seven years. The largest denomination was that of the Foursquare Church.

Costa Rica claimed more than a million in 1960, of whom 90% were nominal Roman Catholics. The total Protestant community numbered 4%, of whom ten thousand counted as communicants.[20] By 1967, there were twelve thousand, a quarter of them Pentecostals.

The population of Nicaragua was a million-and-a-half in 1960, of whom 70% were nominal Roman Catholics, the Protestant community numbering 4%.[21] The Moravians were the largest denomination, generally English-speaking, its community in 1967 rising to 25,000, communicants 10,000.

Less than two million people inhabited Honduras,[22] and of these 80% were Roman Catholic. The Protestant community represented less than two per cent of the population, many being of English-speaking West Indian stock. Communicants doubled in seven years to approximately eighteen thousand.

In 1960, El Salvador reported two-and-a-half million in population, 80% nominal Roman Catholics. Approximately eighteen thousand communicants doubled in seven years, Pentecostals the greatest gainers, numbering two-thirds.[23]

Guatemala in 1960 had a population of three-and-a-half million,[24] of whom about three million were nominal Roman Catholics, a fraction of them practising their faith. There were more Evangelical ministers than Roman clergy in the field. The Protestant community numbered 105,000, a third of whom were communicants, but memberships more than doubled in seven years, the Pentecostals leading.

Mexico's total population in 1960 was 35,000,000,[25] the nominal Roman Catholics 30,000,000. Two per cent made up the Protestant community, but membership was quarter of a million, which approximately doubled in seven years through incessant evangelism, campaigning and pastoring. The Pentecostal denominations represented two-thirds of total communicant membership.

Cuba's population in 1960 was estimated at six-and-a-half million, seven out of eight reputedly a Roman Catholic, though practising Catholics were a fraction of this figure. The Protestant community numbered 3%, or two hundred thousand, fifty thousand communicants served by almost as many ministers as there were Roman clergy on the island. After persecution, church attendance increased again,[26] the young people becoming disillusioned with life in society. At the end of the decade, it was reported that Cuba's many churches were full and growing. Statistics were difficult to collect under dictatorship.

The Republic of Haiti possessed three-and-a-half million inhabitants in 1960, with three-quarters of them claimed as Roman Catholics by statisticians, a great number of whom were actually practitioners of voodoo. The Protestant folk numbered more than 10%, a third of them communicants. During the 1960s, Evangelical membership increased 60% and Pentecostals and Nazarenes multiplied three fold.[27]

The Dominican Republic claimed nearly three million citizens, 90% nominal Roman Catholics. The Protestant community numbered less than 2%, a third of them active members.[28] The 1960s witnessed a steady increase through evangelism, accelerating in the 1970s.

Puerto Rico had less than two-and-a-half million in 1960, 90% nominal Roman Catholic,[29] the Protestant community numbering 7%, a third of them communicants with as many ministers as Roman clergy on the island.[30] It was claimed that Evangelical communicant membership had gained 42% in seven years. Puerto Rico still supplied evangelists with dynamic and ability to the Latin American enterprise.

The success of the Brazilian Baptists' Grand Campaign in 1965, which resulted in a hundred thousand professions of faith, tens of thousands of additions to membership, and the founding of three hundred new churches, inspired the Rev. Rubens Lopes to challenge the Baptists of the other nations of the Western Hemisphere to engage in a Crusade of the Americas.[31] With exception of the American Baptist Convention——whose director of evangelism seemed ideologically lukewarm to evangelism in the historic manner—— the North American Conventions supported the project.

In July 1966, six commissioners of the Southern Baptist Convention and three of the Brazilian Baptist Convention met with representatives, one for each lesser sized body, in Cali's International Baptist Seminary.[32] Plans were made for 1967 and '68 as years of preparation, 1969 the year of proclamation, evangelistic campaigns often called 'revivals.'

Baptists in the Argentine, Uruguay, Paraguay and Chile, numbering less than one tenth of one per cent of the total population, embarked on evangelistic preaching in Spanish, Guarani, and half a dozen European languages in 1969. In Argentina, there were ten thousand professions of faith that year, in Uruguay two thousand, in Paraguay a thousand, in Chile more than seven thousand.[33] The project included the forming of prayer cells, tract distribution, home visitation, radio-television and mass evangelistic campaigns.

In tropical South America, Baptists in Ecuador reported two thousand professions of faith, half as many baptisms and a score of new churches.[34] In Peru, there were more than two thousand professions of faith, a fifth of them in the territory of the Irish Baptist Mission. More than a tenth of those inquiring were baptized in 1969. In Colombia, there were more than a thousand inquirers, great rallies being held in Bogota, Barranquilla, Cali, and the Islands. In the Republic of Venezuela, there were both radio and television broadcasts, as in other countries, and eighteen thousand who attended evangelistic rallies, of whom more than a thousand professed faith, a fifth being baptized in 1969.

In Panama, twelve hundred inquirers professed faith and 6485 church members welcomed 644 new members in 1969. Several hundred people professed faith in Costa Rica, about twelve hundred in Nicaragua, four hundred in El Salvador, a like number in Honduras, eleven hundred in Guatemala, but, in Mexico,[35] there were more than twelve thousand who professed faith, of whom one in seven was baptized in 1969.

That Pentecostalism grew rapidly in Hispanic America was noted by every observer, Roman Catholic or Evangelical. How it grew can best be illustrated in one such denomination. The Assemblies of God began the 1960s with approximately two hundred missionaries distributed throughout the Latin American countries and the West Indies, about nine thousand national workers, and more than seven thousand churches with 670,000 adherents.[36] Most missionaries were of North American origin, but there were many Swedish workers in Brazil. Membership was a number that neither missionary nor national leader could calculate at any given time, the movement growing so rapidly.

Forty years after the Assembly of God missionaries had entered Argentina, after many vicissitudes and little growth, there were eight congregations in Buenos Aires. By 1969, there were eighty, and another sixty in the provinces, with nearly ten thousand adherents.[37]

Carlos Naranjo, an elder in the Christian Brethren—los Hermos Libres who were automatically dissociated from the Hicks campaign because of dispensational doctrine— was distressed when doctors gave up all hope of his wife, Rosalia, dying of an incurable disease.[38] A friend who had been helped in the Hicks campaign persuaded Naranjo to enlist the prayers of Louie Stokes, and Rosalia was healed instantly. The family moved to San Nicholas at the request of Naranjo's employer, and those to whom they witnessed became a nascent congregation. The founding of a steel mill brought thousands of people to the city, doubling to 80,000 in fifteen years; Naranjo's lay pastorate resulted in twenty group meetings and a Christian community of eight thousand. One such group gathered in Villa Pulmon, a suburb where crime, prostitution and drunkenness ran riot, abandoned by the police. Naranjo was mocked and stoned, but preached under a tree in the middle of the slum. A breakthrough to the slum dwellers came when an infant was healed of a head deformity, the head bigger than her body. Many outstanding conversions followed, and the slum was transformed.

Of all the countries of Latin America, the Assemblies of God found Uruguay the most indifferent to the message. In 1961,[39] Salvador Mairena of Argentina campaigned in Fray Bentos, Dolores, Mercedes, and other Uruguayan cities, and in October 1964, Richard Jeffery of Phoenix preached to crowds of between two and three thousand in the city of Melo. By then, there were twenty organized Assemblies.

Paraguay was considered a difficult field by Assembly
of God missionaries, but a dozen churches in 1959 became
two dozen in 1969, indicating a response which raised the
Pentecostal proportion of Protestants to ten per cent.[40]

Pentecostalism was very strong in the Republic of Chile,
but it was a Pentecostalism of wholly indigenous origins,
growing out of Methodism, practising infant baptism which
separated it from the worldwide Pentecostal movement that
uniformly immersed its converts only.[41] Both the Swedish
and American Assemblies of God, as well as the Church of
God (Tennessee-based) and the Foursquare denomination,
offered fraternal help to the Chilean Pentecostals, but they
found too many points of disagreement, and remained to
plant their own churches, which numbered between one and
two thousand communicants in each case, not comparing
with the hundreds of thousands of indigenous Pentecostals
in the larger Chilean denominations, though of course there
were smaller bodies among the hundred groupings reported.
The Methodist Pentecostal denomination counted a hundred-
and-fifty thousand communicants at the end of the 1960s and
built its mother church into a 'cathedral' seating 8000, the
opening ceremonies attended by the President of Chile.[42]

The Assembly of God work in Bolivia had started in 1948
and Pentecostal work there grew rather slowly; but at the
end of 1967, Paul Finkenbinder—better known as Hermano
Pablo—campaigned in La Paz, Cochabamba and Santa Cruz
with crowds up to ten thousand attending.[43] Five thousand
professions of faith were reported, but the membership of
the churches rose from about fourteen hundred to seventeen
hundred, with five thousand adherents, indicating the scope
of the problem of integration into fellowship.[44]

The Assemblies of God had entered Peru in 1923, and by
1964, when the writer lectured in their Bible College, there
were nearly two hundred congregations with twelve thousand
adherents. There had been recurring revivals since 1928.
Five years later, in 1969, there were nearly four hundred
organized churches affiliated with the Assemblies of God in
Peru, ministering to twenty thousand adherents and seven
thousand Sunday School children.[45]

In Ecuador, as in Panama, the Foursquare denomination
was rapidly becoming the leading Evangelical body, its unusual church growth being due to much the same message
and methods as those of the Assemblies of God, activated
in times of obvious revival.[46]

The first Foursquare Pentecostal missionaries were appointed to Ecuador in 1956.[47] The Rev. and Mrs. Arthur Gadberry opened a Bible School in Guayaquil. Their first gospel services attracted an average attendance of fourteen. By 1960, the Sunday School had grown to two hundred.

While the Gadberrys were back in the United States on furlough in 1962, the Rev. Roberto Aguirre of Panama took over the work in Guayaquil. Aguirre cooperated with the other Evangelical pastors in an evangelistic campaign, so he expected that his confreres would cooperate with him in presenting Roberto Espinoza of California for evangelistic-healing meetings and was a little dismayed when they began to back off. So Espinoza and Aguirre and the Sunday School teachers started the campaign on their own.[48]

The meetings were held in an open field, and the people stood for services lasting a couple of hours. The owner of a radio station, who unknown to the leaders had been healed through the prayers of a member of the little congregation of thirty, offered free radio time. The attendance the first night was less than a thousand but news of a dozen healings was broadcast. Attendance the second night was ten thousand, and rose to twenty thousand before the end of the week. As the meetings continued for six weeks, attendances rose to between thirty and forty thousand. Undoubtedly, spectacular healings, broadcast to the public, were a major factor; but the gospel was preached, and fifteen hundred people were baptized one afternoon.[49]

The little Foursquare church could not cater for such a crowd coming from all parts of Ecuador's largest city, so Aguirre appointed his Sunday School teachers as pastors of scattered little congregations, seven in all. The churches thrived, and the new pastors and recent converts witnessed to all and sundry—with such effect that the city marriage license bureau ran out of printed forms, so great was the number who decided to validate common-law marriages.[50]

Within a very few years, the Foursquare Pentecostal Church had overtaken all but one Evangelical denominations in numerical strength.[51] Otherwise, church growth in the Republic of Ecuador was slow, though something of a folk movement developed among the Quichuas of the highlands, and there were sensational conversions among the Auca Indians of the eastern jungles reached by the widows and associates of five martyred missionaries.[52] The HCJB radio station continued its far-flung ministry of evangelism.[53]

At the end of the intensive persecutions in Colombia, the Assemblies of God reported three congregations; ten years later, there were seven thousand adherents gathered, for between 1960 and 1970, the Assemblies of God planted fifty new churches in Colombia; the Foursquare built forty-five, and the Pan-American Mission thirty-five, a total of one hundred and thirty;[54] while the United Pentecostal Church in the same decade started more than three hundred and fifty. The United Pentecostal denomination professed a Sabellian view of the Godhead, baptizing in the name of 'Jesus only' —hence its nickname—and rejecting the Nicean formula; but, while non-Trinitarian, it was not Unitarian as the term is understood, and the doctrine of the deity of Christ was not denied, the necessity of salvation through Christ alone being preached incessantly, with remarkable effect.[55]

Following the Evangelism-in-Depth campaign of 1968 in Colombia, the Jimenez Brothers from Puerto Rico arrived unexpectedly and were hurriedly sponsored by the Assembly of God and Foursquare denominations to conduct campaigns in the open air in the cities of Colombia.[56] The missionaries of other denominations were weary of meetings after an exhausting year, but the Pentecostals were committed and the crowds grew. In Medellín, for example, a poorly organized campaign began with a hundred people but, by the end of the month, the attendance had grown to ten thousand who stood for a couple of hours or more in front of the Bullring. The Assemblies of God established a strong church in Medellín as a result of the campaign.

Late in 1961,[57] Eugenio and Raimundo Jimenez of Puerto Rico campaigned in Venezuela, filling El Nuevo Circo in Caracas. Lorenzo Bolívar, eight years confined to a wheel chair as a result of a fall from a building, was strikingly healed, raising the attendances to 25,000 nightly, with 2000 inquirers counselled. As a result of the impact of the visits of David García and the Jimenez Brothers, the sale of Holy Bibles in Venezuela tripled. The greatest gainers were the Pentecostal denominations, including the Assembly of God, which numbered a little more than three thousand in 1966, having lost to other Pentecostal bodies, including Iglesia Ebenezer, founded through the visit of A. A. Allen.[58]

At the end of the 1960s, Pentecostals in Panama counted more than fifteen thousand as communicants,[59] chiefly in the Foursquare Church, which benefitted by recurring revivals and by the direction of the Edwards family of missionaries.

The Assembly of God work was begun in Costa Rica in 1943; within ten years, four churches were operating; and by 1962, there were sixty churches, mostly in the south of the country.[60] Other Evangelical denominations continued to grow, although their memberships each were less than two thousand, Seventh Day Adventists only a little more.

Meanwhile, the Assembly of God work was growing in El Salvador.[61] Stanley MacPherson with Gilberto Marrero conducted a campaign in Santa Ana, attendance ranging from 1500 to 3000, the scores of inquirers nightly providing a total of six hundred for counsel. Two years later, in 1962, the denomination had 255 organized churches with 12,800 adherents. Undoubtedly the growth was due to the revival movements, Jeffery's meetings of 1956 having produced no less than ten assemblies.

In Honduras, Ruben Castillo was converted following the 1937 earthquake, the Assembly of God missionaries entering three years later. After quarter of a century, there were forty-two organized churches with a hundred members in each, not so great a movement as elsewhere.[62]

After a quarter of a century in Guatemala, the Assembly of God churches numbered 165 in 1962, with 9000 members and 11,000 in Sunday Schools.[63] Two of the main factors in such growth were the spirit of revival and the attraction of the healing campaigns to the masses. By 1969, Assemblies of God in Guatemala claimed twenty thousand adherents in three hundred and fifteen local churches, and twenty-two thousand pupils in Sunday Schools, fully indigenous.[64]

Information from Cuba was difficult to assess, for as persecution extended, churches suffered in the '60s. But in 1970, there were two hundred Assemblies of God operating, and in November of that year, twelve hundred folk gathered in meetings in Camaguey, where revival broke out.[65]

The Assemblies of God had reopened their work in Haiti in 1957, and ten years later there were forty congregations with twenty-five hundred adherents. Membership was much smaller a figure, for the influx of voodoo practioners into the churches posed many problems pastorally.[66]

In early 1962, there was a revival in the Assembly of God churches in the Dominican Republic, the congregation in San Pedro de Macoris baptizing fifty converts with forty others requesting baptism. In thirty years, therefore, the denomination had planted more than sixty churches and had eleven thousand pupils in its Sunday Schools.[67]

The Latin America Mission field in northern Colombia had suffered from the debilitating heat and high humidity of the climate, the solid indifference of the people, and (until recently) the traditional fanaticism of the Roman Catholic Church there. In the 1960s, there came a change.

In the 1950s, Victor Landero, who owned a Bible unused for eight years, was convicted by reading the Gospels and converted alone by the roadside. He released his prostitutes and turned his brothel into a store, settled his marital status, ceased drinking rum, reverenced the Lord's Day, began to tithe, and established daily worship in the home—all as a result of reading the Word.[68]

Landero shared his new-found faith in the villages, and found a ready response. He purchased a tract of land near Montelibano, and founded a model village, Corozal, whose men pioneered their farms on weekdays while pioneering the villages nearby at weekends. The work was indigenous, owing scarcely anything to the occasional visits of mission personnel, none of whom were pentecostal or neo-pentecostal. As they continued studying the New Testament, they noticed that their experience lacked some apostolic manifestations, such as healing and exorcism, about which the missionaries on occasional visits spoke vaguely. They prayed all night, then experienced what they were seeking. Their spiritual power increased, but counterfeit gifts also appeared.[69]

By 1967, thirty-five new congregations were established. When the movement reached the Association of Churches in the area, it caused much controversy, some welcoming it as a work of God and others denouncing it as satanic. At an annual convention, division was avoided; but a series of accidents and problems left the association with only one ordained pastor, so the humble lay preachers began to slip into positions of leadership. In spite of guerrilla activity in the area, these churches continued to grow. By 1970, there were more than eighty congregations founded by the outreach of itinerants of this Río Cauca movement.[70]

Gregorio Landero, a younger brother, established a co-operative—social action, new industries, joint marketing, a health project, savings and loan agencies, and elementary education. Prosperity benefitted church and society alike.[71]

The movement affected other Evangelicals in the area. The number of Presbyterian congregations jumped from fifteen to thirty-six, adult membership increasing by only a third, but the Presbyterian community doubling to 2200.[72]

But the Latin American Pentecostals did not share the horror felt by the Ecumenical Movement regarding church splits, rather attributing to such divisions much of the vast growth of the Pentecostal movement.[73] The Netherlander, J. B. A. Kessler, has presented detailed evidence of such splits in the Republic of Chile, where the Methodist Church in 1909 suffered a secession of the Methodist Pentecostal Church under Hoover, which in 1946 suffered a secession of the Pentecostal Church of Chile under Chavez, which in 1952 suffered a secession of the Pentecostal Church Mission under Pavez—fourteen secessions in half a century. It was no wonder that established denominations feared splits, and resented Pentecostal influence.[74]

The sense of frustration felt by non-Pentecostal leaders regarding the success of their less educated Pentecostal friends or competitors has been well illustrated by Peter Wagner in his friendly survey of Pentecostal success in the Latin American countries.[75] An interdenominational and city wide campaign in Cochabamba sponsored by most churches of Protestant affiliation, including the Pentecostal, drew record-breaking crowds of a thousand to hear the capable Argentine evangelist. There was much expense in publicity and effort in visitation. A couple of weeks later, the same Pentecostals conducted a series of their own, using a vacant lot to present the healing-evangelistic ministry of Raimundo Jimenez of Puerto Rico. Soon they had five thousand people standing patiently throughout the lengthy service. Wagner confessed that he must have suffered from incredulity, envy and 'just plain frustration' to see such throngs result from so little organized effort. He (and other leaders) warned his congregation not to attend, but practically every member attended, and 'as if that wasn't bad enough, some of them were healed!' Wagner and others vented their frustrations in criticisms, and it took a number of years before he could rejoice in his brethren's success.

Contrasting with the rigid attitude of disapproval adopted by certain non-Pentecostal Evangelical denominations and organizations in North America, the same sort of people in Latin America seem to be adopting a more tolerant attitude towards the development of charismatic practices within their fellowships. The Río Cauca indigenous movement led by Victor Landero in Colombia received a wide acceptance, and provoked a willingness to share in such manifestations if these are the price of evangelistic dynamic.

In 1960, the total population of Latin America, exclusive of the former British West Indies, Guyana and Belize, the French Antilles and Guiana, the Netherlands Antilles and Surinam, amounted to approximately 200,000,000; without Brazil and its 70,000,000, there were 130,000,000 in the remainder of Latin America.[76]

At that time, Roman Catholic experts claimed nearly 180,000,000 in the Latin American Catholic community— 120,000,000 without Brazil. The Protestant community was estimated at 10,000,000 for Latin America, of whom half were in Brazil. Communicant Evangelical members were approximately 3,250,000, of whom more than half were in Brazil.[77] Seven years later, Evangelical communicants had increased to nearly 5,000,000, of whom two thirds were in Brazil. This represented approximately a ten per cent increase of Evangelical membership during a four per cent increase in population annually. Protestant community set at 15,000,000, seven years' increase was fifty per cent.

However, it is difficult to estimate such a community in Latin America, for there are many 'believers' who remain unbaptized for social reasons, such as compromised home relationships continuing from the past. But the figures provide an indication of the growing strength of the Evangelical movement, compared with the strength of Roman Catholics who practise their religion. The annual growth rate of the Evangelical memberships has been ten per cent compared with less than four per cent in the general population.[78]

As it appeared impossible to calculate the numbers of practising Roman Catholics in any Latin American country, it is even more impossible to estimate the numbers who became influenced by the Biblical Movement or Charismatic Renewal within the Roman Catholic Church. Evangelicals generally regarded them as brethren with an Evangelical experience and a closer approach to Evangelical faith and practice, a surprising and unexpected development arising from the prayer of John XXIII for the Holy Spirit's work.

24

RENEWAL, POST VATICAN II

During World War II, European Roman Catholics began to develop a genuine interest in Bible study and translation. As in the days of Wycliffe, before the reform of the Church, the liberating influence of the Word began to be experienced. Following 1943, the Pontifical Biblical Commission started to direct the growing activity in Bible study, primarily in Europe. The Roman Catholic authorities aimed definitely to 'restore the living Word of God to its proper place in the daily life of the Church . . . to bring to the common people, whether educated or not, the riches of the Word of God.'[1]

Though twenty years were to pass before the persecution of the people of the Word was to cease, as in Colombia, it was not long before the movement for the study of the Word of God overflowed to privileged parts of Latin America.

So, during the Nazi persecution in 1938, Monsignor John Straubinger, a German priest, fled to Argentina, where he became editor of a number of translations and editions of the Scriptures in Spanish-speaking countries.[2] Clearly, he drew his inspiration from the then developing, scholarly Roman Catholic Biblical Movement officially approved by Pope Pius XII in the Encyclical 'Divino Afflante Spiritu' of 1943. Another Argentine, Jorge Mejia, obtained his doctor of theology degree at the Pontifical Biblical Institute in the Vatican, and returned to the Catholic University of Buenos Aires to undergird pastoral renewal with biblical study.[3]

Thus the Biblical Movement got under way in Argentina, developing quietly in the Church for a whole generation, till Bishop Quauracino of Santo Domingo affirmed in 1965:[4]

> Little by little the Word of God is regaining its primary
> place in the reading, prayer and study of Christian
> people. Much remains to be done, but biblical 'renewal'
> is already on the move.

Other bishops in Latin America encouraged the scholars but, as yet, the movement had little effect upon the attitude of the priesthood toward the Evangelical Christians who so passionately had striven for a hearing of the Word of God.

At the mid-century, when the author visited all of the countries of Latin America, there was little sign of change regarding the study of the Bible. True, there were the few forward-looking missionary priests during the Brazilian Revival of 1952 who wistfully sought for fellowship.[5] Ten years later, during briefer visits to the Latin American republics, one noticed signs of coming changes.

Undoubtedly, the catalyst of change appeared in the choice personality of Angelo Giuseppe Roncalli, raised to the papal throne in 1958. Some who claimed to know insisted that the new pope had experienced an evangelical rebirth, though it would seem that his model was Wycliffe rather than Luther. In 1959, he announced his vision for an ecumenical council, and by 1961, preparations were under way for the Second Vatican Council, which was to revolutionize Catholicism.[6]

Pope John XXIII invited Protestant observers to Vatican discussions, and he did not hesitate to describe them as his 'separated brethren' rather than as 'heretics.' His lead in proclaiming cordial relationship was followed eagerly by Roman Catholics in countries where toleration had grown, more slowly where the hierarchy and clergy were medieval and backward. Meanwhile, the Biblical Movement grew.[7]

One result was a growing number of Bible classes held by laymen under Roman Catholic auspices, and an increase of participation involving Evangelicals—either instruction in the Bible given by visiting Protestant pastors or sharing in Bible study promoted by Protestants. Pope John XXIII's invitation to fellowship with 'separated brethren' ended the years of hostility between Roman Catholics in general and the Evangelical minority in country after country. Faithful Roman Catholics at last felt freer to attend Evangelical services. Some returned to their parish churches fully determined to emulate Protestant practices; others readily decided to join the Evangelical fellowship. As Evangelicals lost their minority complex, they became more ready to recognize the improvements in Roman Catholicism.[8]

John XXIII lived longer than expected, achieving so much that some Church leaders felt a need to slow the movement down, hence their election of a successor more moderate in views. But Paul VI did not repudiate the goodwill towards the 'separated brethren,' nor did he discourage the study of the Scriptures, even though he did not carry the movement forward to a Reformation. The crisis provided opportunity and danger for the Church as an institution.

Kenneth Strachan, so clearly recognized as a leader in the traditional Evangelical mission enterprise, found himself embroiled in controversy with some of his colleagues in other Evangelical missions. When the writer itinerated in Latin America in the early '50s with him, his conversation showed that he was enthusiastic about the dynamic shown in Latin America by the Pentecostal movement,[9] and that he was impressed by the depth of the Biblical renewal in the Roman Catholic Church. He was sure that changes were coming in the Roman Catholic Communion and that a policy of continuing confrontation was no longer valid.

In the 1960s, Strachan disputed the assertions of various colleagues in other missions that Rome never changed. He announced his conviction that missionaries working in Latin America were impressed by the success of the new minority movement in Roman Catholicism that appeared to be Biblio- and Christo-centric, making imperative a new approach on the part of Protestants.[10] Of course, he never for a moment suggested abandonment or compromise of historic Biblical principles. But he urged Evangelicals to pray that Roman Catholic leaders in council at the Vatican might be guided by God. For so saying, he was accused of having a naive attitude to the Roman Church's actions and intentions.

Strachan's colleagues in the Latin America Mission, including those who had suffered in the Violence in Colombia, backed him up in his conclusions.[11] They were encouraged when Vatican II showed that a majority of Roman bishops evidenced liberal sympathies, and were anxious to learn from the Evangelicals, whether by dialogue or fellowship. Where before the Bible had been burned, now it was fully commended for reading by bishops and clergy alike, the Protestant version along with new and better translations made by Roman scholars. In many places, the face of the church exterior and interior was changed, image and gaudy ornament disappearing from some—as one discovered up in the Andes in 1964, where Maryknollers also refused to permit offerings for the dead in certain parish churches.[12] It was confusing to some Protestants to find the Roman priest with a Bible in his hand, and friendship offered instead of invective and persecution. Some decided it was a ruse, and others waited impatiently for devotion to the saints and the Virgin Mary to fall away immediately, instead of rejoicing that the proclamations of the Marian year seemed forgotten and that the trend was seemingly reversed.

The beginning of the Roman Catholic Charismatic movement in the United States has been often told.[13] It paralleled the progress of the unusual ministry of David du Plessis in the historic Protestant denominations. Before long, tens of thousands of charismatic priests and nuns and lay people were gathering at the campus of Notre Dame University in Indiana, and the Catholic Charismatic movement had soon become the most dynamic in the body ecclesiastical.

In 1970, Francis McNutt, a Roman Catholic priest, took off from Miami with two Protestant ministers, Joe Petree and Tom Tyson, to take part in a retreat for little more than a dozen people up in the mountains.[14] The proceedings were in English, so contacts with Costa Ricans were few, and the charismatic priest wondered if he had made a mistake.

McNutt was surprised to receive an invitation to speak to faculty and students in the Latin America Biblical Seminary in San José.[15] Considering the long hostility between Roman Catholics and Evangelicals in Latin America, he accepted, and was pleased with the openness of his reception.

At that time, Templo Biblico—Harry Strachan's church in which the writer had spoken on every visit to San José—was in the spiritual doldrums, Sunday morning attendances having dropped from 600 to 200, Sunday evening from 400 to 40; the trustees even considered selling the property.[16] The visits of Alberto Mottesi and Juan Carlos Ortíz from the Argentine helped, but restoration was still to come.

Ruben Lores, the pastor, attended a meeting in a private home to hear the priest and a psychiatrist speak, and an invitation to pray for the Spirit's fullness was followed by deep emotion. So the priest was invited to preach at the Templo Biblico on Sunday night, and an overflow crowd filled the building. Spontaneously, people began to press forward for the laying-on of hands, and manifestations of a charismatic character occurred.[17]

Juan Carlos Ortíz returned and the movement continued, the church being filled each Sunday, conversions happening regularly. All this happened in a church with a tradition of non-Pentecostal evangelism, but there was no split from its Association of Bible Churches, which shared its joy.[18]

It was most significant that Francis McNutt had flown to Costa Rica to initiate a charismatic work among the Roman Catholics there, but instead started something among the spiritual grandchildren of Harry Strachan, who had felt the heavy hand of Roman persecution all his life.

The Biblical Seminary invited Francis McNutt to speak to them in July 1971, at which time he was able to talk with the Costa Rican President and with Bishop Ignacio Trejos, and to speak to Roman Catholics more than to Protestants, hence a lively spiritual movement began to develop.[19]

Francis McNutt directed a charismatic retreat in Peru, hosted by a Baptist missionary and a Peruvian pastor in a Protestant church, but attended chiefly by priests and nuns and a few others. Out of the visit came the initiation of a prayer meeting for priests in Lima and prayer groups in the slum barriada of Comas.[20]

In January 1971, during a second journey, a couple of hundred people attended a retreat in Lima, most of them North American priests and nuns; then a contingent of local people joined them. Out of this visit came a regular meeting at the Villa Maria and prayer groups around the city for priests and nuns. Another retreat was held in Chimbote, a fishery port, with the Bishop attending.[21]

During the second week of January 1972, three hundred people from all classes of Peruvian society attended another retreat at Villa María in Miraflores. Three days in Spanish were followed by similar ministry in English, the team of ministers being Roman Catholic and Protestant. There was healing reported, some physical but most psychological.[22]

The Rector of the theology department at the Catholic University in Washington, Reginald Masterson, visited the Bolivian city of Cochabamba in January 1969, and shared his experience of renewal.[23] Later in 1969, a prayer group was begun at the Maryknoll sisters' residence.

In May 1970, during the odyssey of Francis McNutt, the Dominicans in Cochabamba sponsored a spiritual retreat, attended by fifty priests and nuns and a few ministers and their wives. A prayer group was begun in Cochabamba, the Catholic Charismatic movement in Bolivia well begun.[24]

In January 1971, another Cochabamba retreat was held, further strengthening the prayer group of priests and nuns. Thus far, the movement seemed to be one among mission personnel rather than among Bolivians.[25]

The growing Catholic Charismatic movement in Bolivia suffered with others in the revolution of August 1971, for seventeen of the hundred priests in Santa Cruz were forced into exile. Efforts were directed towards building up the Bolivian prayer groups in La Paz, Cochabamba and elsewhere, to create national leadership.[26]

In 1973, reliable reports from Bolivia intimated a new phenomenon in the evangelization of its people. Julio César Ruibal, born in 1953, received his primary and secondary education in the La Salle Catholic schools of La Paz and Santa Cruz, and won a scholarship to study abroad. He enrolled in a pre-medical course at Pasadena City College in California, but became increasingly involved in the occult. Some Christian friends began to pray for him; he attended a healing service directed by Kathryn Kuhlman, and was converted in a private home in November 1971 in a power encounter between spirits demonic and divine. Ruibal came into contact with the Catholic Charismatic movement and with other neo-Pentecostal leaders in the United States.[27]

Returning to Bolivia in September 1972, his course set, Ruibal commenced preaching to friends among the upper-class—nominally Roman Catholic professional people—the homes made available being utterly overcrowded. Roman Catholic nuns from the United States welcomed the crowds to their premises. In December, two meetings were held in the basketball coliseum, attended by a thousand people, and daily meetings continued in the park. Ruibal exercised a healing ministry even in a Roman Catholic church until inhibited by its priest.[28] President Hugo Banzer's lady was reportedly healed and made confession of faith in a private meeting in her home, whereupon Bolivia's president made a soccer stadium available without charge, this being filled with twenty thousand people inside and twenty thousand outside on its plaza on two occasions.[29]

Ruibal's preaching was Christ-centered, and an absence of references to the Virgin Mary provoked antagonism in some Roman Catholic circles, leading to denunciation and repudiation by some authorities. Protestant leaders were taken unawares by the response to Ruibal's ministry, but they heartily welcomed the overflow in daily morning and evening services, and a new suburban church with only four members found itself with two hundred attending meetings. In Cochabamba, Ruibal's meetings attracted between thirty and sixty thousand hearers.[30]

Sales of Scriptures in Bolivia were unprecedented during the movement, according to the Bible Society. Interest in the evangelist was general among the population, while the Evangelicals and Catholic Charismatics approved the work. It seemed that Ruibal, though considered a Catholic layman, was an Evangelical at heart, refusing Roman discipline.[31]

In Colombia,[32] the charismatic work commenced among Roman Catholics through a radio priest, Rafael García, in Bogotá, quite apart from the movement at large, of which García Herrero had no knowledge. North American people in Colombia were stirred by the visit of Francis McNutt in 1972, and the two movements flowed together, touching various Colombian cities, including Cali.[33]

Julio César Ruibal began ministry modestly in Bogotá, the Colombian capital, where fifty people met him in a home. Soon he addressed three thousand in a public square, then ten thousand from the steps of a Roman Catholic church in Medellín, where a paralytic abandoned his wheelchair and a deaf-mute began to shout 'Jesus.' Two days later, seventy thousand (one in twenty of the city's population)[34] attended a rally in the soccer stadium. In Cali, twelve thousand came to meetings, and in the gatherings in all three cities, a call for repentance and conversion was given.[35] The measure of opposition from Roman Catholics in Bolivia was absent in Colombia, the Archbishop of Medellín giving permission for Ruibal's appearances, though sounding a cautious note about the accompanying phenomena, while the charismatics of the Roman Church were enthusiastic supporters. Most Evangelicals rejoiced in the soundness of the Gospel thus presented and in the validity of the healings, but some were uneasy about the implications of Roman Catholic support. A newspaper presented an objective account of the healings, interviews, case histories, names of family doctors and the like, as well as assessments by a psychologist and a doctor who did not deny the healings but attributed them to mass suggestion or hypnosis.[36]

A Venezuelan priest, considering leaving the priesthood, took leave of absence in the United States to think it over, but there his life was transformed. This so impressed his bishop, Archbishop Crispulo Benitez, that he made his way with five priests and forty lay people to observe the Aguas Buenas community in Puerto Rico. His auxiliary bishop, Eduardo Herrera, also shared the charismatic experience. David du Plessis visited the Archbishop in December 1973.[37]

When the first National Charismatic Rally was held in Venezuela at Barquisimeto, in January 1976, twenty-five thousand attended, not all of them Catholic Charismatics. The rally was addressed by Archbishop Crispulo Benitez, time divided between prayer and rally speakers, including Francis McNutt and Barbara Shlemon.[38]

The renewal movement began in Ecuador through circles of prayer.[39] In November of that year, 1970, the Cardinal Archbishop appointed a Jesuit, Francisco Ramos, as the director of the movement. The first retreat was held in 1972, with Roman Catholic religious and Protestant pastors participating. In April 1973, a spring convention was held in Quito, initiated by Monsignor Antonio Gonsalez, auxiliary bishop of Quito.[40]

The first charismatic conference for Roman Catholics was held in Chile in February 1972, seventy attending, the great majority of them missionaries. The chief visitor was Francis McNutt, and out of this retreat held in a suburb of Santiago came the prayer groups of the movement.[41]

The charismatic renewal that began among the Chilean Roman Catholics in February 1972 attracted the attention of the hierarchy, for within a year there were fifteen local prayer groups in Santiago, and others in Concepcion, Talca, Talcahuano, Temuco, Osorno, and the like. The Bishops in conference asked the national committee to keep in touch.[42]

Argentina had already been convulsed by the phenomenon of Tommy Hicks in the 1950s, not only the Evangelicals but the Roman Catholic community. In the 1960s, the churches of the Pentecostals grew rapidly, and in the '60s, the Bible Renewal progressed among the Roman Catholics. The stage being set for a charismatic movement in the Church, it was not long before there were eighty or more charismatic prayer groups among Roman Catholic Argentines.[43]

Not only was Puerto Rico a recruiting ground for dynamic evangelists in the Evangelical and Pentecostal movements, but it became a fruitful field for the Catholic Charismatics. An 'explosion of power' began in Roman Catholic circles in November 1971, when a Roman Catholic-Protestant team visited the island. A Redemptorist priest, Thomas Forrest, emerged to leadership, the Bishop of Arecibo backing him. Before long, one of the prayer groups attracted a thousand people, forty groups in all operating, so that it was said that prayer meetings surpassed politics as a topic of conversation. The movement published a Spanish periodical.[44]

In 1975, during an international conference, a thousand filled an Aguas Buenas parish church, two thousand outside, and two days later five thousand filled the plaza for praise and testimony, seven thousand gathering at the Municipal Stadium at Bayamon. There was a startling healing of a girl with a club foot, and the enthusiasm became intense.[45]

Early in April 1971, Francis McNutt—and the American psychiatrist, Mrs. Barbara Shlemon—conducted a retreat in Santo Domingo for Dominican nuns and a few lay people, priests and nuns of other orders. A prayer group began, of only eight people, but before long there were twenty-two such groups operating in the backward island.[46]

The Dominican nuns in Santo Domingo promoted prayer groups for Roman Catholic lay women, including teachers, graduates and parents belonging to Colegio Santo Domingo, proceeding cautiously 'because of cultural differences and religious superstition.'[47]

The Catholic Charismatic movement in the Dominican Republic owed much to the ministry of a French-Canadian priest, Emiliano Tardif, who had served in the Caribbean island for fifteen years when he developed pulmonary tuberculosis. In a Canadian hospital, a charismatic group prayed for him, and he was healed. In 1974, he was back in parish ministry in Nagua, a town of fifteen thousand inhabitants. In a local prayer meeting, he invited people to seek healing, as did a fellow Canadian priest, Raymond Audet. Many folk were healed. Response posed problems for the three local priests who could not shepherd so many inquirers, so fifty prayer groups were formed in the barrios with between fifty and a hundred in each, a regular weekly attendance of three thousand coming to the central meetings, sometimes as many as forty thousand. Trained catechists were used to keep contact between priests and people.[48]

The hierarchy in Panama lent assistance to the work of renewal, encouraging the circles of prayer.[49] There were manifestations of physical healing as well as of other gifts of the Spirit. Antagonism to the Foursquare Pentecostals, the 'salva-cuatros,' dwindled.

In Guatemala, the renewal movement began with prayer groups in English arranged by Maryknoll missionaries in 1972. In December 1973, Harold Cohen directed a retreat out of which came five Spanish-speaking groups. One of the leaders was Bishop José Ramiro Pellecer, Guatemala City, who was encouraged by Cardinal Casariego.[50]

Bishop Nicolas D'Antonio, of Olancho in Honduras,[51] was warned in a prophecy given in Rome in 1975 of trouble that was coming. Little did he know that an uprising a month or so later would kill two of his priests and several laymen— driving the Bishop into exile. Prayer groups continued in a time of upheaval.

In Mexico, the first charismatic retreat attracted only thirty people in January 1971.[52] Before long, five hundred were gathering for instruction. Because of 'problems with Protestants,' the work was designated Christian Renovation in the Holy Spirit, to avoid the title Catholic Pentecostals.

A Jesuit priest, Harold Cohen, a leader in the Catholic Charismatic community in New Orleans, conducted a series of meetings in Mexico at the invitation of the Archdiocese, with the goodwill of Cardinal Miranda. The sponsor, Carlos Talavera, maintained a prayer group for fellow-priests and others interested, the beginning of a strong charismatic movement in the Republic of Mexico.[53]

Also in 1972, visitors from the Melodyland Christian Center in Southern California visited Mexico City to set up a charismatic clinic, priests and seminarians coming even a thousand miles from Yucatán to attend. By then, there were twenty prayer communities in Mexico City, including officials high in the Mexican hierarchy.[54]

In Mexico City, 18th to 21st September 1972, no less than twelve hundred Mexican Roman Catholics participated in the first Congress of Christian Renewal in the Holy Spirit. Besides a team of Roman Catholic Americans taking part, a Baptist from Georgia, Ruth (Carter) Stapleton participated. The chapel used was overcrowded throughout.[55]

A Congress on Spiritual Renewal was also held in Mexico City late in November 1972, attended by a thousand people, chiefly Roman Catholics, to hear Hermano Pablo (the radio missionary, Paul Finkenbinder) and a team from Melodyland in California. By then, the Catholic Charismatic prayer groups in Mexico City numbered thirty.[56]

There seemed to be official suspicion of the Protestants. So strong did the Catholic Charismatic movement become in Mexico, that the Archbishop of Mexico issued guidelines in consultation with the Vatican; commending its good points, a directive warned against illuminism, anti-intellectualism and irrationalism, and cautioned against undue Protestant influence. The clergy were urged to help.[57]

In 1968, ten years after the end of the Violence in the Colombian Republic, Pope Paul VI visited the country, an event which aroused exuberant patriotism among the people. Six hundred thousand people rallied in Bogotá. Evangelicals no longer dreaded such a rally, for there was little likelihood of the enthusiasm being directed into anti-Evangelical rage such as had disgraced the country prior to Vatican II.[58]

In the Revival in Brazil in 1952, occasional fellowship had been sought by Roman Catholic priests, both missionary and national, as when a group of American mission priests invited the visiting evangelist and local pastors to the local presbytery to learn something of the secret of the power in the preaching in Campo Grande.[59] But a majority of foreign mission priests, generally European by birth, had shown hostility. True, the action of Pope Pius XII in 1943 had set off a movement of Bible study, but while this diminished the traditional anti-Bible zeal of priests in the hinterlands, it did not produce fellowship for many years.

The vision of Pope John XXIII and its realization at the Second Vatican Council released a far-reaching surge of energy in Roman Catholicism. Through the charismatic renewal, many devout Roman Catholics were appreciating an experience of conversion and the filling of the Spirit in a way unknown by confirmation and disciplined devotions. The official papal encouragement of fellowship with the 'separated brethren,' and the enjoyment of an experience of common comprehension immediately lowered barriers between devout Roman Catholics and Evangelical people.[60]

Although the Roman Catholic Church and Pentecostals had been in touch for generations, the charismatic renewal seemed to reach the older body through the movements in the historic Protestant churches in Brazil.

The Roman Catholic Church in Paraíba sent observers to study the outbreak of charismatic phenomena in the Congregational Church in Campina Grande, and the local bishop decided that the Renewal was related to scripture, hence merited special consideration.[61]

Again, the young folk of the Good Shepherd Presbyterian Church in Anápolis were out carolling on Christmas Eve, and decided to visit the home of the Roman Catholic Bishop. They were received graciously, and the Bishop expressed much interest in their renewal. George Kosicki, a priest from the charismatic fellowship in Ann Arbor, Michigan, came south to hold a prayer workshop in Goiânia, attended by more than fifty priests, nuns, monks, and a bishop.[62]

Then in 1972, Kevin Ranaghan's treatise on the Catholic Pentecostals was translated into Portuguese and published in Brazil.[63] Thus it seemed as if Brazilian Roman Catholics were more affected by the Renewal movement of the late 'sixties and early 'seventies than by Pentecostalism of the denominational pattern.

Hence, in the early 1970s, the Charismatic Renewal in the Roman Catholic Church in Brazil began to spread. In 1973, Dr. David du Plessis spent three weeks as the guest of Paulo Evaristo, Cardinal Archbishop of São Paulo. He addressed the senate of priests and several other groups, including Protestant missionaries.[64]

In Brazil, a National Service Committee for the Catholic Charismatic Renewal was formed in 1973. By 1975, when three hundred prayer group leaders from ten Brazilian states met from 10th to 12th January at the Jesuit Seminary in the state of São Paulo, the movement was spreading rapidly. In 1973, Silvestre Scandian became the committee coordinator, but in 1974 he became Bishop of Araçuai. His superior, the Cardinal Archbishop of São Paulo, warmly endorsed the Renewal and noted that most of the Brazilian bishops were open to the movement.[65]

It is worth noting that the Charismatic Renewal in the Roman Catholic Church in Brazil caused no schisms, while in the historic Protestant denominations there were several expulsions or secessions. The difference cannot be attributed to the greater enthusiasm of the Roman Catholics for things spiritual, but rather to the organizational structure of the respective Churches. That archbishops and bishops were 'open' to the movement is not surprising considering the attitude demonstrated in the Vatican at that time. In the days of Pius XII, charismatic Catholics would have been excommunicated, and, at the grass-roots level of the local priest, muted persecution would have followed.

Some Protestants were baffled by the obvious changes. The ardent Pentecostal Brazilian, Manoel de Melo, gave an urgent warning to fellow-Evangelicals:[66]

> No Protestant should sin against the Holy Spirit by doubting that these changes in the Catholic Church are the real thing. The Holy Spirit is powerful enough to change and renew even the Catholic Church. . . all churches should rejoice in this fact.

But the euphoria of persecution giving way to tolerance and tolerance giving way to fellowship did not alter the fact that Brazil, the land of the future, was still a vast country of need, the spiritual need far greater than the physical, with its poverty and disease and illiteracy. The promise of better times lay in the hope of increased preaching of the Word of God, the work of Christ, and the direction of the Holy Spirit among His people.

It is possible to survey the growth of the Roman Catholic Charismatic movement through its international congresses. In February of 1973, a new development was reported in the formation of the Encuentro Carismatico Catolico Latino-Americano—E.C.C.L.A.—by a couple of dozen priests and nuns and a layman, from eight countries, the most exciting news being of 'the young Catholic evangelist,' Julio César Ruibal attracting a crowd of thirty thousand in La Paz, and of whole parishes being renewed in Puerto Rico.[67]

The second E.C.C.L.A. Congress met in Bogotá late in January 1974, with 250 leaders from eighteen countries participating, a tenfold increase. The congress was hosted by the radio priest, Rafael Garcia.[68]

The third E.C.C.L.A. Congress was held in Puerto Rico, at the end of January 1975, 1250 representatives attending sessions in Aguas Buenas. There were 400 prayer groups in Peru, 200 in Puerto Rico, 190 in Venezuela, 150 in the Dominican Republic, 82 in Argentina, 22 in Costa Rica, and hundreds in other countries. One bishop had attended the second Congress, but eight participated in the third.[69]

By January of 1976, the fourth E.C.C.L.A. Conference was held in Mexico City, three hundred leaders attending from all over Latin America, three thousand people at the first service in the Basílica of Guadalupe. Cardinal Miguel Miranda presided, and bishops from as far away as the Argentine participated.[70] The emphasis of the conference in 1976 was on the influence of charismatic renewal on social liberation, a subject recurring in the movement's agenda from the beginning in Latin America.[71]

Spread of the Charismatic movement through the Roman Catholic Church did much more than promote tolerance. It had been difficult during the first fifty years of the twentieth century to imagine two religious bodies farther apart than the Roman Catholics and the Pentecostals, but such became the eagerness of the more spiritual Roman Catholics to learn about 'the things of the Spirit' that they sought out Pentecostal pastors and people also to come and share their insights and expertise with them.[72] David du Plessis and the other international neo-Pentecostal leaders received warm welcomes from various Roman Catholic clergy and laity. Some who enjoyed a 'charismatic experience' later joined Pentecostal churches, but most remained Roman Catholic. It seemed that the Catholic Charismatic movement would remain within the Roman Catholic fold.

Such Roman Catholic Charismatics could not reasonably call themselves either Protestant or Evangelical, because of the denominational significance of such terms. Hence these Evangelicals—in practice and largely in doctrine—identified themselves as Catholic Charismatics, and maintained an open attitude to fellowship with other Evangelicals, especially charismatic. One of their greatest contributions came from their singing, their choruses of praise being often transliterated from the Psalms and other portions of Scripture, happily contrasting with some of the sentimental doggerel of modern evangelical 'rock-music.'[73]

The fraternal fellowship caused concern in not only the conservative Roman Catholic circles but in the Protestant. A vast majority of Latin American Evangelicals have been either converts from Roman Catholicism, or the children or grandchildren of such converts. The rapid growth of the Biblical Movement and the Charismatic Fellowship among Roman Catholics, with little opposition from the Hierarchy, has had the effect of encouraging converted Roman Catholic people to remain in the Church of their fathers. Despite the visions of well-meaning people, and the wishful thinking of others, the Biblical and Charismatic renewals seem likely to grow unchecked in the Roman Communion, for they are the two most dynamic sectors of that ancient institution.

An Evangelical who talked with fifty prelates among the hundred and sixty Bishops and seven Cardinals attending the 1968 meeting of the Hierarchy in Medellin observed:

> Unless the Holy Spirit comes upon Evangelicals in Latin America and elsewhere, another Martin Luther will emerge from within Catholicism and take with him the products of Protestant missions.[74]

Evangelical Latin American theologians conceded that most Catholic Charismatics evidenced a Christ-centered theology, and that they appropriated the Word of God to the unsophisticated laity, besides practising a fellowship of the Spirit; some complained that they were undergirded by the values of the middle class, that they were too often moved by untested prophecy and revelation; and that they were not sufficiently interested in reformation, without which renewal was apt to be dissipated.

As early as 1952,[75] Dr. John A. Mackay returned from a tour of Central and South America and declared: 'The future of the Gospel in Latin America is in the hands of the Roman Catholics and the Pentecostals.' Who believed him?

Summary and Conclusion

The ongoing evangelization of the peoples of that vast segment of the world's land mass known as Latin America is one of the wonders of the progress of Christianity. And the twentieth century has proved to be the significant epoch. Such is the inevitable conclusion drawn from the collation of records brought up to date.

The nineteenth century witnessed the evangelization of the anglophone peoples of the Caribbean and continguous areas, seemingly an extension of the work achieved in the countries farther north and accelerated by the same great evangelical revivals.

What of the work of the Roman Catholic missionaries in the centuries following Columbus? All due respect must be paid to Bartolomeo de las Casas and a minority of heroic men who strove against the force of Hispanic subjugation to care for the souls and bodies of indigenous peoples; but it has been emphasized by Protestant missionaries and conceded by Roman Catholic writers that the evangelization of the aboriginal peoples was 'superficial in the extreme.' It could never have been said that there were enough priests to care for the nominally Roman Catholic population, even if it were not true that the Word of God was not made known to the people by the Roman clergy.

After the abortive mission of the Scot, James Thomson, Evangelical Christianity gained an entrance to the Latin American lands of the South through immigration. It was not long before this beach head was expanded by colporteur and missionary, in evangelism bitterly contested.

Still, at the end of the nineteenth century, the work of the pioneers had produced only a handful of converts in a few countries, still bitterly persecuted—though less so in Brazil than in other countries. Spontaneous movements of the Spirit were unknown, except for rarest revivals among Protestant immigrants. Evangelism in the New Testament sense and in the scope known in the Protestant world since Whitefield was severely restricted or entirely unknown. In Protestant schools, appreciated for their excellent quality, there was no great movement to evangelical faith.

In the light of the cordial cooperation of Roman clergy with their 'separated brethren' since the days of the saintly Pope John XXIII and the Second Vatican Council, it is an embarrassment even to read the records of the persecution visited by a professedly Christian establishment upon those who ever so sincerely disagreed with its dogma and practice. But the records are true. Who can deny that Evangelicals in Mexico were murdered at a rate of one a week in 1893 ?

Nor were all non-Roman churches agreed on evangelism. Interdenominational missionary cooperation till 1910 was generally evangelical in its direction. The accession of the 'High Church' participants brought about a change, and the Edinburgh World Missionary Conference thus was limited to societies that operated among non-Christian people only, effectively excluding Latin America from the agenda.

If the growth of sturdy Evangelical Churches numbering millions of communicating Christians and belated recognition of their success by objective Roman Catholic scholars be a test, it could be said that the Holy Spirit 'disregarded' the decisions made regarding Latin America by the Anglo-Catholic leaders. Those decisions were protested by the Evangelicals led by Dr. Robert E. Speer, a rump session at Edinburgh resulting in the Committee on Cooperation in Latin America and its Panama Congress in 1916.

But it could not be said that an organized Protestant project became the main factor in subsequent Evangelical growth throughout the Latin republics; the main factor was an evangelism initiated and expanded by evangelical revival in the sending and receiving churches.

It was at the end of the nineteenth century and the beginning of the twentieth that the veteran Methodist missionary, T. B. Wood, made a remarkable prophecy, already cited:

> The signs of the times point to the coming of great sweeping revivals. All the work thus far is providentially preparatory to them. And when they once get started among these impulsive peoples, the mighty changes that will follow fast and far throughout this immense homogeneous territory promise to surpass anything of the kind hitherto known.

In the seventy-five years, or three generations, since the missionary prophet made his prediction, his words in fact have come true in a way unparalleled in any other part of the world. In every case, revival movements preceded widespread evangelization.

The era of great sweeping movements in Latin America predicted by T. B. Wood had a modest beginning in the 1900s in the wake of the Welsh Revival of 1905. Revival was felt in Brazil, Chile and Mexico on a scale hitherto unknown, even in tiny minorities of the population.

During the next decade, the energetic Canadian Scot, Harry Strachan, began his series of continental campaigns of evangelism, enjoying much success and encountering recurring opposition. His mastery of Spanish was such that his ministry could be reckoned an indigenous one, though he raised his support in Canada and the United States. No other missionary made such an impact upon the masses.

An increasing number of national evangelists arose in their respective countries to pursue a vigorous ministry within the national boundaries, but it was not until the end of World War II that Spanish-speaking evangelists began to exercise a truly international ministry. At the same time, Billy Graham and his associates attracted great crowds in campaigns of limited duration. Evangelism-in-Depth, the concept of Kenneth Strachan, developed in the 1960s as a moblization of the spiritual resources of the churches for evangelism— it was evangelism, rather than revival, as some have suggested. The mantle of Harry Strachan fell in the late 1960s upon an Argentinian, Luis Palau, who was greatly influenced by Billy Graham's methods.

Meanwhile, in the wake of the Welsh Revival, a dynamic Pentecostalism began in Latin America, particularly Chile, in which it was indigenous, and Mexico, where it was carried by missionaries, and in Brazil, where it made its greatest advances by missionary initiation and indigenization. In the 1950s and '60s, the influx of gifted but impetuous North American healing-evangelists gave the Pentecostal work a tremendous fillip, huge crowds gathering in many places. A disposition of the Latin American towards the miraculous in religion—hitherto exploited—encouraged him to support the ministry of these healing-evangelists whose work was attested by enough miraculous healings to create a vast interest. Thus the Pentecostal churches thrived through an extraordinary movement of the masses.

In the '50s, there was a significant movement of revival in Brazil, preceded by a movement of prayer, sparked by the visit of an overseas evangelist, and carried on in both revival and evangelism by Brazilians for years. All the denominations shared in the movement.

About the same time, a revival movement generally of Pentecostal impulse, swept Cuba just before the Communist revolution under Castro. All the while, incredible violence was sweeping Colombia, with severest persecution of the Evangelicals. And before the 1950s had ended, Argentina had been moved by the ministry of a novice evangelist, the incredible Tommy Hicks, a movement with many failings which nevertheless proved of great significance to the work of almost every Evangelical body in the country.

The efforts of Evangelical pioneers in education and in other social welfare bore fruit, especially in disposing many leaders in national life to regard the Evangelical cause with appreciation. Without the movements of revival and evangelization, this factor would have played a lesser part in the growth of the churches.

Although the greatest evangelists, from Harry Strachan to Luis Palau, were usually non-Pentecostal in conviction, the Pentecostal churches everywhere surged ahead through such evangelism as well as their own indefatigable efforts. In 1900, there were only 50,000 Protestants in all of Latin America, none of them Pentecostal. By 1970, there were 20,000,000 Protestants, two-thirds of them Pentecostal.

The neo-Pentecostal movement, or charismatic renewal, met with a very mixed reception among the Latin American Protestant denominations, splits occurring in Brazil in the Baptist, Congregational, Methodist and Presbyterian bodies without inhibiting the movement. In other countries, the movement encountered less opposition. The same renewal surprisingly penetrated the Roman Catholic Church in one country after another, and, following upon the spread of the Biblical movement, helped change the attitude of the Roman Catholic clergy to evangelical religion. In the 1970s, the Roman Catholics everywhere seemed free to attend great meetings of evangelism, and the years of persecution and confrontation had apparently passed into history. Without doubt, the Roman Catholic Church was being evangelicalized and pentecostalized from within and without with what effect upon dogma none could hazard a guess.

Latin American political life is still in a state of flux and the 'great sweeping movements' of Evangelical religion are still continuing. The foregoing accounts of these movements are happily incomplete.

Notes on Chapter 1: THE NEW WORLD AND THE OLD GOSPEL

1 Stephen C. Neill, A HISTORY OF CHRISTIAN MISSIONS, p. 141.
2 Kenneth Scott Latourette, A HISTORY OF THE EXPANSION OF CHRISTIANITY, Volume III, p. 85.
3 Stephen C. Neill, A HISTORY OF CHRISTIAN MISSIONS, p. 389.
4 Kenneth Scott Latourette, Volume III, p. 89.
5 See COLECION DE LAS OBRAS DE BARTOLOME DE LAS CASAS, Volume I, 'Relación breve de la destrucción de América.'
6 Marcel Brion, BARTOLOME DE LAS CASAS, pp. 1-40.
7 Stephen C. Neill, A HISTORY OF CHRISTIAN MISSIONS, p. 169.
8 Kenneth Scott Latourette, A HISTORY OF THE EXPANSION OF CHRISTIANITY, Volume III, p. 161.
9 Pannier & Mondain, L'EXPANSION FRANCAISE OUTRE-MER, pp. 10-23.
10 MISSIONARY REVIEW OF THE WORLD, 1910, p. 920 (J.I. Good)
11 Braga & Grubb, THE REPUBLIC OF BRAZIL, p. 47.
12 E.R. Hasse, THE MORAVIANS, p. 16; J.T. Hamilton, MISSIONS OF THE MORAVIAN CHURCH, pp. 2-3.
13 J.E. Hutton, A HISTORY OF MORAVIAN MISSIONS, pp. 14-49.
14 J.T. Hamilton, MISSIONS OF THE MORAVIAN CHURCH, p. 6.
15 See MISSIONARY REVIEW OF THE WORLD, 1897, pp. 811ff (Schweinitz), & J.T. Hamilton, pp. 38-42.
16 Morgan Godwyn, THE NEGRO'S & INDIAN'S ADVOCATE, p. 137.
17 J.T. Hamilton, MISSIONS OF THE MORAVIAN CHURCH, p. 38.
18 J.E. Hutton, A HISTORY OF MORAVIAN MISSIONS, pp. 50-56.
19 John Clark, THE VOICE OF JUBILEE, pp. 30-36.

Notes on Chapter 2: AWAKENINGS AND PIONEERS, I

1 Kenneth Scott Latourette, A HISTORY OF THE EXPANSION OF CHRISTIANITY, Volume III, p. 454; W.W. Sweet, THE STORY OF RELIGION IN AMERICA, p. 224.
2 See J. Edwin Orr, THE EAGER FEET, pp. 14-15; 52-53; 89-90.
3 J. Edwin Orr, Chapter 2, pp. 13ff.   4 Chapter 3, pp. 28ff.
5 J. Edwin Orr, Chapter 4, pp. 32ff.
6 Chapter 13, pp. 86ff. & Chapter 25, pp. 179ff.
7 J. Edwin Orr, THE EAGER FEET, pp. 52-53.
8 J. Edwin Orr, Chapters 7-9, pp. 51-70.   9 pp. 92-95.
10 Peter Samuel, WESLEYAN METHODIST MISSIONS IN JAMAICA AND HONDURAS, pp. 11-13.
11 See D.A. McGavran, CHURCH GROWTH IN JAMAICA, p. 10.
12 Cf. Peter Samuel, WESLEYAN METHODIST MISSIONS, pp. 25ff.
13 George Smith, HISTORY OF WESLEYAN METHODISM, Volume II, p. 460.   14 E.A. Payne, FREEDOM IN JAMAICA, p. 19.
15 George Smith, Volume II, pp. 462-463; 506-507.
16 METHODIST MAGAZINE, London, 1816, p. 874 (Shipman).
17 George Smith, Volume III, pp. 138-140.
18 J.T. Hamilton, MISSIONS OF THE MORAVIAN CHURCH, p. 104.
19 E.A. Payne, FREEDOM IN JAMAICA, pp. 27-31; and Peter Samuel, WESLEYAN METHODIST MISSIONS, pp. 60-70.
20 John Harris, A CENTURY OF EMANCIPATION, pp. 3ff.
21 E.A. Payne, FREEDOM IN JAMAICA, p. 49.
22 J.H. Hinton, A MEMOIR OF WILLIAM KNIBB, pp. 301ff.
23 J.T. Hamilton, MISSIONS OF THE MORAVIAN CHURCH, p. 106.
24 REPORTS of the Wesleyan Methodist Missionary Society.

25 See W. S. Robertson, THE RISE OF THE SPANISH REPUBLICS.
26 J. L. Mecham, CHURCH AND STATE, pp. 45ff. (Latin America)
27 See M. W. Williams, DOM PEDRO THE MAGNANIMOUS.
28 Kenneth Scott Latourette, A HISTORY OF THE EXPANSION OF
    CHRISTIANITY, Volume V, p. 70.
29 See H. C. Lea, HISTORY OF THE INQUISITION IN SPAIN.
30 J. Edwin Orr, 'Evangelical Awakenings in Collegiate Communities,'
    doctoral dissertation, U.C.L.A., or CAMPUS AFLAME, popular
    edition, pp. 32-34.
31 William Corston, THE LIFE OF JOSEPH LANCASTER, p. 16.
32 H. C. Barnard, A HISTORY OF ENGLISH EDUCATION, pp. 56ff.
33 David Salmon, editor, LANCASTER AND BELL, introduction.
34 J. Edwin Orr, CAMPUS AFLAME, p. 34.
35 D. R. Mitchell, 'The Evangelical Contribution of James Thomson
    to South American Life, 1818-25,' unpublished Th.D. dissertation,
    Princeton Theological Seminary, 1972, pp. 73-74.
36 D. R. Mitchell, 'James Thomson,' pp. 11 & 14.
37 British and Foreign School Society, London, Minute 14 May 1818.
38 45th REPORT, British and Foreign School Society, 1849.
39 D. R. Mitchell, 'James Thomson,' pp. 72-73.
40 J. Edwin Orr, CAMPUS AFLAME, p. 42.
41 Cf. J. J. Johnson, POLITICAL CHANGES IN LATIN AMERICA,
    p. 16; & Evaristo Iglesias, LA ESCUELA PUBLICA, pp. 36-37.
42 D. R. Mitchell, 'James Thomson,' p. 108.
43 James Thomson, LETTERS ON THE MORAL AND RELIGIOUS
    STATE OF SOUTH AMERICA, p. 1.
44 D. R. Mitchell, 'James Thomson,' p. 114.
45 EVANGELICAL CHRISTENDOM, Volume I, 1847 (James Thomson)
    & 16th REPORT, British and Foreign School Society, 1820, p. 125.
46 GACETA DE BUENOS AIRES, 30 May 1821, p. 503.
47 James Thomson, LETTERS, p. 4.
48 AURORA DE CHILE, Santiago, 1813, p. 46.
49 James Thomson, LETTERS, pp. 6ff.
50 EVANGELICAL CHRISTENDOM, Volume I, 1847, p. 287; see
    James Thomson, LETTERS, pp. 33-34, 70-71.
51 James Thomson, LETTERS, pp. 84ff.
52 James Thomson, LETTERS, pp. 236ff.
53 See Richard Herr, THE EIGHTEENTH CENTURY REVOLUTION
    IN SPAIN, pp. 11-13; cf. A.P. Whitaker, editor, LATIN AMERICA
    AND THE ENLIGHTENMENT.
54 James Thomson, LETTERS, p. 163.
55 Domingo Amunategui, EL SISTEMA DE LANCASTER, p. 36.
56 EVANGELICAL CHRISTENDOM, Volume I, 1847, p. 316.
57 James Thomson, LETTERS, p. 66.
58 James Thomson, LETTERS, pp. 101-103.
59 EVANGELICAL CHRISTENDOM, Volume I, 1847, p. 317.
60 Henry Denzinger, THE SOURCES OF CATHOLIC DOGMA, p. 400.
61 D. R. Mitchell, 'James Thomson,' p. 263.
62 24th REPORT, British and Foreign School Society, 1828, p. 14.
63 Evaristo Iglesias, LA ESCUELA PUBLICA, p. 238.
64 James Thomson, LETTERS, p. 278.
65 HISTORIA, I, Santiago, 1961 (Jaime Eyzaguirre).
66 L. A. Cabello, 'El Sistema Monitorial,' 1946 unpublished doctoral
    dissertation, Universidad de San Marcos, Lima.
67 D. R. Mitchell, 'James Thomson,' p. 321.
68 THE AMERICAS, April 1966, XXII: 4.

Notes on Chapter 3: AWAKENINGS AND PIONEERS, II

1   J. Edwin Orr, THE FERVENT PRAYER, Chapters I-VI.
2   J. Edwin Orr, THE FERVENT PRAYER, Chapters VII-XII.
3   J. E. Hodder-Williams, SIR GEORGE WILLIAMS, pp. 187, 203.
4   J. Edwin Orr, THE FERVENT PRAYER, Chapter XVIII.
5   See F. C. MacDonald, BISHOP STIRLING OF THE FALKLANDS.
6   G. P. Despard, HOPE DEFERRED, NOT LOST, London, 1854.
7   See Arnoldo Canclini, HASTA LO ULTIMO DE LA TIERRA.
8   Robert Young, FROM CAPE HORN TO PANAMA, p. 61.
9   F. C. MacDonald, BISHOP STIRLING OF THE FALKLANDS.
10 E. F. Every, TWENTY-FIVE YEARS IN SOUTH AMERICA, p. 81;
    J. M. Drysdale, 100 YEARS IN BUENOS AIRES; & Robert Young,
    pp. 123ff; J. A. Mackay, THE OTHER SPANISH CHRIST, p. 234.
11 See J. G. Guerra, SARMIENTO, SU VIDA Y SUS OBRAS, passim.
12 A. H. Luiggi, SIXTY-FIVE VALIANTS, pp. 17, 35ff.
13 J. B. Zubiar, SINOPSIS DE LA EDUCACION EN LA REPUBLICA
    ARGENTINA, pp. 31-44.
14 Browning, Ritchie & Grubb, THE WEST COAST REPUBLICS OF
    SOUTH AMERICA, pp. 27ff, 79ff.
15 J. A. Mackay, THE OTHER SPANISH CHRIST, p. 240.
16 J. H. McLean, HISTORIA DE LA IGLESIA PRESBITERIANA EN
    CHILE, pp. 58ff.
17 'The work was too charismatic,' stated Chilean Pentecostals.
18 See W. B. Grubb, A CHURCH IN THE WILDS, passim.
19 William Taylor, OUR SOUTH AMERICAN COUSINS, p. 96.
20 THE CHRISTIAN WORLD, Volume XXIV, p. 77.
21 F. G. Penzotti, SPIRITUAL VICTORIES IN SOUTH AMERICA.
22 A. J. Brown, ONE HUNDRED YEARS, pp. 792-793.
23 Braga & Grubb, THE REPUBLIC OF BRAZIL, p. 50.
24 William Canton, A HISTORY OF THE BRITISH AND FOREIGN
    BIBLE SOCIETY, Volume II, p. 84; & Braga & Grubb, p. 74.
25 See H. C. Tucker, THE BIBLE IN BRAZIL, passim.
26 See Fortunato Luz, A IGREJA EVANGELICAL FLUMINENSE.
27 P. S. Landes, ASHBEL GREEN SIMONTON.
28 V. Themudo Lessa, PADRE JOSE MANOEL DA CONCEICAO;
    W. R. Wheeler, MISSIONS IN CHILE AND BRAZIL, pp. 344-345.
29 Wilhelm Schlatter, GESCHICHTE DER BASLER MISSION, 1815-
    1915, Volume I, p. 90.
30 W. R. Wheeler, pp. 344-345.
31 P. E. Buyers, HISTORIA DE METODISMO, São Paulo, 1945.
32 A. R. Crabtree, BAPTISTS IN BRAZIL, p. 35.
33 W. R. Read, CHURCH GROWTH IN BRAZIL, pp. 186ff.
34 A. B. Kinsolving, BIOGRAFIA DE L. L. KINSOLVING, passim.
35 W. R. Wheeler, MODERN MISSIONS IN CHILE AND BRAZIL,
    Chapter IX; cf. Braga & Grubb, THE REPUBLIC OF BRAZIL.
36 q. in W. E. Browning, THE RIVER PLATE REPUBLICS, p. 72.
37 MISSIONARY REVIEW OF THE WORLD, 1889, p. 635.
38 MISSIONARY REVIEW OF THE WORLD, 1888, p. 225.
39 MISSIONS OF THE EPISCOPAL CHURCH, 1927, VII, Mexico.
40 Camargo & Grubb, RELIGION IN THE REPUBLIC OF MEXICO,
    pp. 87-88.
41 See Melinda Rankin, TWENTY YEARS AMONG THE MEXICANS,
    pp. 88-89.   42 Melinda Rankin, pp. 36ff.
43 MISSIONARY REVIEW OF THE WORLD, 1888, p. 377.
44 MISSIONARY REVIEW OF THE WORLD, 1887, pp. 683-685.

Notes on Chapter 4: CARIBBEAN AWAKENING, 1860—

1 EVANGELICAL CHRISTENDOM, 2 February 1863, p. 100 (Clark of Savanna-la-Mar)
2 MISSIONARY NOTICES, Wesleyan Methodist Missionary Society, 10 December 1858 & 17 February 1859.
3 EVANGELICAL CHRISTENDOM, 1 January 1861, p. 32.
4 THE FREEMAN, 5, 12, 19, & 26 December 1860.
5 J. T. Hamilton, HISTORY OF THE MORAVIAN CHURCH, p. 457.
6 EVANGELICAL CHRISTENDOM, 1 January 1861, p. 32.
7 Sonderman, EVANGELICAL CHRISTENDOM, p. 34.
8 28 September 1860, diary.   9 1 October 1860, diary.
10 Claydon, 1 January 1861, p. 33.   11 4 October 1860, diary.
12 1 January 1861, p. 32.   13 20 November 1860, letter.
14 Sibley, 1 January 1861, p. 33.   15 Gordon, p. 33.
16 Independent, 1 January 1861, p. 33.   17 Claydon, p. 33.
18 Claydon, 1 January 1861, p. 34.   19 Sibley,   p. 32.
20 J. B. Ellis, THE DIOCESE OF JAMAICA, pp. 139ff; see also S. C. Neill, A HISTORY OF CHRISTIAN MISSIONS, p. 309.
22 E. A. Payne, FREEDOM IN JAMAICA, pp. 88ff.
23 EVANGELICAL CHRISTENDOM, 1 January 1861, p. 35.
24 Clark, 2 February 1863, pp. 99-100.
25 Richard Lovett, THE HISTORY OF THE LONDON MISSIONARY SOCIETY, Volume II, pp. 376-396.
26 United Presbyterian MISSIONARY RECORD, June 1862.
27 REPORT of the Wesleyan Methodist Missionary Society, April 1861, p. 102.   28 April 1861, p. 108.
29 April 1861, p. 105.   30 April 1861, p. 106.
31 April 1861, p. 103.   32 Reports of April 1861 & April 1862.
33 April 1863, p. 139.   34 April 1863, p. 141.
35 William Canton, A HISTORY OF THE BRITISH AND FOREIGN BIBLE SOCIETY, Volume IV, p. 150.
36 EVANGELICAL CHRISTENDOM, 1 January 1861, p. 35.
37 1 August 1861, p. 498.   38 1 August 1861, p. 499.
39 William Canton, Volume IV, p. 150.
40 EVANGELICAL CHRISTENDOM, 1 August 1861, p. 498.
41 E. A. Payne, FREEDOM IN JAMAICA, p. 88.
42 J. E. Hutton, A HISTORY OF MORAVIAN MISSIONS, pp. 224ff.
43 G.G. Findlay & W.W. Holdsworth, HISTORY OF THE WESLEYAN METHODIST MISSIONARY SOCIETY, Volume II, p. 374.
44 See G. E. Henderson, GOODNESS AND MERCY, p. 104.
45 EVANGELICAL CHRISTENDOM, 1 August 1861, p. 498.
46 1 January 1861, p. 31.   47 1 January 1861, p. 33.
48 Leonard Tucker, "GLORIOUS LIBERTY," pp. 76ff.
49 William Canton, Volume IV, p. 150.
50 REPORT, Wesleyan Methodist Missionary Society, April 1861, p. 88.   51 April 1862, p. 120.
52 Thelma Good, MORAVIAN MISSIONS IN BLUEFIELDS, p. 8.
53 MISSIONARY REVIEW OF THE WORLD, 1888, p. 230.
54 Thelma Good, MORAVIAN MISSIONS IN BLUEFIELDS, pp. 10ff.
55 MISSIONARY REVIEW, 1888, p. 230.   56 1895, p. 214.
57 Richard Lovett, Volume II, pp. 318ff, 389ff.
58 M. C. Kahn, DJUKA: THE BUSH NEGROES OF DUTCH GUIANA.
59 MISSIONARY REVIEW, 1896, pp. 520ff, and 1897, p. 814.
60 See EVANGELICAL CHRISTENDOM, 2 February 1863, p. 100; & MISSIONARY REVIEW, 1897, p. 814; 1896, pp. 522ff.

Notes on Chapter 5: MISSIONARY RESURGENCE, 1890—

1   J. C. Pollock, A CAMBRIDGE MOVEMENT, pp. 59-60.
2   J. Edwin Orr, CAMPUS AFLAME, 'The Student Volunteers.'
3   MISSIONARY REVIEW OF THE WORLD, issues of the 1890s.
4   Stephen Neill, A HISTORY OF CHRISTIAN MISSIONS, p. 389.
5   MISSIONARY REVIEW, 1894, p. 216.   6 1896, p. 214.
7   The Rev. Manuel J. Gaxiola called attention to Moody's visit.
8   MISSIONARY REVIEW, 1895, pp. 447ff.   9 Bishop Juan Pascoe.
10 MISSIONARY REVIEW, 1907, p. 472.   11 1911, p. 386.
12 See ANNUAL REPORT, American Bible Society, 1888, p. 95.
13 A. J. Brown, ONE HUNDRED YEARS, p. 825.
14 K. G. Grubb, RELIGION IN CENTRAL AMERICA, pp. 33ff.
15 MISSIONARY REVIEW, 1895, p. 215.   16 1895, pp. 214-215.
17 MISSIONARY REVIEW, 1895, pp. 215-216.   18 1897, p. 197.
19 Cf. J. S. Stowell, BETWEEN THE AMERICAS, pp. 128ff.
20 MISSIONARY REVIEW, 1896, p. 215.   21 1887, pp. 232ff.
22 1888, p. 634.   23 1897, p. 198.   24 1897, p. 199.
25 E. A. Odell, IT CAME TO PASS, p. 14.
26 MISSIONARY REVIEW OF THE WORLD, 1899, p. 257.
27 H. B. Grose, ADVANCE IN THE ANTILLES, pp. 208ff.
28 C. F. Pascoe, CLASSIFIED DIGEST: RECORDS, S.P.G., pp. 208.
29 CANADIAN PRESBYTERIAN MISSION, TRINIDAD, passim.
30 C. F. Pascoe, TWO HUNDRED YEARS OF THE S.P.G., pp. 223ff.
31 BRITISH GUIANA, London, 1920, p. 33.
32 MISSIONARY REVIEW OF THE WORLD, 1897, p. 815.
33 ANNUAL REPORT, American Bible Society, 1888, p. 94.
34 A. J. Brown, ONE HUNDRED YEARS, pp. 829-831.
35 MISSIONARY REVIEW OF THE WORLD, 1900, p. 723.
36 THE GOSPEL MESSAGE, Kansas City, February 1896.
37 MISSIONARY REVIEW OF THE WORLD, 1900, p. 67.
38 Interview with Jerome Altig, Artesia, California (Donald Dilworth)
39 W. F. Jordan, ECUADOR: MISSION ACHIEVEMENT, passim.
40 Browning, Ritchie & Grubb, WEST COAST REPUBLICS, p. 78.
41 THE GOSPEL IN ALL LANDS, 1895, p. 404 (T. B. Wood).
42 J. B. A. Kessler, PROTESTANT MISSIONS IN PERU AND CHILE,
    pp. 38-39, 158-159.   43 Peters, Jarret & Stark, R. B. M. U.
44 THE GOSPEL IN ALL LANDS, 1899, pp. 131-132 (T. B. Wood)
45 ANNUAL REPORT, British & Foreign Bible Society, 1828, p. 112.
46 Browning, Ritchie & Grubb, pp. 173-174.
47 MISSIONARY REVIEW OF THE WORLD, 1911, p. 222.
48 See ECHOES OF SERVICE, January 1966 & H. E. Stillwell,
    PIONEERING IN BOLIVIA, pp. 83ff.   49 Stephen Neill, p. 391.
50 MISSIONARY REVIEW OF THE WORLD, 1898, pp. 810-812.
51 J. B. A. Kessler, PROTESTANT MISSIONS (Peru & Chile), p. 243.
52 Arno Enns, MAN, MILIEU AND MISSION IN ARGENTINA, p. 145.
53 Methodist Episcopal Missionary Society, ANNUAL REPORT, 1901,
    pp. 266ff.   54 SALVATION ARMY YEAR BOOK, 1976, p. 175.
55 A. R. Crabtree, BAPTISTS IN BRAZIL, pp. 40ff.
56 MISSIONARY REVIEW, 1892, p. 159; 1894, p. 475.
57 William Canton, A HISTORY OF THE BRITISH AND FOREIGN
    BIBLE SOCIETY, Volume III, pp. 125-142; Volume IV, pp. 322ff.
58 There were such revivals among bilingual second generation folk.
59 J. B. A. Kessler, PROTESTANT MISSIONS (Peru & Chile), p. 89.
60 See H. T. Beach, editor, PROTESTANT MISSIONS IN SOUTH
    AMERICA, article by T. B. Wood, pp. 195ff (see p. 211).

Notes on Chapter 6: THE FIFTH GENERAL AWAKENING

1 See J. Edwin Orr, THE FLAMING TONGUE, Chapters 1-25, for an account of the Fifth General Awakening and fuller documentation of the details.
2 On 1st July 1916, the Ulster Division was decimated in the battle of the Somme.
3 F. C. Ottman, J. WILBUR CHAPMAN, p. 272.
4 MISSIONARY REVIEW OF THE WORLD, 1903, pp. 20ff.
5 For an account of the prisoner-of-war awakenings, see Chapter 15, 'The Mission of Peace,' pp. 121ff.
6 J. Edwin Orr, THE FLAMING TONGUE, Chapter 23, 'Taikyo Dendo in Japan.'
7 MISSIONARY REVIEW OF THE WORLD, 1903, pp. 20ff.
8 On the ministry of Gipsy Rodney Smith, see Chapter 15, 'The Mission of Peace' in South Africa, pp. 125-129.
9 J. Edwin Orr, THE FLAMING TONGUE, Chapters 1-3.
10 J. Vyrnwy Morgan, THE WELSH RELIGIOUS REVIVAL: A RETROSPECT AND A CRITICISM, pp. 248ff.
11 Keir Hardie, converted in the Fourth General Awakening, active as a Christian throughout his trade union career, died in 1915.
12 THE RECORD, 16 June 1905; THE WITNESS, 17 February 1905; and other British journals reported Anglican support.
13 J. Edwin Orr, THE FLAMING TONGUE, Chapter 4, 'Irish and Scottish Awakenings.'
14 'Awakening in Scandinavia,' THE FLAMING TONGUE, Chapter 7.
15 J. Edwin Orr, THE FLAMING TONGUE, Chapter 8, European continental reports.
16 STATESMAN'S YEARBOOK, 1905 & 1909 figures.
17 J. Edwin Orr, THE FLAMING TONGUE, Chapters 9-12, giving North American accounts.
18 'The 1905 American Awakening,' pp. 74-75; 'Impact on Church and State,' pp. 93-94; in THE FLAMING TONGUE.
19 THE FLAMING TONGUE, pp. 76-79; and passim.
20 'The 1905 American Awakening,' pp. 79-80.
21 J. Edwin Orr, THE FLAMING TONGUE, p. 80.
22 STATESMAN'S YEARBOOK, 1905 & 1911 data.
23 'The Mission of Peace,' p. 133, following.
24 J. Edwin Orr, THE FLAMING TONGUE, Chapters 17-20, giving an account of Awakenings in India.
25 92nd ANNUAL REPORT, American Baptist Missionary Union, pp. 99 & 119; cf. 93rd ANNUAL REPORT.
26 'The Korean Pentecost,' Chapter 22, THE FLAMING TONGUE.
27 CHINA MISSION YEAR BOOK, 1915.
28 ATLAS OF PROTESTANT MISSIONS, 1903; and WORLD ATLAS OF CHRISTIAN MISSIONS, 1911.
29 J. Edwin Orr, THE FLAMING TONGUE, Chapter 13, 'Latin American Quickening.'
30 'The African Awakenings,' Chapter 16, following.
31 J. Edwin Orr, THE FLAMING TONGUE, Chapter 24, 'The Pentecostal Aftermath.'
32 WESLEYAN METHODIST MAGAZINE, 1905, p. 65; CHRISTIAN ADVOCATE, 6 January 1906.
33 J. Edwin Orr, THE FLAMING TONGUE, pp. 97ff.
34 K. S. Latourette, A HISTORY OF THE EXPANSION OF CHRISTIANITY, Volume IV, Chapter 11.

Notes on Chapter 7: THE QUICKENING IN BRAZIL, 1905—

1 Cf. L. L. Kinsolving, in THE EAST AND THE WEST, 1903, pp. 134ff, justifying establishment of an Anglican diocese.
2 MISSIONARY REVIEW OF THE WORLD, 1903, p. 548.
3 A. G. Horton, AN OUTLINE OF LATIN AMERICAN HISTORY, p. 237.   4 MISSIONARY REVIEW, 1907, p. 811.
5 SOUTHERN BAPTIST CONVENTION ANNUAL, 1900, p. 76.
6 MISSIONARY REVIEW, 1907, p. 810.   7 1907, p. 392.
8 This hymn was sung everywhere during the movement of 1952.
9 SOUTHERN BAPTIST CONVENTION ANNUAL, 1900, p. 76.
10 MISSIONARY REVIEW, 1903, pp. 148-149.
11 G. C. Lenington, in MISSIONARY REVIEW, 1906, pp. 199ff.
12 MISSIONARY REVIEW, 1906, p. 200.   13 1906, p. 200.
14 G. C. Lenington, MISSIONARY REVIEW, 1906, p. 200.
15 F. C. Edwards, 'The First Brazilian Evangelical Awakening,' in THE ROLE OF THE FAITH MISSION: A BRAZILIAN CASE STUDY, pp. 6-7.
16 See W. R. Wheeler, MODERN MISSIONS IN CHILE AND BRAZIL, Chapter IX.
17 q. in W. E. Browning, THE RIVER PLATE REPUBLICS, p. 72.
18 MISSIONARY REVIEW OF THE WORLD, 1906, p. 805; RECORD OF CHRISTIAN WORK, p. 983; & ANNUALS, Southern Baptist Conventions.
19 MISSIONARY REVIEW OF THE WORLD, 1906, p. 805.
20 Solomon Ginsburg, A MISSIONARY ADVENTURE, pp. 135ff; cf. EVANGELICAL CHRISTENDOM, 1907, p. 74 & 1909, p. 46.
21 SOUTHERN BAPTIST CONVENTION ANNUALS; cf. Solomon Ginsburg, A MISSIONARY ADVENTURE, pp. 216ff.
22 MISSIONARY REVIEW OF THE WORLD, 1912, p. 863.
23 See P. E. Pierson, A YOUNGER CHURCH IN SEARCH OF MATURITY, pp. 50-51.
24 O PURITANO, 5 May 1910; 25 May 1911; 26 May 1911; Mario Neves, MEIO SECULO, p. 29; & J. A. Ferreira, HISTORIA DA IGREJA PRESBITERIANA DO BRASIL, p. 149.
25 P. E. Pierson, A YOUNGER CHURCH, p. 51.
26 Lauro Bretones, REDEMOINHOS DO SUL, p. 12; Archives of Igreja Presbiteriana, Governador Valadares.
27 O PURITANO, 17 May 1917.
28 E. G. Leonard, O PROTESTANTISM BRASILEIRO, pp. 152-153; cf. W. R. Read, CHURCH GROWTH IN BRAZIL, pp. 56-57; & Microfilm Letter, W. E. Finley, 29 August 1903, Philadelphia.
29 See W. R. Read, NEW PATTERNS OF CHURCH GROWTH IN BRAZIL, pp. 110ff; cf. Microfilm Letter, G. A. Landes, report of statistics, 3 September 1906.
30 F. C. Edwards, THE ROLE OF THE FAITH MISSION.
31 See E. G. Conde, HISTORIA DAS ASSEMBLEIAS DE DEUS NO BRASIL, pp. 11ff.
32 W. R. Read, CHURCH GROWTH IN BRAZIL, pp. 22ff.
33 E. G. Conde, ASSEMBLEIAS DE DEUS NO BRASIL, pp. 12-25.
34 W. R. Read, CHURCH GROWTH IN BRAZIL, p. 120.
35 See REVISTA DAS MISSÕES NACIONAES, November 1912; cf. W. R. Read, CHURCH GROWTH IN BRAZIL, pp. 25-26, 120-121.
36 CONVENCÃO BATISTA BRASILEIRO, Statistics.
37 W. R. Read, CHURCH GROWTH IN BRAZIL, pp. 112-113.
38 W. R. Read, CHURCH GROWTH IN BRAZIL, p. 119.

Notes on Chapter 8: SOUTHERN SOUTH AMERICA, 1905—

1 H. P. Beach, ed., PROTESTANT MISSIONS IN SOUTH AMERICA, article by T. B. Wood, pp. 211 & 201.
2 THE CHRISTIAN, London, 3 August 1905.
3 Arno Enns, MAN, MILIEU AND MISSION IN ARGENTINA, p. 146.
4 William Payne, PIONEERING IN BOLIVIA, pp. 8-9.
5 Arno Enns, MAN, MILIEU AND MISSION IN ARGENTINA, p. 147.
6 ECHOES OF SERVICE, 1904; William Payne, p. 7.
7 Orestes Marotta, DR. SIDNEY McFARLAND SOWELL, passim.
8 Letter of J. L. Hart, 1909, Archives of Southern Baptist Foreign Board, Richmond, Virginia.
9 LOS BAUTISTAS DEL RIO DE LA PLATA, passim.
10 Kramer, Beckman & Fehlauer, EVANGELISCHE LUTERISCHE KIRCHE IN ARGENTINA, passim.
11 J.B.A. Kessler, PROTESTANT MISSIONS AND CHURCHES IN PERU AND CHILE, pp. 73, 91, 260, & 248 (graphs).
12 J.B.A.Kessler, p. 105.
13 See I. H. LaFetra, THE CHILE MISSION OF THE METHODIST EPISCOPAL CHURCH, p. 84.
14 Goodsil Arms, HISTORY OF THE WILLIAM TAYLOR SELF-SUPPORTING MISSION, pp. 141ff.
15 W. C. Hoover, HISTORIA DEL AVIVAMIENTO PENTECOSTAL EN CHILE, p. 11.
16 W. C. Hoover, HISTORIA, p. 10.
17 ALLIANCE WEEKLY, New York, 1907, p. 2.
18 ALLIANCE WEEKLY, 1908, pp. 175-176.
19 Arturo Oyarzun, LA OBRA EVANGELICA EN CHILE, p. 71.
20 LA VOZ BAUTISTA, Santiago, 30 November 1932.
21 MISSIONARY REVIEW OF THE WORLD, 1909, p. 344.
22 See J. Edwin Orr, EVANGELICAL AWAKENINGS IN SOUTHERN ASIA, pp. 144-146; cf. W. C. Hoover, HISTORIA, p. 14.
23 W. C. Hoover, in WORLD DOMINION, 1932, p. 155.
24 W. C. Hoover, HISTORIA, p. 17.
25 W. C. Hoover, HISTORIA, pp. 19ff.
26 Arturo Oyarzun, LA OBRA EVANGELICA EN CHILE, p. 50.
27 See EL CRISTIANO, Santiago, 20 September 1909.
28 J.B.A.Kessler, p. 121.
29 J.B.A.Kessler, p. 110.
30 W. C. Hoover, HISTORIA, passim.
31 W. C. Hoover, HISTORIA, pp. 35ff.
32 Donald Gee, THE PENTECOSTAL MOVEMENT, p. 57.
33 J.B.A. Kessler, p. 131.
34 W. C. Hoover, HISTORIA, p. 83.
35 CHILE PENTECOSTAL, Concepcion, 1 July 1912.
36 J.B.A. Kessler, p. 292.
37 CHILE PENTECOSTAL, Concepcion, 9 February 1912.
38 FUEGO DE PENTECOSTES, Santiago, May 1948. The late Dr. Kenneth Strachan and the writer in 1951 witnessed great open-air marches of Pentecostal Methodists, and addressed their rally.
39 S. C. Neill, A HISTORY OF CHRISTIAN MISSIONS, p. 391.
40 MISSIONARY REVIEW OF THE WORLD, 1910, pp. 574ff.
41 See Tron & Ganz, HISTORIA DE LAS COLONIAS VALDENSES SUDAMERICANAS, 1858-1958, passim.
42 W. O. Bullis, 'A History of the Southern Baptists in Uruguay, M.A. Thesis, Baylor University, 1965.

1　H. E. Stillwell, PIONEERING IN BOLIVIA, p. 133.
2　N. H. Dabbs, DAWN OVER THE BOLIVIAN HILLS, p. 74.
3　Mrs. William Payne, Sucre, 29 June 1901, letter in ECHOES OF SERVICE, 1901, p. 338.
4　See C. P. Wagner, THE PROTESTANT MOVEMENT IN BOLIVIA, pp. 37 & 56, citing several factors.
5　H. E. Stillwell, PIONEERING IN BOLIVIA, p. 139.
6　Paul McCleary, 'The Methodist Church in Bolivia,' p. 2, cited in C. P. Wagner, p. 56.
7　See B. L. Goddard, ENCYCLOPEDIA OF MODERN CHRISTIAN MISSIONS, passim; cf. Margarita Allan Hudspith, RIPENING FRUIT, passim.
8　J. B. A. Kessler, PROTESTANT MISSIONS AND CHURCHES IN PERU AND CHILE, p. 159.
9　See John Ritchie, THE INDIGENOUS CHURCH IN PERU.
10　See Autobiography of Alfonso Munoz, MIS MEMORIAS; & J. B. A. Kessler, pp. 171ff.
11　Browning, Ritchie & Grubb, THE WEST COAST REPUBLICS OF SOUTH AMERICA, p. 86.
12　J. B. A. Kessler, p. 90.
13　CHRISTIAN HERALD, London, 27 April 1905.
14　MISSIONARY REVIEW OF THE WORLD, 1899, pp. 842-843.
15　MISSIONARY REVIEW, 1903, p. 387.　　16　1910, p. 22.
17　John Aberly, AN OUTLINE OF MISSIONS, p. 27.
18　MISSIONARY REVIEW, 1912, pp. 803-804.
19　See Tom Watson, T. J. BACH: A VOICE FOR MISSIONS.
20　The writer enjoyed a long friendship with T. J. Bach.
21　See C. O. Butler, 'Protestant Growth and a Changing Panama,' M. A. Thesis, Perkins School of Theology, Dallas, 1964.
22　MISSIONARY REVIEW, 1911, p. 386.　　23　1912, p. 861.
24　P. C. Enyart, 'Friends in Central America,' M.A. Thesis, 1970, School of World Mission, Pasadena, California.
25　MISSIONARY REVIEW, 1912, p. 861.　　26　1905, p. 229.
27　Vicente Mendoza, interviewed by the Rev. Manuel Gaxiola, in the later years of his life.
28　MISSIONARY REVIEW, 1907, p. 472.　　29　1911, p. 386.
30　MISSIONARY REVIEW, 1910, p. 313.　　31　1905, p. 467.
32　THE CHRISTIAN, 16 March & 30 November 1905; MISSIONARY REVIEW, 1906, p. 643; & ALLIANCE WEEKLY, 1906, p. 364; and various other periodicals.
33　MISSIONARY REPORTS, Wesleyan Methodist Missionary Society, 1907, pp. 132ff & 150.
34　See 93rd REPORT, 1907, Wesleyan Methodist Missionary Society, London, p. 138.
35　92nd REPORT, 1906, pp. 146-147.
36　91st REPORT, 1905, p. 123.
37　MISSIONARY REVIEW, 1913, p. 221.
38　cf. ATLAS OF PROTESTANT MISSIONS, 1903; WORLD ATLAS OF CHRISTIAN MISSIONS, 1911.
39　World Missionary Council, 4th Meeting, 12 March 1908, Minute 45, p. 28; cf. W. R. Hogg, ECUMENICAL FOUNDATIONS.
40　Silas McBee, 'Catholic Episcopalian,' editor of THE CHURCHMAN, seemed to be spokesman for the 'exclude Latin America' lobby; cf. W. R. Hogg, ECUMENICAL FOUNDATIONS, pp. 119, 131-133.

Notes on Chapter 10: THE DECLINE IN THE WEST

1   W. A. Beahm, 'Factors in the Development of the Student Volunteer Movement for Foreign Missions,' unpublished Ph.D. dissertation, University of Chicago, 1941, pp. 14-15.
2   C. H. Hopkins, Y. M. C. A. IN NORTH AMERICA, pp. 642-645.
3   Author's analysis, repeated from EVANGELICAL AWAKENINGS IN COLLEGIATE COMMUNITIES (U.C.L.A. Ed.D. dissertation), popular version published as CAMPUS AFLAME.
4   F. P. & M. S. Wood, YOUTH ADVANCING, London, 1961.
5   J. Edwin Orr, 'The Progression of Revivals of New Testament Christianity in Modern Times,' unpublished typescript, Melbourne.
6   C. W. Malcolm, TWELVE HOURS IN THE DAY, pp. 87-103.
7   See Chapter 13, 'Empire Evangelist,' pp. 115-126; & pp. 127ff.
8   Harold Murray, SIXTY YEARS AN EVANGELIST (Gipsy Smith's biography), London, 1937.
9   R. E. Garrett, WILLIAM EDWARD BIEDERWOLF, passim.
10 W. T. Ellis, BILLY SUNDAY: THE MAN AND HIS MESSAGE.
11 See W. G. McLoughlin, MODERN REVIVALISM, pp. 432ff.
12 Homer Rodeheaver, TWENTY YEARS WITH BILLY SUNDAY, pp. 145-146.
13 Stated by Homer Rodeheaver, 1942, in the writer's hearing.
14 W. G. McLoughlin, BILLY SUNDAY WAS HIS REAL NAME, p. 271.   Sunday died 6 November 1935.
15 L. A. Loetscher, editor, TWENTIETH CENTURY ENCYCLOPEDIA OF RELIGIOUS KNOWLEDGE, Volume II, p. 973.
16 E. E. Ham, FIFTY YEARS ON THE BATTLE FRONT WITH CHRIST, 1950.   17 ZION'S HERALD, 19 January 1916.
18 J. Edwin Orr, ALWAYS ABOUNDING, pp. 89-90.
19 Faith Mission, FROM CIVIL WAR TO REVIVAL VICTORY, p. 1.
20 S. W. Murray, W. P. NICHOLSON: FLAME FOR GOD IN ULSTER, pp. 5ff.   21 FROM CIVIL WAR TO REVIVAL VICTORY, p. 2.
22 S. W. Murray, W. P. NICHOLSON, pp. 12ff.
23 GENERAL ASSEMBLY OF THE PRESBYTERIAN CHURCH IN IRELAND, Report of the State of Religion Committee, 1923.
24 S. W. Murray, W. P. NICHOLSON, pp. 23-24.
25 Archibald Irwin, 'Is There a Revival in Ulster?', THE WITNESS, Belfast, 24 November 1922.
26 No one denied the vulgarities, but many made excuses for them.
27 S. W. Murray, W. P. NICHOLSON, pp. 35-36.
28 A. R. Gesswein, 'The Norwegian Revival of 1934 Onward,' paper read at the Oxford Reading and Research Conference, 1974.
29 J. Edwin Orr, ALWAYS ABOUNDING, pp. 71-75; PROVE ME NOW, pp. 77ff; Stuart-Watt, DYNAMITE IN EUROPE, pp. 144ff.
30 E. Stuart-Watt, DYNAMITE IN EUROPE, pp. 52-56.
31 See J. Edwin Orr, EVANGELICAL AWAKENINGS IN AFRICA, pp. 159-164.   32 pp. 160-162.
33 pp. 165-166.   34 pp. 163-164.   35 pp. 167-168.
36 C. W. Malcolm, TWELVE HOURS IN THE DAY, pp. 150-161; & Bishop A. J. Appasamy, WRITE THE VISION, pp. 91ff.
37 W. J. Hollenweger, THE PENTECOSTALS, pp. 126ff.
38 See J. Edwin Orr, EVANGELICAL AWAKENINGS IN SOUTHERN ASIA, pp. 161-169.
39 See J. Edwin Orr, EVANGELICAL AWAKENINGS IN EASTERN ASIA, pp. 46-56.
40 pp. 57-63.   41 pp. 64-91.   42 pp. 92-96.

Notes on Chapter 11: THIRTY YEARS, POST-PANAMA

1   W. R. Hogg, ECUMENICAL FOUNDATIONS, pp. 120-121, 131ff.
2   CHRISTIAN WORK IN LATIN AMERICA, Volume I, pp. 27ff.
3   MISSIONARY REVIEW OF THE WORLD, 1916, pp. 397ff.
4   CHRISTIAN WORK IN LATIN AMERICA, Volume I, p. 79.
5   pp. 79 & 89.   6 pp. 80, 83 & 89.   7 pp. 80 & 90-91.
8   pp. 81-82, 94-95 & 100.
9   Susan B. Strachan, 'Latin American Evangelization Campaign,'
    unpublished typescript, 1941, Latin American Mission, pp. 7ff.
10 'Latin American Evangelization Crusade,' pp. 33-36.
11 MISSIONARY REVIEW OF THE WORLD, 1924, p. 291.
12 'Latin American Evangelization Crusade,' pp. 37-49.
13 MISSIONARY REVIEW OF THE WORLD, 1924, p. 291.
14 'Latin American Evangelization Crusade,' pp. 50-52.
15 pp. 57-60.   16 pp. 61-77.   17 p. 78.
18 p. 79.   19 pp. 79-80.   20 p. 81.
21 MISSIONARY REVIEW OF THE WORLD, 1924, p. 291.
22 John Christansen, UNDER THE SOUTHERN CROSS, p. 151.
23 See MISSIONARY REVIEW OF THE WORLD, 1928, p. 881; &
    1929, p. 67.   24 1929, pp. 461ff (G. T. B. Davis).
25 1927, p. 636.   26 1935, pp. 459-461.
27 1927, pp. 277ff.   28 1927, p. 399.   29 1936, p. 330.
30 q. in H. P. Beach, PROTESTANT MISSIONS IN SOUTH AMERICA.

Notes on Chapter 12: EVANGELICAL BRAZIL, 1916-1946

1   Braga & Grubb, THE REPUBLIC OF BRAZIL, cf. MISSIONARY
    REVIEW OF THE WORLD, 1924, pp. 337ff.
2   1915, p. 717.   3 1915, p. 865.   4 1916, p. 795.
5   See P. E. Pierson, A YOUNGER CHURCH IN SEARCH OF
    MATURITY, p. 48.
6   Daniel Berg, ENVIADO POR DEUS; PENTECOSTAL EVANGEL,
    25 June & 24 September 1961 (Jubilee of Assemblies of God)
7   W. R. Read, CHURCH GROWTH IN BRAZIL, p. 120.
8   G. F. Atter, "THE THIRD FORCE," p. 216; W. R. Read, pp. 22ff.
9   W. R. Read, CHURCH GROWTH IN BRAZIL, p. 29.
10 J. Edwin Orr, THE FLAMING TONGUE,, passim.
11 MISSIONARY REVIEW OF THE WORLD, 1924, p. 753.
12 P. E. Pierson, A YOUNGER CHURCH, p. 128.
13 W. R. Read, CHURCH GROWTH IN BRAZIL, pp. 74-75.
14 A. R. Crabtree, BAPTISTS IN BRAZIL, p. 188.   15 p. 189.
16 Braga & Grubb, THE REPUBLIC OF BRAZIL, pp. 54-57.
17 MISSIONARY REVIEW OF THE WORLD, 1931, p. 117.
18 75 ANOS DE EXISTENCIA DO SINODO RIO-GRANDENSE, 1886—
19 E. T. Bachmann, LUTHERANS IN BRAZIL, pp. 46ff.
20 MISSIONARY REVIEW OF THE WORLD, 1929, p. 399.
21 1924, pp. 892ff.   22 1931, p. 117.
23 WORLD DOMINION, 1934, p. 97.
24 J. Merle Davis, HOW THE CHURCH GROWS, pp. 93ff.
25 W. R. Read, CHURCH GROWTH IN BRAZIL, p. 188.
26 'Latin American Evangelization Campaign,' pp. 254ff.
27 LATIN AMERICAN EVANGELIST, April 1931, p. 3.
28 G. W. Ridout, SHOWERS OF BLESSING, Louisville, 1932.
29 J. W. Tarboux, in G. W. Ridout, p. 6.
30 W. G. Borchers, in G. W. Ridout, p. 23.

31 G. W. Ridout, p. 11.   32 G. W. Ridout, p. 9.
33 W. G. Borchers, in G. W. Ridout, pp. 23-24.
34 G. W. Ridout, pp. 12, 15 & 25.   35 G. W. Ridout, p. 18.
36 J. W. Tarboux, in G. W. Ridout, p. 5.   37 G. W. Ridout, p. 6.
38 See A. R. Crabtree, BAPTISTS IN BRAZIL, cf. MISSIONARY
    REVIEW OF THE WORLD, 1935, p. 86.
39 See WORLD DOMINION, October 1933, p. 418; & MISSIONARY
    REVIEW OF THE WORLD, 1935, p. 204.
40 Walter Ermel, O ESTANDARTE, Sao Paulo, 31 July 1953.

Notes on Chapter 13: THE SOUTHERN REPUBLICS, 1916-1946.

1   16,052,765, 1947 Argentine Census.
2   Philip Raine, PARAGUAY, pp. 195ff.
3   Cf. J.J.Considine, THE CHURCH IN LATIN AMERICA, p. 174.
4   W. J. Coleman, LATIN AMERICAN CATHOLICISM, p. 26.
5   Cf. J. J. Considine, NEW HORIZONS IN LATIN AMERICA, in
    statistics, pp. 328 & 331.
6   J. J. Considine, pp. 328 & 331.
7   Margaret Bates, THE LAY APOSTOLATE, p. 49; J.J. Considine,
    NEW HORIZONS IN LATIN AMERICA, p. 328.
8   Cf. J. J. Considine, NEW HORIZONS, pp. 328ff.
9   Yorke Allen, A SEMINARY SURVEY, p. 485.
10 WORLD ATLAS OF CHRISTIAN MISSIONS, 1911, p. 96.
11 WORLD MISSIONARY ATLAS, 1916, p. 72.
12 W. E. Browning, THE RIVER PLATE REPUBLICS, p. 53.
13 Arno Enns, MAN, MILIEU AND MISSION IN ARGENTINA, p. 148.
14 See ECHOES OF SERVICE, 1920-1930.
15 G. M. J. Lear, UN EXPLORADOR VALIENTE, Lanus, p. 142.
16 ECHOES OF SERVICE, 1924, passim.
17 Arno Enns, p. 150.   18 Arno Enns, p. 152.
19 D. M. Carroll, 'Baptist Work in Argentina,' D. R. E. Dissertation,
    Southwestern Baptist Theological Seminary, Fort Worth, 1960.
20 Arno Enns, p. 170.   21 Arno Enns, p. 89.
22 CHRISTIAN CHURCHES YEARBOOK, 1916 & 1945.
23 C. W. Conn, WHERE THE SAINTS HAVE TROD, pp. 155-162.
24 Lutheran Church, Missouri Synod, STATISTICAL YEARBOOKS.
25 Cf. Statistical table in Arno Enns, p. 184.
26 See EVANGELICAL HANDBOOK OF LATIN AMERICA, p. 120.
27 MISSIONARY REVIEW, 1936, p. 150.   28 1918, p. 225.
29 CHILE PENTECOSTAL, Santiago, October 1917.
30 EL HERALDO CRISTIANO, 2 October 1924.
31 J. B. A. Kessler, PROTESTANT MISSIONS AND CHURCHES IN
    PERU AND CHILE, p. 300.
32 J. T. Nicholls, PENTECOSTALISM, p. 166.
33 J. B. A. Kessler, pp. 303 & 307.
34 Cf. Ignacio Vergara, EL PROTESTANTISMO EN CHILE, p. 173.
35 MISSIONARY REVIEW OF THE WORLD, 1927, pp. 715 & 864.
36 MISSIONARY REVIEW OF THE WORLD, 1929, p. 399.
37 LATIN AMERICAN EVANGELIST, q. in MISSIONARY REVIEW
    OF THE WORLD, 1929, p. 67.
38 MISSIONARY REVIEW OF THE WORLD, 1929, p. 79.
39 'Latin American Evangelization Campaign,' pp. 234ff.
40 R. E. Speer, MISSIONS IN SOUTH AMERICA, p. 64.
41 J. B. A. Kessler, p. 223.,
42 MISSIONARY REVIEW OF THE WORLD, 1936, p. 166.

Notes on Chapter 14: TROPICAL SOUTH AMERICA, 1916-1946

1 Cf. J.J.Considine, NEW HORIZONS IN LATIN AMERICA, p. 328.
2 Yorke Allen, A SEMINARY SURVEY, pp. 480 & 487.
3 Methodist Episcopal Church, ANNUAL REPORT, 1946.
4 Canadian Baptist Foreign Mission Board, REPORTS, 1916 & 1946.
5 N. H. Dabbs, DAWN OVER THE BOLIVIAN HILLS, p. 144.
6 Cf. WORLD CHRISTIAN HANDBOOK, 1952.
7 General Conference, Seventh Day Adventists, Statistics.
8 S. B. Strachan, pp. 216ff.   9 p. 222.   10 pp. 222-223.
11 INTERNATIONAL REVIEW OF MISSIONS, April 1928, p. 286.
12 See Richard Pattee, EL CATOLICISMO, pp. 379-380.
13 MISSIONARY REVIEW OF THE WORLD, 1924, pp. 171 & 753.
14 Cf. J. J. Considine, NEW HORIZONS, pp. 328 & 331.
15 K. S. Latourette, CHRISTIANITY IN A REVOLUTIONARY AGE,
   Volume V, pp. 204-205.
16 Methodist Episcopal Church, ANNUAL REPORT, 1916, pp. 391ff.
17 SOUTH AMERICA, E.U.S.A., November-December 1922, p. 84.
18 John Ritchie, INDIGENOUS CHURCH PRINCIPLES, p. 46.
19 R. B. Clark, UNDER THE SOUTHERN CROSS, p. 208.
20 J. B. A. Kessler, PROTESTANT MISSIONS AND CHURCHES IN
   PERU AND CHILE, pp. 280-281.   21 pp. 63ff.
22 CHILE PENTECOSTAL, April 1927.
23 L. F. Sumrall, THROUGH BLOOD AND FIRE, p. 72.
24 FUEGO DE PENTECOSTES, January 1929.   25 March 1936.
26 J. B. A. Kessler, pp. 283ff.
27 K. E. Hamilton, CHURCH GROWTH IN THE HIGH ANDES, p. 29.
28 J. B. A. Kessler, pp. 230-231,   &   K. E. Hamilton, pp. 46-47.
29 Herbert Money, LA REFORMA DEL ARTICULO CUARTO DE
   LA CONSTITUCION DEL PERU, 1915, pp. 13-16.
30 J. B. A. Kessler, p. 230.
31 R. G. Winans, GOSPEL OVER THE ANDES, p. 22.
32 DeLong & Taylor, 50 YEARS OF NAZARENE MISSIONS, p. 237.
33 MISSIONARY REVIEW OF THE WORLD, 1931, p. 862.
34 WORLD DOMINION, April 1934, p. 208.
35 MISSIONARY REVIEW OF THE WORLD, 1931, p. 862; & S. B.
   Strachan, p. 241.   36 pp. 242-253.
37 MISSIONARY REVIEW OF THE WORLD, 1927, p. 788.
38 K. S. Latourette, Volume V, p. 202.
39 MISSIONARY REVIEW, 1924, p. 890.   40 1924, 886ff, 891.
41 LATIN AMERICAN EVANGELIST, 1931 (May); 1932 (November).
42 MISSIONARY REVIEW OF THE WORLD, 1931, p. 635.
43 K. S. Latourette, Volume V, p. 200.
44 See CATHOLIC HISTORICAL REVIEW, XXVI,   pp. 215ff.
45 Cf. J. J. Considine, NEW HORIZONS, p. 328.
46 S. B. Strachan, pp. 107ff.
47 MISSIONARY REVIEW OF THE WORLD, 1923, p. 319.
48 S. B. Strachan, pp. 126ff.   49 pp. 137ff.   50 pp. 140ff.
51 T. B. Hall, 'The Progress of Protestantism in Colombia,' M.S.
   thesis, Kansas State College, 1959, pp. 52-56, 67-68; R. B. Clark,
   UNDER THE SOUTHERN CROSS, 1938, p. 140.
52 Cf. K. G. Grubb, THE NORTHERN REPUBLICS OF SOUTH
   AMERICA; & WORLD DOMINION, January 1935, p. 46.
53 Gomez was father of many illegitimate children.
54 J. L. Mecham, CHURCH AND STATE IN LATIN AMERICA,
   pp. 110ff; cf. J. J. Considine, NEW HORIZONS, p. 328.

55 S. B. Strachan, pp. 143ff.
56 John Christiansen, UNDER THE SOUTHERN CROSS, pp. 153ff.
57 MISSIONARY REVIEW OF THE WORLD, 1928, p. 194.
58 S. B. Strachan, pp. 283ff.

Notes on Chapter 15: THE CARIBBEAN COUNTRIES, 1916-1946

1 J. Edwin Orr, 'A Survey of Evangelism in the Caribbean Area,'
    B.D. thesis, Northern Baptist Theological Seminary, 1942.
2 United States Department of Commerce, 1940, p. 171.
3 Richard Pattee, EL CATOLICISMO, p. 177.
4 MISSIONARY REVIEW OF THE WORLD, 1919, p. 66.
5 J. Edwin Orr, Survey, p. 13.
6 American Baptist Home Mission Society, 1940 REPORT, p. 49;
    Southern Baptist Convention, 1940 HANDBOOK, p. 337; and
    MISSIONARY REVIEW OF THE WORLD, 1936, p. 262.
7 cf. J. M. Davis, THE CHURCH IN PUERTO RICO'S DILEMMA,
    p. 9; J. Edwin Orr, Survey, p. 27.
8 MISSIONARY REVIEW OF THE WORLD, 1917, p. 222.
9 MISSIONARY REVIEW OF THE WORLD, 1921, p. 208.
10 'Latin American Evangelization Campaign,' pp. 195ff.
11 LA IMPARCIAL, San Juan, quoted pp. 203-207.
12 MISSIONARY REVIEW OF THE WORLD, 1935, pp. 224 & 437.
13 J. L. Lugo, in WEEKLY EVANGEL, 25 November 1916.
14 S. H. Frodsham, WITH SIGNS FOLLOWING, 1946, p. 219.
15 Cf. J. J. Considine, NEW HORIZONS, pp. 290ff.
16 MISSIONARY REVIEW OF THE WORLD, 1921, pp. 182ff.
17 'Latin American Evangelization Campaign,' pp. 209ff.
18 Cf. J. J. Considine, NEW HORIZONS, p. 330.
19 J. Edwin Orr, Survey, p. 23.
20 MISSIONARY REVIEW OF THE WORLD, 1927, p. 141.
21 MISSIONARY REVIEW, 1929, p. 398 & 1930, p. 181.
22 J. Edwin Orr, Survey, p. 24.
23 Cf. MISSIONARY REVIEW OF THE WORLD, 1938, p. 504.
24 LATIN AMERICAN EVANGELIST, July 1927.
25 J. Edwin Orr, Survey, p. 35; cf. J. M. Davis, THE CHURCH
    IN THE NEW JAMAICA, p. 32.
26 Northern Baptist Convention YEARBOOK, 1941, p. 677; and
    J. Edwin Orr, Survey, pp. 33-34.
27 E. A. Payne, FREEDOM IN JAMAICA, p. 116.
28 Notes and Recollections, J. Edwin Orr.
29 Cf. J. P. Hickerton, CARIBBEAN KALLALOO, pp. 73-79.
30 Cf. J. J. Considine, NEW HORIZONS IN LATIN AMERICA, p. 329;
    & J. Edwin Orr, Survey, p. 42.
31 See Read, Monterroso & Johnson, LATIN AMERICAN CHURCH
    GROWTH, p. 139.
32 United States Department of Commerce, p. 65.
33 Costa Rica is called 'the Switzerland of the Americas.'
34 Cf. J. J. Considine, NEW HORIZONS, p. 329.
35 'Latin American Evangelization Campaign,' pp. 224ff.
36 Cf. MISSIONARY REVIEW OF THE WORLD, 1927, p. 637.
37 'Latin American Evangelization Campaign,' pp. 224ff (228).
38 'Latin American Evangelization Campaign,' p. 226.
39 MISSIONARY REVIEW OF THE WORLD, 1927, p. 863.
40 J. Edwin Orr, Survey, p. 48.
41 LATIN AMERICAN EVANGELIST, 1956,, p. 37.

42 S. B. Strachan, pp. 176ff. 43 pp. 176ff. 44 232ff.
45 LATIN AMERICAN EVANGELIST, March & May 1933.
46 WORLD DOMINION, April 1934, p. 313.
47 United States Department of Commerce, p. 98.
48 Cf. J. J. Considine, NEW HORIZONS, p. 329.
49 MISSIONARY REVIEW, 1935, p. 86 & 1930, p. 15.
50 United States Department of Commerce, p. 106; J. Edwin Orr, Survey, p. 40; cf. J. J. Considine, NEW HORIZONS, p. 329.
51 Northern Baptist Convention YEARBOOK, 1941, p. 50.
52 United States Department of Commerce, p. 88.
53 Cf. J. J. Considine, NEW HORIZONS, p. 329.
54 J. Edwin Orr, Survey, 1940.
55 Paul C. Enyart, FRIENDS IN CENTRAL AMERICA, p. 56; and THE HARVESTER, 1918 issues.
56 THE HARVESTER, October 1918. 57 Oct & Nov. 1918.
58 Paul C. Enyart, FRIENDS IN CENTRAL AMERICA, pp. 56-57.
59 See M. P. Holleran, CHURCH AND STATE IN, GUATEMALA, pp. 221ff; & Yorke Allen, A SEMINARY SURVEY, p. 463.
60 S. B. Strachan, pp. 91ff. 61 pp. 94-96. 62 pp. 102ff.
63 MISSIONARY REVIEW OF THE WORLD, 1927, p. 787.
64 MISSIONARY REVIEW OF THE WORLD, 1935, p. 253.
65 LATIN AMERICAN EVANGELIST, 1932, pp. 9-10.
66 R. H. Glover, THE PROGRESS OF WORLD-WIDE MISSIONS, edited by J. Herbert Kane, 1960, p. 410.

Notes on Chapter 16: REVOLT AND REVIVAL IN MEXICO

1 C.C. Cumberland, MEXICO: THE STRUGGLE FOR MODERNITY.
2 W. H. Calcott, LIBERALISM IN MEXICO, pp. 245ff. & pp. 351ff.
3 Wilfrid Parsons, MEXICAN MARTYRDOM, pp. 14ff.
4 Murders of Evangelicals for their faith, often on priestly instigation, had exceeded sixty a year during the late nineteenth century.
5 W. H. Calcott, pp. 353-377.
6 WORLD STATISTICS OF CHRISTIAN MISSIONS, p. 74.
7 American Bible Society REPORTS, 1917 & 1918.
8 Cf. MISSIONARY REVIEW OF THE WORLD, 1921, p. 353.
9 1923, p. 204. 10 1923, p. 205. 11 1923, p. 206.
12 J. G. Dale, KATHERINE NEEL DALE, p. 99.
13 Methodist Episcopal Church, ANNUAL REPORT, 1925.
14 MISSIONARY REVIEW, 1929, p. 975. 15 1924, p. 170.
16 1930, pp. 183ff. 17 1931, p. 148. 18 1931, p. 542.
19 See C. S. MacFarland, CHAOS IN MEXICO, pp. 139-151.
20 500 stated in J. L. Mecham, CHURCH AND STATE, pp. 404-405.
21 MISSIONARY REVIEW, 1934, p. 147. 22 1935, p. 579.
23 1936, p. 117. 24 1935, p. 253. 25 1935, pp. 85 & 581.
26 N. W. Taylor. 27 N. W. Taylor. 28 MISSIONARY REVIEW, 1936, p. 330. 29 1938, p. 123. 30 1938, p. 124.
31 WORLD DOMINION, January 1939, p. 98.
32 MISSIONARY REVIEW, 1938, pp. 123ff. 33 N. W. Taylor.
34 WORLD DOMINION, July 1937, pp. 278ff.
35 MISSIONARY REVIEW OF THE WORLD, 1938, pp. 354ff.
36 WORLD DOMINION, July 1937, p. 278ff.
37 R. H. Glover, PROGRESS OF WORLD-WIDE MISSIONS, p. 405.
38 Richard Patté , THE CATHOLIC REVIVAL IN MEXICO, p. 60.
39 Yorke Allen, A SEMINARY REVIEW, p. 463.
40 N. W. Taylor, Misión Presbiteriana en México, 26 October 1940.

Notes on Chapter 17: POST WORLD WAR II AWAKENING

1 See J. Edwin Orr, EVANGELICAL AWAKENINGS IN EASTERN ASIA, Chapter 18, 'The Curtain Falls in China.'
2 Andrew Woolsey, DUNCAN CAMPBELL: A Biography, Chapters 13-15, pp. 112-138.
3 'Post War Evangelism in Japan,' EVANGELICAL AWAKENINGS IN EASTERN ASIA, Chapter 16, pp. 103-108.
4 'The 1947 Quickening in Korea,' Chapter 17, pp. 109-119.
5 'Taiwan, Hong Kong, and Overseas,' Chapter 20, pp. 135-139.
6 J. Edwin Orr, EVANGELICAL AWAKENINGS IN SOUTHERN ASIA, Chapter 24, 'Evangelical Resurgence in India,' pp. 177-190.
7 See J. Edwin Orr, EVANGELICAL AWAKENINGS IN AFRICA, pp. 167-168.   8 'The Winds of Change,' Chapter 20, pp. 181-183.
9 Chapter 20, pp. 184-187; & Chapter 19, 'Evangelism in Tension,' pp. 174-175.   10 Chapter 20, pp. 189-191.
11 J. Edwin Orr, EVANGELICAL AWAKENINGS IN THE SOUTH SEAS, p. 201.
12 Chapter 23, 'Other Island Groups,' pp. 198-200.
13 Chapter 23, pp. 194-195.
14 'Movements in Independent Indonesia,' Chapter 22, pp. 177-193; & G. W. Peters, INDONESIA REVIVAL.
15 See Kenneth Cragg, CHRISTIANITY IN WORLD PERSPECTIVE, p. 66 & N. A. Horner, editor, PROTESTANT CROSS-CURRENTS IN MISSIONS, p. 39.
16 Ralph D. Winter, THE TWENTY-FIVE UNBELIEVABLE YEARS, William Carey Library, South Pasadena, 1970.
17 T. B. Wood in H. P. Beach, editor, PROTESTANT MISSIONS IN SOUTH AMERICA, Chicago, 1900.
18 J. Edwin Orr, GOOD NEWS IN BAD TIMES, passim; see also E. L. R. Elson, AMERICA'S SPIRITUAL RECOVERY.
19 A. R. Gesswein, 'The Mid-Thirties Revival in Norway,' paper read at the Oxford Reading and Research Conference, Regent's Park College, University of Oxford, 1975.
20 J. Edwin Orr, GOOD NEWS IN BAD TIMES, 'Preachers to Prayer,' Chapter 2.
21 J. Edwin Orr, CAMPUS AFLAME, Evangelical Awakenings in Collegiate Communities, Chapter 19, 'Mid-Century Resurgence.'
22 Chapter 19, pp. 170-171.
23 See D. V. Benson, HENRIETTA MEARS, p. 252; J. C. Pollock, BILLY GRAHAM, pp. 52-53; J. Edwin Orr, FULL SURRENDER, Introduction by Billy Graham.
24 J. Edwin Orr, CAMPUS AFLAME, passim.
25 Cf. M. E. Marty, THE NEW SHAPE OF AMERICAN RELIGION, pp. 10ff 'The Revival of Interest in Religion.'
26 David du Plessis, in PENTECOST, December 1950, p. 5.
27 Editorial, HIS Magazine, January 1956, pp. 1-4.
28 D. E. Harrell, ALL THINGS ARE POSSIBLE, The Healing and Charismatic Revivals in Modern America, passim.
29 An example of the former is Oral Roberts, founder of the Tulsa university; for the latter, see D. E. Harrell, pp. 140ff, 233ff.
30 C. J. Hahn, Director, Inter-American Missionary Society in Brazil, 'Spiritual Awakening in Latin America,' THE CHRISTIAN, London, November 1952, quoted in PENTECOST, December.
31 LATIN AMERICAN EVANGELIST, 1951, p. 61.
32 C. J. Hahn, 'Spiritual Awakening in Latin America.'

Notes on Chapter 18: REAVIVAMENTO EVANGELICO BRASILEIRO

1 Rodolfo Anders, Secretary General, Evangelical Confederation of Brazil, 'Brazil's Spiritual Awakening,' UNITED EVANGELICAL ACTION, 15 February 1953, pp. 10 & 13.
2 Rodolfo Anders, 'Brazil's Spiritual Awakening.'
3 See W. R. Read, NEW PATTERNS OF CHURCH GROWTH IN BRAZIL, pp. 29 & 120; cf. WORLD CHRISTIAN HANDBOOK.
4 Rodolfo Anders, 'Brazil's Spiritual Awakening.'
5 See ANNUAL REPORT, 1955, British and Foreign Bible Society, p. 127; ANNUAL REPORT, 1953, American Bible Society, p. 226; statistics of distribution, 1951-1954 (shortage of paper in 1953).
6 ANNUAL REPORT, 1953, Bible Society of Brazil (C.H. Morris).
7 See INTERNATIONAL REVIEW OF MISSIONS, January 1954, & (editor) WORLD DOMINION, September-October 1953, p. 317.
8 Rodolfo Anders, 'Brazil's Spiritual Awakening.'
9 P.E. Pierson, A YOUNGER CHURCH IN SEARCH OF MATURITY, pp. 234-235 & J.E. Bear, MISSION TO BRAZIL, p. 218.
10 Rodolfo Anders, 'Brazil's Spiritual Awakening.'
11 See Lauro Bretones, REDEMOINHOS DO SUL: Um Ano de Reavivamento no Brasil com o Dr. J. Edwin Orr, passim.
12 Walter Ermel, Rector of São Paulo Faculty of Theology, 'Brazilian Spiritual Revival,' in O JORNAL BATISTA, 26 June 1952.
13 News Bulletin on Evangelism, VI (1952),, issued by N. W. Taylor, q. Dr. Synval Moraes, Reavivamento Brasileiro, Minas Gerais.
14 O JORNAL BATISTA, 5 June 1952, E. S. Freitas, Campinas.
15 Walter Ermel, O JORNAL BATISTA, 26 June 1952.
16 Bulletin, Reavivamento Espiritual Brasileiro, 31 May 1952.
17 BOOK OF REPORTS, Southern Baptist Convention, 1953, p. 69.
18 Because of pressure from a non-cooperative minority (nicknamed 'Casca-duras'), Prof. Alberto Mazoni's report was not published till 30 April 1953, in O JORNAL BATISTA.
19 See O VIDA PRESBITERIANA, an illustrated supplement of O PURITANO, 25 October 1952, p. 20; & ANNUAL REPORT, 1953, Presbyterian Church in the United States, pp. 65-66 with pp. 43-44, 'The Awakening in Brazil,' Milton Daugherty.
20 News Bulletin on Evangelism, VI (1952), issued by N. W. Taylor, q. Dr. Synval Moraes, Reavivamento Brasileiro, Minas Gerais.
21 O PURITANO, 'Noticias do Reavivamento,' 10 September 1952.
22 See 'Spiritual Awakening in Latin America,' C.J. Hahn, in THE CHRISTIAN, London, 15 November 1952.
23 Lauro Bretones, REDEMOINHOS DO SUL, p. 51.
24 See A. Baird Fanstone, MISSIONARY ADVENTURE IN BRAZIL; & Lauro Bretones, REDEMOINHOS DO SUL, p. 50.
25 BOOK OF REPORTS, Southern Baptist Convention, 1953, p. 65; & ANNUAL REPORT, 1953, Board of World Missions, Presbyterian Church in the United States, p. 73.
26 O PURITANO, 'Noticias do Reavivamento,' 10 September 1953.
27 Lauro Bretones, REDEMOINHOS DO SUL, Chapter 5, pp. 57-58.
28 Report of Floyd Grady, Presbyterian superintendent missionary.
29 Lauro Bretones, REDEMOINHOS DO SUL, Chapter 6, pp. 60-61.
30 UNITED EVANGELICAL ACTION, 1 November 1952; & Lauro Bretones, REDEMOINHOS DO SUL, Chapter 6, pp. 63-64.
31 Prof. Alberto Mazoni in O JORNAL BATISTA, 30 April 1953.
32 Lauro Bretones, REDEMOINHOS DO SUL, Chapter 7, pp. 64ff.
33 Not published by O JORNAL BATISTA until 30 April 1953.

34   Lauro Bretones, REDEMOINHOS DO SUL, Chapter 7, p. 67.
35   See Clyde W. Taylor, 'Acts of the Holy Spirit in Missions,' in UNITED EVANGELICAL ACTION, 15 February 1953.
36   'Por Quem os Sinos Dobram,' DIARIO DA BAHIA, 3 September; cf. CRUZ DE MALTA, April 1953, 'The Blessing of the Bells.'
37   Hercilio Arandas, First Baptist Church, Salvador, in a report sent to O JORNAL BATISTA, but unpublished. It was signed by Independent, Methodist, Pentecostal and Presbyterian pastors and seven Baptist ministers, including the veteran, Dr. M. G. White.
38   O JORNAL BATISTA, telegram published 30 April 1953.
39   O PURITANO, 'Noticias do Reavivamento,' 10 September 1952.
40   Lauro Bretones, REDEMOINHOS DO SUL, Chapter 8, pp. 70ff.
41   Letter of J. Edwin Orr to Rev. Boanerges Ribeiro, 30 September 1952; cf. Lauro Bretones, REDEMOINHOS DO SUL, p. 73.
42   Rev. James Cook, in THE LIFE OF FAITH, November 1952.
43   Lauro Bretones, REDEMOINHOS DO SUL, p. 77.
44   Silvia de Magalhães Lima, of course, was the infant daughter of Dr. Durval and Mrs. Else Lima, taken to a revival meeting in 1931 and dedicated by George Ridout to the hope of revival in Brazil.
45   It would take a volume to chronicle the activities of the various evangelists already busy or called to service in the awakening, including Brazilian missionaries working out of Brazil.
46   Rodolfo Anders, 'Brazil's Spiritual Awakening.'
47   CRUZ DE MALTA, April 1953, 'O Homem que Sacudiu o Brasil.'
48   Rodolfo Anders, 'Brazil's Spiritual Awakening.'
49   Only a minority of 'casca-dura' Baptists disputed the high percentage of cooperation in the denomination, this being finally established by Prof. Alberto Mazoni and the historic Baptist Convention in 1953 (Salvador) which overwhelmingly supported his propositions.
50   Rodolfo Anders, 'Brazil's Spiritual Awakening.'
51   See BOOK OF REPORTS, Southern Baptist Convention, 1953, p. 67. In view of the main attack upon interdenominational co-operation, it is significant that Edwin Orr, as a member of an executive commision, addressed the Baptist World Alliance of 1970 upon 'Baptists, Great Awakenings, and Christian Cooperation.' O JORNAL BATISTA, after enthusiastic commendations of the movement, succumbed to the pressure of a minority of critics and published attacks on the character of the movement and of its leading evangelist. This was censured by a great majority in the 1953 Brazilian Baptist Convention, terminating a news black-out lasting months. The last word in the controversy was given by Professor Alberto Mazoni in an article, 'The Prophet's Reward,' 30 April. Bretones dealt with the controversy in a chapter entitled, 'Alexander the Coppersmith,' and correspondence showed that the conspiracy to discredit the Reavivamento Brasileiro began in Belo Horizonte.
52   Lauro Bretones, REDEMOINHOS DO SUL, pp. 93-94.
53   Rodolfo Anders, 'Brazil's Spiritual Awakening.'
54   P. E. Pierson, A YOUNGER CHURCH, p. 235.
55   See W. R. Read, CHURCH GROWTH IN BRAZIL, p. 18, etc.
56   Quoted by Bishop A. J. Appasamy, WRITE THE VISION, p. 194.
57   ANNUAL REPORT, 1953, Board of World Missions, Presbyterian Church in the United States, p. 10.
58   Lauro Bretones, REDEMOINHOS DO SUL, passim.
59   ANNUAL REPORT, 1953, American Bible Society, p. 253; cf. ANNUAL REPORT, 1956, BWM, PCUS, 1956.
60   THE CHRISTIAN, London, 6 September 1957.

Notes on Chapter 19: HISPANIC SOUTH AMERICA, 1950—

1 Kenneth Strachan to Edwin Orr, 5 October 1951.
2 Latin American Mission, EVANGELISM IN DEPTH, Chapter 2.
3 INTERNATIONAL REVIEW OF MISSIONS, 1953, p. 51.,
4 W. D. Roberts, REVOLUTION IN EVANGELISM, p. 21.
5 M. R. Bradshaw, CHURCH GROWTH THROUGH EVANGELISM
   IN DEPTH, p. 3.
6 Letters of Kenneth Strachan to Edwin Orr, dated 8 October 1952;
   2 May 1953; 14 January 1954; 27 April 1960; etc.
7 See Tommy Hicks, MILLIONS FOUND CHRIST: HISTORY'S
   GREATEST RECORDED REVIVAL, pp. 7-8; cf. C. P. Wagner,
   LOOK OUT! THE PENTECOSTALS ARE COMING, pp. 19ff.
8 See Louie & Lillian Stokes, THE PENTECOSTAL MOVEMENT
   IN ARGENTINA, p. 24; and Tommy Hicks, p. 10.
9 Tommy Hicks, MILLIONS FOUND CHRIST, p. 13; C. P. Wagner,
   p. 20.   10 Tommy Hicks, pp. 14-15.
11 Arno Enns, MAN, MILIEU AND MISSION IN ARGENTINA, q.
    Hilton Merritt who interviewed Tommy Hicks.
12 E. R. Miller, THY GOD REIGNETH, p. 35. (Miller claimed
    that Juan Perón was healed of excema, which Hicks denied.)
13 See Read, Monterroso & Johnson, LATIN AMERICAN CHURCH
    GROWTH, p. 90.
14 See Arno Enns, p. 77; cf. Tommy Hicks, pp. 20-23.
15 BUENOS AIRES HERALD, 25 May 1954.
16 Arno Enns, pp. 77-78.
17 PENTECOST, London, September 1954, q. David du Plessis.
18 Pablo Polischuk, 'The Hicks Phenomenon,' unpublished paper.
19 Reports of Subsecretaria de Cultos no Catolicos, 1954-55.
20 Buenos Aires newspapers estimated 200,000, Arno Enns, p. 77.
21 At a breakfast in Los Angeles in 1954.
22 CHRISTIAN CENTURY, Chicago, 7 July 1954, pp. 814-815.
23 J. D.! Montgomery, DISCIPLES OF CHRIST IN ARGENTINA,
    pp. 157-158; D. R. Acenelli, YO FUI TESTIGO, Buenos Aires,
    1954; INTERNATIONAL REVIEW OF MISSIONS, 1955, p. 61.
24 Tommy Hicks, MILLIONS FOUND CHRIST, Fontana, 1956.
25 Los Angeles, 1954.   26 See Arno Enns, p. 206.
27 See Read, Monterroso & Johnson, p. 381.
28 PENTECOST, June 1955, & J. D. Montgomery, p. 158.
29 Reported to the writer by Kenneth Strachan.
30 PENTECOSTAL EVANGEL, 9 January 1955, p. 8; & Arno Enns,
    MAN, MILIEU AND MISSION, pp. 79 & 90.
31 PENTECOST, December 1965-February 1966.
32 M. C. Voth, 1967, quoted in Arno Enns.
33 Arno Enns, p. 152.   34 p. 169.   35 p. 138.
36 LATIN AMERICAN EVANGELIST, 1955, pp. 100, 117.
37 O. J. Smith, WORLD-WIDE EVANGELISM, pp. 66-71.
38 p. 65.   39 PENTECOSTAL EVANGEL, 25 December 1960.
40 See Read, Monterroso & Johnson, pp. 93-94.
41 O. J. Smith, WORLD-WIDE EVANGELISM, pp. 63-64.
42 WORLD CHRISTIAN HANDBOOK, 1957, p. 143.
43 Read, Monterroso & Johnson, p. 99: estimated 13,000.
44 EVANGELICAL CHRISTENDOM, London, January 1953, p. 25.
45 PENTECOSTAL EVANGEL, 27 April 1952, p. 10; PENTECOST,
    June 1953.
46 EVANGELICAL CHRISTENDOM, London, January 1953, p. 25.

47 EVANGELICAL CHRISTENDOM, London, January 1953, p. 25.
48 PENTECOSTAL EVANGEL, 18 May 1952, pp. 8-9.
49 INTERNATIONAL REVIEW OF MISSIONS, 1954, p. 54.
50 LATIN AMERICAN EVANGELIST, 1953, p. 193.
51 See Graphs, Read, Monterroso & Johnson, pp. 103 & 105.
52 O. S. Smith, WORLD-WIDE EVANGELISM, pp. 65-66.
53 Read, Monterroso & Johnson, pp. 104-105.
54 C. P. Wagner, PROTESTANT MOVEMENT IN BOLIVIA, pp. 121ff.
55 Read, Monterroso & Johnson, pp. 109-112.
56 C. P. Wagner, p. 50.   57 pp. 63ff.   58 pp. 81ff.
59 LATIN AMERICAN EVANGELIST, 1953, p. 182.
60 PENTECOSTAL EVANGEL, 16 March 1952, p. 8.
61 PENTECOSTAL EVANGEL, 1 November 1953, p. 6.
62 C. P. Wagner, pp. 130 & 141.
63 Read, Monterroso & Johnson, p. 113.
64 J. B. A. Kessler, PROTESTANT MISSIONS AND CHURCHES IN
    PERU AND CHILE; Read, Monterroso & Johnson, pp. 114-116.
65 PENTECOSTAL EVANGEL, 28 January & 17 December 1950.
66 PENTECOST, London, September 1958, quoting Herbert Money.
67 LATIN AMERICAN EVANGELIST, 1953, p. 182.
68 Read, Monterroso & Johnson, pp. 118-122.
69 See Elizabeth Elliot, THROUGH GATES OF SPLENDOR.
70 J. A. Rippy, LATIN AMERICA: A MODERN HISTORY, p. 430.
71 T. B. Hall, 'The Progress of Protestantism in Colombia,' M.S.
    thesis, Kansas State College, Pittsburg, 1959, p. 90.
72 Clyde W. Taylor, 'The Fate of Protestants in Colombia,' Parts I
    & II, CHRISTIANITY TODAY, 28 October & 11 November 1957;
    PENTECOSTAL EVANGEL, 22 June 1952, p. 9.
73 PENTECOST, March 1950.
74 See ACTAS DE LA SEGUNDA ASAMBLEA GENERAL DE LA
    CONFEDERACION EVANGELICA DE COLOMBIA, August 1952.
75 PENTECOST, June 1953.
76 CEDEC BULLETIN, 8 May 1956; cf. C. W. Taylor, 'The Fate of
    Protestants in Colombia,' CHRISTIANITY TODAY, 23 October &
    11 November 1957.
77 LATIN AMERICAN EVANGELIST, 1960, May-June.
78 LATIN AMERICAN EVANGELIST, 1960, September-October.
79 Eduardo Espinoza, S. J., quoted by C. W. Taylor; see T. B. Hall,
    'The Progress of Protestantism in Colombia,' pp. 96-97.
80 WORLD DOMINION, London, May-June 1953, p. 189; October
    1956, pp. 265ff. & EL TIEMPO, Bogotá, 17 September 1957.
81 See INTERNATIONAL REVIEW OF MISSIONS, 1954, p. 56 &
    PENTECOSTAL EVANGEL, 8 July 1956, p. 13.
82 PENTECOST, June 1954, June 1955 & September 1956.
83 PENTECOSTAL EVANGEL, 26 October 1958, p. 14.
84 T. B. Hall, 'The Progress of Protestantism in Colombia,' pp. 96ff.
85 PENTECOSTAL EVANGEL, 21 February 1960, pp. 16-17.
86 LATIN AMERICAN EVANGELIST, 1961, May-June.
87 Read, Monterroso & Johnson, p. 125.
88 President Juan Vicente Gomez capitalized on the oil revenues.
89 LATIN AMERICAN EVANGELIST, 1952, p. 116.
90 Read, Monterroso & Johnson, pp. 131-132.
91 PENTECOSTAL EVANGEL, 8 June; PENTECOST, September,
    1952; cf. Read, Monterroso & Johnson, pp. 136-137.
92 Read, Monterroso & Johnson, pp. 136-137; and PENTECOSTAL
    EVANGEL, 17 May 1953, p. 6 & 18 March 1956, p. 10.

93 PENTECOST, London, March 1957.
94 The independent healing evangelist posed a problem for the long-established Pentecostal denominations at home and abroad because of their lack of discipline. See D. E. Harrell, ALL THINGS ARE POSSIBLE, pp. 112-116.
95 C. P. Wagner, Chapter 1, 'Phenomenal Growth of Pentecostalism,' in LOOK OUT! THE PENTECOSTALS ARE COMING.

Notes on Chapter 20: THE CARIBBEAN IN THE 'FIFTIES

1 PENTECOSTAL EVANGEL, 3 June 1950, p. 7.
2 THE CUBAN CALL, issues of January-June 1950.
3 Morris Eiffert, School of World Mission, interview with the Rev. John Nickolson.
4 PENTECOST, December 1951 & March 1954.
5 See PENTECOSTAL EVANGEL, 25 March 1951, pp. 8-9; & PENTECOST, March 1954.
6 PENTECOSTAL EVANGEL, 25 October 1953, p. 8.
7 PENTECOST, June 1951.
8 PENTECOSTAL EVANGEL, 25 March 1951, pp. 8-9; 21 October 1951, pp. 6-7.
9 J. L. Gonzalez, THE DEVELOPMENT OF CHRISTIANITY IN THE LATIN CARIBBEAN, p. 92.
10 Morris Eiffert, interview with the Rev. John Nickolson.
11 LATIN AMERICAN EVANGELIST, 1957, p. 37.
12 WORLD CHRISTIAN HANDBOOK, 1957, p. 162.
13 En route from Hamburg to New Orleans.
14 WORLD CHRISTIAN HANDBOOK, 1957, p. 136.
15 PENTECOSTAL EVANGEL, 26 September 1954, p. 8.
16 PENTECOSTAL EVANGEL, 29 May 1955, p. 6.
17 D. L. Platt, 'New Hope for Santo Domingo,' M.A. thesis, School of World Mission, Pasadena, 1975, unpublished, pp. 63ff.
18 Darryl Platt, quoting Thomas Woodward, Princeton thesis, 1972, regarding the impact of Garcia's ministry.
19 PENTECOSTAL EVANGEL, 26 April 1959, p. 6.
20 WORLD CHRISTIAN HANDBOOK, 1957, p. 145.
21 J. L. Gonzalez, THE DEVELOPMENT OF CHRISTIANITY IN THE LATIN CARIBBEAN, pp. 109-111.
22 D. A. McGavran, CHURCH GROWTH IN JAMAICA, p. 16.
23 Baptism in infancy and confirmation at puberty provide statistics little related to active membership.
24 D. A. McGavran, CHURCH GROWTH IN JAMAICA, p. 13.
25 The controversy was particularly acute during the between-wars period, in many places besides Jamaica.
26 LATIN AMERICAN EVANGELIST, 1953, pp. 218-219, 232-233.
27 G. H. Montgomery, 'A Lying Spirit in the Mouth of the Prophets,' INTERNATIONAL HEALING MAGAZINE, April 1962.
28 PENTECOSTAL EVANGEL, 22 April 1956.
29 LATIN AMERICAN EVANGELIST, 1952, p. 116.
30 LATIN AMERICAN EVANGELIST, 1954, pp. 38-39.
31 LATIN AMERICAN EVANGELIST, 1956, p. 54.
32 W. D. Roberts, REVOLUTION IN EVANGELISM, pp. 30-31; & CHRISTIANITY TODAY, 17 February 1958, p. 32.
33 CHRISTIANITY TODAY, 17 February 1958, p. 32.
34 CHRISTIANITY TODAY, 25 November 1957 & 3 March 1958.
35 Report of Norman W. Taylor, Mexico City.

36   See Read, Monterroso & Johnson, LATIN AMERICAN CHURCH GROWTH, p. 139.
37   LATIN AMERICAN EVANGELIST, 1951, pp. 5, 6-7, 23, 26; & 1952, p. 108.
38   PENTECOSTAL EVANGEL, 11 May 1952, p. 11.
39   Kenneth Strachan to Edwin Orr, 8 October 1952.
40   See Read, Monterroso & Johnson, LATIN AMERICAN CHURCH GROWTH, p. 145.
41   LATIN AMERICAN EVANGELIST, 1958, pp. 45-46.
42   LATIN AMERICAN EVANGELIST, 1950, pp. 6-7, 20, 38.
43   PENTECOSTAL EVANGEL, 8 April 1956; 27 January 1957.
44   See Read, Monterroso & Johnson, LATIN AMERICAN CHURCH GROWTH, p. 147.
45   PENTECOSTAL EVANGEL, 8 April 1951, p. 8.
46   PENTECOST, June 1953 & PENTECOSTAL EVANGEL, 8 March 1953, p. 8.
47   PENTECOSTAL EVANGEL, 1 April 1956, p. 12.
48   G. F. Atter, "THE THIRD FORCE," p. 207.
49   See Read, Monterroso & Johnson, LATIN AMERICAN CHURCH GROWTH, p. 156.
50   LATIN AMERICAN EVANGELIST, 1953, p. 182.
51   PENTECOSTAL EVANGEL, 10 May 1953, p. 7.
52   PENTECOST, June & September 1953.
53   PENTECOSTAL EVANGEL, 7 November 1954, p. 7.
54   PENTECOSTAL EVANGEL, 7 November 1954, p. 7.
55   See Read, Monterroso & Johnson, LATIN AMERICAN CHURCH GROWTH, pp. 157-161.
56   R. D. Winter, editor, THEOLOGICAL EDUCATION BY EXTENSION, 'Milestones in a Movement.' Part I: Guatemala: Laboratory for Experiment.
57   PENTECOSTAL EVANGEL, 20 May 1956, p. 13.
58   LATIN AMERICAN EVANGELIST, 1958, pp. 45-46.
59   PENTECOST, December 1957.
60   LATIN AMERICAN EVANGELIST, 1958, pp. 45-46.
61   J. C. Bridges, 'A Study of the Protestant Population in Mexico,' M.A. thesis, unpublished, University of Florida, 1969.
62   D. A. McGavran, CHURCH GROWTH IN MEXICO, 1963; See WORLD CHRISTIAN HANDBOOK, 1962, p. 122.
63   R. P. Rivera, INSTITUCIONES PROTESTANTES EN MEXICO, pp. 25-27.
64   See Read, Monterroso & Johnson, LATIN AMERICAN CHURCH GROWTH, pp. 165-166.
65   Assembly of God and other Pentecostals, pp. 168-169.
66   PENTECOST, December 1949.
67   See Read, Monterroso & Johnson, LATIN AMERICAN CHURCH GROWTH, p. 169.
68   See Read, Monterroso & Johnson, LATIN AMERICAN CHURCH GROWTH, p. 170.
69   BOOK OF REPORTS, Southern Baptist Convention, 1960, p. 44.
70   Report of Norman W. Taylor; cf. ETERNITY, April 1958.
71   LATIN AMERICAN EVANGELIST, 1958, pp. 45-46.
72   In Mexico, the Federal District possessed the largest number of Evangelical church buildings, 329, followed by Tamaulipas (242), Vera Cruz (214), Coahuila (193), Nuevo Leóne (186), Chihuahua (178), Yucatán (163), Sonora (158), Baja California (147), and Sinaloa (118), six of these being border states.

Notes on Chapter 21: BRAZIL IN THE 'SIXTIES

1   See issue of BRASIL PRESBITERIANO, September 1960.
2   Paul N. Lewis, 'Renewal in the Brazilian Church,' M.A. project, Wheaton College, 1972, pp. 41-43.
3   See A. J. Reasoner, 'Evangelical Awakening in Brazil, 1930-1966, unpublished paper, School of World Mission, Pasadena.
4   BRASIL PRESBITERIANO, December 1961.
5   En route to Baptist World Alliance, meeting in Rio de Janeiro.
6   BRASIL PRESBITERIANO, May 1959.
7   Cf. A. J. Appasamy, WRITE THE VISION, pp. 193-194; Lauro Bretones, REDEMOINHOS DO SUL, Chapter XII.
8   P. E. Pierson, A YOUNGER CHURCH IN SEARCH OF MATURITY, pp. 234-235.   9   BRASIL PRESBITERIANO, December 1963.
10 P. E. Pierson, pp. 234-235.
11 CHRISTIANITY TODAY, 11 November 1957, p. 33, & O. J. Smith, WORLD-WIDE EVANGELISM, pp. 60-61.
12 CHRISTIANITY TODAY, 26 October, 23 November 1962.
13 BRASIL PRESBITERIANO, Issues of 1960—.
14 Prof. Alberto Mazzoni, O JORNAL BATISTA, 30 April 1953.
15 See W. R. Read, NEW PATTERNS OF CHURCH GROWTH IN BRAZIL, pp. 188-192.
16 Issues of O JORNAL BATISTA, 1965-1966; THE COMMISSION, September 1965 & April 1966.
17 THE COMMISSION, 'Revival in Brazil,' September 1965.
18 See Read, Monterroso & Johnson, LATIN AMERICAN CHURCH GROWTH, pp. 73-74. Statistics of the gains of 1969 among the Baptists are derived from the Crusade of the Americas reports of 14 April 1970, conference at Leesburg, Florida.
19 PENTECOSTAL EVANGEL, 18 January & 22 February 1953.
20 Read, Monterroso & Johnson, p. 68.
21 Cf. C. P. Wagner, LOOK OUT! THE PENTECOSTALS ARE COMING, p. 61.
22 PENTECOSTAL EVANGEL, 25 April 1954.
23 FOURSQUARE MAGAZINE, November 1955, pp. 13-15.
24 W. A. Ermel, O ESTANDARTE, 31st July 1953.
25 FOURSQUARE MAGAZINE, November 1955, pp. 13-15.
26 'The Brazil Story,' FOURSQUARE MAGAZINE, November 1955.
27 FOURSQUARE MAGAZINE, November 1962, pp. 9 & 28.
28 Erickson's ministry reported in PENTECOSTAL EVANGEL.
29 Again,, the healing ministry attracted the crowds.
30 See J. Philip Hogan, BRAZIL, p. 6 & passim; PENTECOSTAL EVANGEL, 24 September 1961.
31 FOURSQUARE MAGAZINE, November 1962, pp. 9 & 28.
32 PENTECOSTAL EVANGEL, 18 June 1967.
33 W. R. Read, pp. 19ff; Read, Monterroso & Johnson, p. 69.
34 J. B. Lyra, ORIENTAÇÃO EVANGÉLICA, Niterói, 1960.
35 W. R. Read, p. 145.
36 W. R. Read, p. 151.
37 Read, Monterroso & Johnson, p. 65.
38 Cf. Eneas Tognini, O PREÇO DA GRANDE BENÇÃO, published in São Paulo, 1960, and P. N. Lewis, 'Renewal in the Brazilian Church,' M.A. project, Wheaton College, 1972. (p. 30, q. Tognini)
39 Rosalee Appleby, 'As Seeing Him Who is Invisible,' unpublished autobiography.
40 See PLENA SUBMISSÃO, Evangelical Confederation, 1952.

41 See W. R. Read, pp. 165-166; cf. P. N. Lewis, cited.
42 Antônio Elias, cited by P. N. Lewis, chapter viii.
43 José Rego de Nascimento, cited by P. N. Lewis.
44 The pressure encountered is better understood by reading articles
    of Prof. Alberto Mazzoni in O JORNAL BATISTA, 1953.
45 P. N. Lewis, pp. 62-64.
46 Rosivaldo Araujo, in P. N. Lewis, p. 96.
47 P. N. Lewis, pp. 25-26.
48 Antônio Elias, cited in P. N. Lewis, p. 54; see pp. 35-37.
49 W. R. Read, 'A Charismatic Stream Flows in Brazil,' unpublished
    paper, p. 8; P. N. Lewis, pp. 37-40; 55-57.
50 P. N. Lewis, pp. 55-57; W. R. Read, p. 8.
51 P. N. Lewis, p. 25; W. R. Read, p. 8.
52 Gerson Barbosa, cited in P. N. Lewis, pp. 41-43; 153-155.
53 P. N. Lewis, pp. 43-49; 58-60.
54 W. R. Read, pp. 8-9; p. n. lewis, p. 60.
55 P. N. Lewis, p. 74.
56 W. R. Read, pp. 1-7; P. N. Lewis, pp. 4-41; 57-58.
57 Read Monterroso & Johnson, pp. 78-79.
58 W.R. Read, NEW PATTERNS OF CHURCH GROWTH IN BRAZIL,
    pp. 166.
59 P. N. Lewis, pp. 60-61; 76-77.
60 W. R. Read, NEW PATTERNS, p. 200, citing Evangelical Con-
    federation of Brazil.
61 There seemed to be little support at the Lausanne Congress on
    World Evangelization in 1974 among the Brazilian representatives
    for the social activist emphasis among the Spanish-speaking folk.
62 Several denominations have sent missionaries out of the country,
    cf. CHRISTIANITY TODAY, 19 July 1963, p. 19.
63 CHRISTIANITY TODAY, 19 July 1963, p. 19.
64 There was unofficial interest in the meetings of the Reavivamento
    Brasileiro in 1952, official in the Graham meetings in 1962.
65 See H. A. Johnson, 'Authority over the Spirits: Brazilian Spiritism
    and Evangelical Church Growth,' unpublished M. A. thesis, School
    of World Mission, Pasadena, 1969.

Notes on Chapter 22: HISPANO-AMERICAN EVANGELIZATION

1   See C. P. Wagner, LOOK OUT! THE PENTECOSTALS ARE
    COMING, p. 25.
2   LATIN AMERICAN CHURCH GROWTH, p. 54.
3   Latin America Mission, EVANGELISM-IN-DEPTH.
4   Issues of CHRISTIANITY TODAY, 1958-1962.
5   J. Edwin Orr. The article had been written for LIFE Magazine.
6   Cf. LATIN AMERICAN EVANGELIST, May-June 1962, pp. 10-11,
    Associated Press release, New York, 24 April 1957.
7   Issues of CHRISTIANITY TODAY, 1962.
8   Servicio Evangélico Noticioso de America, San José, 15 February,
    TIME Magazine, 23 February 1962, p. 56.
9   CHRISTIANITY TODAY, 19 February 1962, p. 56, & S.E.N.D.A.
10 TIME Magazine, 23 February 1962, p. 56, & S.E.N.D.A.
11 S.E.N.D.A., 15 February 1962.
12 TIME Magazine, 23 February 1962, p. 56.
13 S.E.N.D.A., 15 February 1962.
14 TIME Magazine, 23 February 1962, p. 56.
15 CHRISTIANITY TODAY, 2 March 1962, & S.E.N.D.A.

16 CHRISTIANITY TODAY, 2 March 1962. See ERCILLA and other Santiago periodicals and newspapers.
17 CHRISTIANITY TODAY, 9 November 1962.
18 2 March 1962.
19 News Release, CRISTO PARA TODOS, Asuncion. CHRISTIANITY TODAY, 26 October 1962.
20 CHRISTIANITY TODAY, 26 October & 9 November 1962.
21 Bulletin, Montevideo; CHRISTIANITY TODAY, 23 November 1962.
22 CHRISTIANITY TODAY, 26 October 1962.
23 Reports of 9 November 1962, CHRISTIANITY TODAY.
24 CHRISTIANITY TODAY, 23 November 1962.
25 Reports of 9 & 23 November 1962, CHRISTIANITY TODAY.
26 CHRISTIANITY TODAY, 23 November 1962.
27 Reports of 23 November 1962, CHRISTIANITY TODAY.
28 W. D. Roberts, STRACHAN OF COSTA RICA, p. 82.
29 See R. Kenneth Strachan, THE INESCAPABLE CALLING, 1968.
30 Cf. M. R. Bradshaw, CHURCH GROWTH AND EVANGELISM-IN-DEPTH, p. 95.
31 C. P. Wagner, PROTESTANT MOVEMENT IN BOLIVIA, p. 169.
32 W. D. Roberts, REVOLUTION IN EVANGELISM, pp. 38ff.
33 Introduction, EVANGELISM-IN-DEPTH, pp. 7-12.
34 LATIN AMERICAN EVANGELIST, September-October 1968.
35 EVANGELISM-IN-DEPTH, pp. 77-78.
36 LATIN AMERICAN EVANGELIST, September-October 1968.
37 W. D. Roberts, REVOLUTION IN EVANGELISM, pp. 33-35.
38 LATIN AMERICAN EVANGELIST, September-October 1968; cf. W. D. Roberts, REVOLUTION IN EVANGELISM, pp. 56ff.
39 Reports of January-February, March-April 1963, Guatemala, in LATIN AMERICAN EVANGELIST.
40 LATIN AMERICAN EVANGELIST, May-June 1963, September-October, 1964.
41 Report, January-February 1965, LATIN AMERICAN EVANGELIST.
42 W. D. Roberts, REVOLUTION IN EVANGELISM, pp. 68ff; and LATIN AMERICAN EVANGELIST, January-February, May-June, 1965.
43 W. D. Roberts, STRACHAN OF COSTA RICA, pp. 122 & 154-155; LATIN AMERICAN EVANGELIST, May-June 1965.
44 CHRISTIANITY TODAY, 17 October 1965; and W. D. Roberts, REVOLUTION IN EVANGELISM, pp. 111ff.
45 C. P. Wagner, PROTESTANT MOVEMENT IN BOLIVIA, p. 164.
46 C. P. Wagner, p. 165.
47 LATIN AMERICAN EVANGELIST, May-June 1966.
48 Notes and Recollections.
49 LATIN AMERICAN EVANGELIST, September-October 1968.
50 Report of July-August 1967, LATIN AMERICAN EVANGELIST.
51 ALLIANCE WEEKLY, 17 January & 6 November 1968; LATIN AMERICAN EVANGELIST, January-February, March-April 1968.
52 LATIN AMERICAN EVANGELIST, May-June, July-August 1967.
53 September-October 1968, LATIN AMERICAN EVANGELIST.
54 LATIN AMERICAN EVANGELIST, Reports of September-October, November-December 1968; January-February 1969.
55 LATIN AMERICAN EVANGELIST, September-October, 1968; & January-February 1969.
56 September-October 1970, LATIN AMERICAN EVANGELIST.
57 CHRISTIANITY TODAY, 12 March 1971; and LATIN AMERICAN EVANGELIST, March-April 1971.

58 CRUZADA: Story of the Luis Palau Evangelistic Crusades, p. 3. CHILD EVANGELISM, May 1972, p. 5.

59 See CHRISTIAN TIMES, Wheaton, Illinois, 31 March 1968; and CRUZADA, p. 3.

60 Overseas Crusades Prayer Letter, 15 September 1966; see also CRUZADA, pp. 6 & 27.

61 Overseas Crusades Prayer Letter, December 1967; and Statistical Summaries, CRUZADA, p. 27.

62 CHRISTIAN TIMES, 31 March; Overseas Crusades Prayer Letter, 15 September; LATIN AMERICAN EVANGELIST, November 1968; CRUZADA, p. 27.

63 CRUZADA, pp. 7 & 27; Overseas Crusades Prayer Letters.

64 CRUZADA, p. 7; Report of Jaime Gonsalez, Quito, 6 August 1974; Evangelical Press News Release.

65 See ALUMNI WORLD, Multnomah School of the Bible, July 1969; CRUZADA, p. 10-11; Overseas Crusades CABLE, September-October, 1969; EL NORTE, Monterrey, Mexico, 31 March 1969, and other issues.

66 CRUZADA, p. 11; Overseas Crusades Prayer Letter, April 1970; INFORMADOR, Mexico, Release of Cruzada Mexico.

67 It has not been possible to list the results of all the Mexican series which included Coatzacoalcos, Villahermosa, Reynosa, Ciudad Obregon and several Mexico City campaigns; CRUZADA, pp. 8-9, and Overseas Crusades Prayer Letters.

68 See Evangelical Press News Release, 18 March 1974; CRUZADA, p. 22 and Statistical Summaries, p. 27.

69 CRUZADA, p. 7; Overseas Crusades Prayer Letters; Statistical Summaries, CRUZADA, p. 27.

70 See Luis Palau, Overseas Crusades Letter; and CRUZADA, p. 17; cf. THE NEWS, Mexico City, 20 February 1971, p. 13.

71 GRAFICO, Guatemala City, 11 March; MISSIONARY CRUSADER, July 1972; Central American Mission BULLETIN, September & October 1971; Quezaltenango Cruzada News, 30 September 1972; CRUZADA, pp. 14, 17, & 27.

72 CRUZADA, p. 16 & 27; LA NACION, San José, 11 February; Evangelical Press News Release, 5 February & 4 March 1972; & LATIN AMERICAN EVANGELIST issues.

73 See CRUZADA, pp. 12-13 & 27; Evangelical Press News Release, 29 January 1972.

74 LISTIN DIARIO, Santo Domingo, 5 & 10 March 1973; EL CARIBE, 10 March; CRUZADA, pp. 19 & 27; Overseas Crusades CABLE, Summer 1973.

75 See COMERCIO, Santa Cruz, LA PATRIA, Oruro, LOS TIEMPOS, Cochabamba, October 1974; ANDEAN OUTLOOK, December 1974.

76 See TODAY'S CHRISTIAN, Los Angeles, April 1974.

77 INFORMADOR, November 1974, Cruzada Bolivia.

78 LATIN AMERICAN EVANGELIST, January 1976.

79 CHRISTIANITY TODAY, 19 December 1975.

80 CHRISTIANITY TODAY, 19 December 1975; RELIGIOUS BROAD-CASTING, Quito, January 1976; and EVANGELICAL MISSIONS QUARTERLY, April 1976.

81 Edward Plowman, associate editor, CHRISTIANITY TODAY, 19 November 1975; MULTNOMAH MINIATURE, November 1975; & NOVEDADES, Managua, 14 November 1975.

82 Overseas Crusades CABLE, Fall 1976; & San Jose MERCURY-NEWS, 5 February 1977.

1   Ignacio Vergara, EL PROTESTANTISMO EN CHILE, p. 227.
2   See Read, Monterroso & Johnson, LATIN AMERICAN CHURCH
    GROWTH, pp. 48-49.
3   CHRISTIANITY TODAY, 19 July 1963, W. M. Nelson, 'Evangelical
    Surge in Latin America,' Survey of Catholics and Protestants in
    Latin America, based on THE WORLD ALMANAC, 1961 and on
    ANNUARIO PONTIFICO, 1960 & Clyde Taylor and Wade Coggins,
    PROTESTANT MISSIONS IN LATIN AMERICA, 1961; cf. Read,
    Monterroso & Johnson, pp. 82ff.
4   See Luis Villalpando, 'Misión de Cien Anos,' Methodist Council,
    Buenos Aires, 1966, mimeograph.
5   C.P. Wagner, LOOK OUT! THE PENTECOSTALS ARE COMING,
    pp. 161-162.   6   C.P. Wagner, quoting A. W. Cook, p. 163.
7   Juan Carlos Ortiz participated in the World Congress, Lausanne.
8   C.P. Wagner, p. 164.
9   Read, Monterroso & Johnson, pp. 93-95.
10 CHRISTIANITY TODAY, 19 July 1963, p. 9; Read, Monterroso
    & Johnson, pp. 96-99.
11 CHRISTIANITY TODAY, 19 July 1963, p. 9.
12 Read, Monterroso & Johnson, p. 103.
13 Cf. ANNUARIO PONTIFICO, 1960 & WORLD ALMANAC, 1961.
14 Read, Monterroso & Johnson, pp. 109-112.   15 pp. 112ff.
16 CHRISTIANITY TODAY, 19 July 1963, p. 9; Read, Monterroso
    & Johnson, pp. 118ff.
17 ANNUARIO PONTIFICO, 1960; cf. Read, Monterroso & Johnson,
    pp. 125ff.,
18 Read, Monterroso & Johnson, pp. 131ff.
19 CHRISTIANITY TODAY, 19 July 1963, p. 9; Read, Monterroso
    & Johnson, pp. 139-142.
20 Read, Monterroso & Johnson, pp. 142-146.
21 CHRISTIANITY TODAY, 19 July 1963, p. 9; Read, Monterroso
    & Johnson, pp. 147-149.
22 Cf. ANNUARIO PONTIFICO, 1960, Read, Monterroso & Johnson,
    pp. 154-157.   23 Read, Monterroso & Johnson, p. 151.
24 WORLD ALMANAC, 1961, CHRISTIANITY TODAY, 19 July 1963,
    p. 9, & Read, Monterroso & Johnson, pp. 157ff.
25 ANNUARIO PONTIFICO, 1960; R. P. Rivera, INSTITUCIONES
    PROTESTANTS EN MEXICO, pp. 25-27; & Read, Monterroso &
    Johnson, pp. 164ff.
26 LATIN AMERICAN EVANGELIST, May-June 1967; May-June 1969.
27 H. A. Johnson, 'The Protestant Movement in Haiti,' unpublished
    project, School of World Mission, Pasadena, 1969.
28 CHRISTIANITY TODAY, 19 July 1963, p. 9; D. L. Platt, 'New
    Hope for Santo Domingo,' M.A. thesis, School of World Mission,
    Pasadena, 1975, unpublished.
29 E. E. Carver, 'Showcase for God: a Study of Evangelical Church
    Growth in Puerto Rico,' M.A. thesis, School of World Mission,
    Pasadena, 1972, unpublished.
30 CHRISTIANITY TODAY, 19 July 1963, p. 9.
31 H. E. Peacock, Crusade of the Americas, São Paulo, Brazil.
32 F. K. Means, Crusade of the Americas, Richmond, Virginia, 1967.
33 S. O. Libert, Regional Coordinator, Southern Cone, Leesburg, Fla.
34 Manuel Calderon, Regional Coordinator, Bolivarian Region, 1970.
35 E. E. Hastey, Regional Coordinator, Mexico & Central America.

36 PENTECOSTAL EVANGEL, 28 May 1961.
37 Cf. Read, Monterroso & Johnson, p. 89, and PENTECOSTAL
    EVANGEL, 21 December 1969, pp. 21-22.
38 Edgardo Silvoso, 'When the Wind of the Spirit Blows,' unpublished
    paper on Argentina, School of World Mission, Pasadena, 1974.
39 PENTECOSTAL EVANGEL, 7 May 1961 & 11 October 1964.
40 PENTECOSTAL EVANGEL, 18 August 1963 & 9 February 1969.
41 See Read, Monterroso & Johnson, LATIN AMERICAN CHURCH
    GROWTH, p. 105.
42 The older church, when the writer ministered in Chile, seated only
    five thousand people.
43 PENTECOSTAL EVANGEL, 21 January 1968.
44 There were then seventy-five Assemblies in Bolivia.
45 PENTECOSTAL EVANGEL, 27 April 1969.
46 Read, Monterroso & Johnson, p. 122.
47 See Wayne Weld, AN ECUADOREAN IMPASSE, passim.
48 PENTECOSTAL EVANGEL, 16 February 1964, pp. 14-15; cf.
    C. P. Wagner, LOOK OUT! THE PENTECOSTALS ARE COMING,
    pp. 50-51.
49 FOURSQUARE MAGAZINE, January 1964, pp. 12-13.
50 C. P. Wagner, pp. 53-56.
51 Read, Monterroso & Johnson, p. 122.
52 See Elizabeth Elliot, THROUGH GATES OF SPLENDOR.
53 World Radio Missionary Fellowship.
54 See PENTECOSTAL EVANGEL, 15 June 1969, pp. 19-20; and
    C. P. Wagner, pp. 56-57.
55 Donald Palmer, 'Growth of Pentecostal Churches in Colombia,'
    unpublished M.A. thesis, Trinity Evangelical Divinity School, 1972;
    C. P. Wagner, pp. 37-39.
56 See Arnold Cook, 'Religious Freedom and Revival Fire in Latin
    America,' unpublished paper, School of World Mission, Pasadena,
    1975. These are the writer's own observations.
57 PENTECOSTAL EVANGEL, 19 November 1961, pp. 20-21.
58 Read, Monterroso & Johnson, pp. 136-137.
59 THE BRIDAL CALL, FOURSQUARE, August 1932, p. 11; Read,
    Monterroso & Johnson, p. 139.
60 PENTECOSTAL EVANGEL, 25 March 1962, p. 26.
61 PENTECOSTAL EVANGEL, 30 October 1960; 25 February 1962.
62 PENTECOSTAL EVANGEL, 24 June 1962.
63 PENTECOSTAL EVANGEL, 31 December 1961.
64 PENTECOSTAL EVANGEL, 19 October 1969.
65 PENTECOSTAL EVANGEL, 28 March 1971.
66 PENTECOSTAL EVANGEL, 19 November 1967.
67 PENTECOSTAL EVANGEL, 4 February & 30 September 1962.
68 See David Howard, HAMMERED AS GOLD, pp. 105ff.
69 C. P. Wagner, p. 153.
70 David Howard, pp. 150-175.
71 C. P. Wagner, p. 155.
72 Charles Bennett, in CHURCH GROWTH BULLETIN, VII: 1.
73 J. B. A. Kessler, A STUDY OF THE OLDER PROTESTANT
    MISSIONS AND CHURCHES IN PERU AND CHILE, p. 318.
74 C. P. Wagner, pp. 73-74.
75 C. P. Wagner, pp. 122-123.
76 CHRISTIANITY TODAY, 19 July 1963, p. 9.
77 Read, Monterroso & Johnson, p. 49.
78 Read, Monterroso & Johnson, p. 49.

Notes on Chapter 24: RENEWAL, POST VATICAN II

1 See J. J. Considine, editor: THE RELIGIOUS DIMENSION IN THE NEW LATIN AMERICA: Jorge Mejia, 'Biblical Renewal in Latin America,' p. 209.
2 Jorge Mejia, 'Biblical Renewal in Latin America,' pp. 205ff.
3 W. M. Nelson, in LATIN AMERICAN EVANGELIST, May-June 1963, p. 7.
4 Jorge Mejia, 'Biblical Renewal in Latin America,' p. 211.
5 Occasionally, American missionary priests sought fellowship or Brazilian national priests showed friendliness, but other priests, generally European by birth, were aloof or antagonistic.
6 For an Evangelical prospect of the Second Vatican Council, see W. D. Roberts, STRACHAN OF COSTA RICA,, pp. 128ff.
7 LATIN AMERICAN EVANGELIST, May-June 1963.
8 Note the perceptive paper given by Dr. José Miguez Bonino at the Third Evangelical Congress of Latin America, Buenos Aires, 1969, cited by W. D. Roberts, pp. 130ff.
9 Kenneth Strachan was particularly impressed by the dynamic of the Chilean Pentecostals, and commented upon it to the writer in Chile; he had little or no knowledge of Pentecostals in Brazil.
10 W. D. Roberts, p. 99, citing Strachan's address at the National Association of Evangelicals Convention, 1961.
11 W. D. Roberts, pp. 132ff.
12 One found Maryknollers in Peru renovating the church interiors, removing offensive decorations, and objecting to Christo-pagan practices, so much so that the 'faithful' called them Protestants, and a bishop transferred them to less protesting parishioners.
13 Kevin Ranaghan, THE CATHOLIC PENTECOSTALS; Edward D. O'Connor, THE PENTECOSTAL MOVEMENT IN THE CATHOLIC CHURCH, pp. 38ff.
14 Francis McNutt in NEW COVENANT, November 1971, pp. 1ff.
15 A. W. Cook, Research paper, Latin American Biblical Seminary, San José, Costa Rica, 1972.
16 C. P. Wagner, LOOK OUT! THE PENTECOSTALS ARE COMING, pp. 167ff.
17 Prof. Victor Monterroso, quoted by C. P. Wagner.
18 C. P. Wagner, pp. 167ff.
19 Francis McNutt in NEW COVENANT, November 1971, p. 7.
20 NEW COVENANT, November 1971, p. 2.
21 Francis McNutt in NEW COVENANT, November 1971, p. 4.
22 NEW COVENANT, May 1972, p. 22.
23 NEW COVENANT, February 1972, p. 12.
24 Francis McNutt in NEW COVENANT, November 1971, p. 3.
25 Francis McNutt in NEW COVENANT, November 1971, p. 6.
26 NEW COVENANT, June 1972, p. 20.
27 Milton Robinson, 'Awakenings in Southern Hispanic South America since 1914,' unpublished paper, School of World Mission, 1973.
28 C. P. Wagner in CHRISTIAN LIFE, 16 March 1973.
29 Cf. NEW COVENANT, August 1973, p. 26.
30 C. P. Wagner in CHRISTIAN LIFE, 16 March 1973.
31 Subsequent events have confirmed this opinion, for Julio Ruibal enrolled at Multnomah School of the Bible in Portland, Oregon, and described himself as a Catholic-born Evangelical.
32 NEW COVENANT, February 1973, p. 20.
33 NEW COVENANT, February 1973, pp. 20-21.

34 CHRISTIAN LIFE, 7 December 1973.
35 Milton Robinson, unpublished paper, 1973.
36 CHRISTIAN LIFE, 7 December 1973.
37 ALABARE, Aguas Buenas, Puerto Rico, April-May 1974, p. 21.
    NEW COVENANT, May 1976, pp. 24-25.
38 NEW COVENANT, April 1976, p. 20.
39 Francis McNutt in NEW COVENANT, November 1971, p. 4.
40 ALABARE, February-March 1974, pp. 30-31.
41 NEW COVENANT, May 1972, p. 23.
42 Humberto Muñoz in NEW COVENANT, September 1973, p. 22.
43 NEW COVENANT, April 1975, p. 26.
44 ALABARE, February-March 1974, pp. 31-32; NEW COVENANT,
    February 1972, p. 12; April 1973, pp. 23ff; November 1973, p. 21.
45 NEW COVENANT, April 1975, pp. 26-27.
46 Francis McNutt in NEW COVENANT, November 1971, pp. 6-7.
47 NEW COVENANT, February 1972, p. 12.
48 ALABARE, October-November 1974, pp. 9-10; Gary Seromik in
    NEW COVENANT, May 1976, pp. 32-33.
49 Bishop José Cedeno of Panama at E.C.C.L.A. Congress, 1976.
50 ALABARE, April-May, p. 10; October-November 1974, pp. 28-30;
    NEW COVENANT, May 1976, p. 24.
51 NEW COVENANT, May 1976, p. 26; ALABARE, April-May 1974.
52 ALABARE, February-March 1974, p. 32.
53 NEW COVENANT, November 1971, p. 9.
54 Dick Mishler in NEW COVENANT, November 1972, p. 26.
55 NEW COVENANT, February 1973, p. 20.
56 'Congress in Mexico,' NEW COVENANT, April 1973, p. 27.
57 NEW COVENANT, August 1973, p. 27.
58 See PENTECOSTAL EVANGEL, 24 November 1968, pp. 8-9.
59 Notes and Recollections.
60 CHRISTIANITY TODAY, 19 July 1963, p. 19; LATIN AMERICAN
    EVANGELIST, March-April 1977, pp. 12-14.
61 P. N. Lewis, 'Renewal in the Brazilian Church,' unpublished M.A.
    project, Wheaton College, 1972, p. 59.
62 Cf. ALABARE, February-March 1974, p. 30; LATIN AMERICAN
    EVANGELIST, March-April 1977, p. 14; P. N. Lewis, p. 75.
63 P. N. Lewis, p. 167.
64 NEW COVENANT, June 1972, p. 21; March 1974, p. 22.
65 ALABARE, January 1975, pp. 8-9; NEW COVENANT, May 1975,
    pp. 25-26.
66 See G. H. Anderson & T. F. Stransky, EVANGELIZATION, p. 154;
    CHRISTIANITY TODAY, 2 July 1976, 'Catholic Charismatics: An
    Age of Revolution.'
67 NEW COVENANT, August 1973, pp. 26-27.
68 E.C.C.L.A. II, NEW COVENANT, April 1974, pp. 20-21.
69 ALABARE, January 1975, pp. 3-4.
70 E.C.C.L.A. IV, NEW COVENANT, May 1976, pp. 38-39.
71 Cf. Francis McNutt in NEW COVENANT, 1971, p. 2; & NEW
    COVENANT, May 1976, pp. 38-39.
72 Cf. LATIN AMERICAN EVANGELIST, March-April 1977, p. 13.
73 LATIN AMERICAN EVANGELIST, March-April 1977, p. 13, an
    observation shared by the writer regarding the contribution of the
    Catholic Charismatics to the hymnody of the general movement.
74 LATIN AMERICAN EVANGELIST, January-February 1969, p. 12.
75 Dr. John Mackay was of the same opinion when he shared ministry
    with the writer and Dr. Bob Jones, Junior (!) at Forest Home, 1954.

SELECT BIBLIOGRAPHY

Acenelli, D. R., YO FUI TESTIGO, Buenos Aires, 1954.
Amaunategui, D., EL SISTEMA DE LANCASTER, Santiago, 1895.
Appasamy, Bishop A. J., WRITE THE VISION, Madras, 1964.
Arms, Goodsil, HISTORY OF THE WILLIAM TAYLOR SELF-
  SUPPORTING MISSIONS IN SOUTH AMERICA, New York, 1921.
Azevedo, Fernando, BRAZILIAN CULTURE, New York, 1951.
Atter, G. F., "THE THIRD FORCE," Peterborough, Ontario, 1965.
Bachmann, E. T., LUTHERANS IN BRAZIL, Minneapolis, 1970.
Barnard, H. C., HISTORY OF ENGLISH EDUCATION, London, 1947.
Beach, Harlan P., PROTESTANT MISSIONS IN SOUTH AMERICA,
  Chicago, 1900.
Bear, J. E., MISSION TO BRAZIL, Nashville, 1961.
Bennett, Charles, TINDER IN TABASCO, Grand Rapids, 1968.
Benson, D. V., HENRIETTA MEARS, Glendale, California, 1966.
Berg, Daniel, ENVIADO POR DEUS, São Paulo, no date.
Bradshaw, M. R., CHURCH GROWTH THROUGH EVANGELISM-IN-
  DEPTH, South Pasadena, 1969.
Braga & Grubb, THE REPUBLIC OF BRAZIL, London, 1932.
Bretones, Lauro, REDEMOINHOS DO SUL: Um Ano de Reavivamento
  no Brasil com o Dr. J. Edwin Orr, Teresópolis, 1953.
Brown, A. J., ONE HUNDRED YEARS, New York, 1936.
Browning, Ritchie & Grubb, THE WEST COAST REPUBLICS OF
  SOUTH AMERICA, London, 1930.
Browning, W. E., THE RIVER PLATE REPUBLICS, London, 1938.
Buyers, P. E., HISTORIA DE METODISMO NO BRASIL, São Paulo,
  1945.
Camargo & Grubb, RELIGION IN THE REPUBLIC OF MEXICO,
  London, 1935.
Canclini, Arnoldo, HASTA LO ULTIMO DE LA TIERRA, Buenos
  Aires, 1951.
Canton, William, A HISTORY OF THE BRITISH AND FOREIGN
  BIBLE SOCIETY, Volumes II, III & IV, London, 1904-1910.
Chambers, T. W., THE NOON PRAYER MEETING, New York, 1858.
Christiansen, John, UNDER THE SOUTHERN CROSS, Chicago, 1932.
Clark, R. B., UNDER THE SOUTHERN CROSS, Harrisburg, 1938.
Coleman, W. J., LATIN AMERICAN CATHOLICISM, New York, 1958.
Conant, W. C., NARRATIVE OF REMARKABLE CONVERSIONS,
  New York, 1858.
Conde, E. G., HISTORIA DAS ASSEMBLEIAS DE DEUS NO BRASIL,
  Rio de Janeiro, 1960.
Conn, C. W., WHERE THE SAINTS HAVE TROD, Cleveland, 1959.
Considine, J. J., NEW HORIZONS IN LATIN AMERICA, New York,
  1958.
Considine, J. J., THE CHURCH IN THE NEW LATIN AMERICA,
  Notre Dame, Indiana, 1964.
Considine, J. J., THE RELIGIOUS DIMENSION IN THE NEW LATIN
  AMERICA, Notre Dame, Indiana, 1966.
Corston, W., THE LIFE OF JOSEPH LANCASTER, London, 1861.
Crabtree, A. R., BAPTISTS IN BRAZIL, Rio de Janeiro, 1950.
Dabbs, N. H., DAWN OVER THE BOLIVIAN HILLS, Toronto, 1952.
Davis, J. M., THE CHURCH IN THE NEW JAMAICA, New York,
  1952.
Davis, J. M., THE CHURCH IN PUERTO RICO'S DILEMMA, New
  York, 1942.

Davis, J. M., HOW THE CHURCH GROWS IN BRAZIL, New York, 1953.

DeLong & Taylor, FIFTY YEARS OF NAZARENE MISSIONS, Kansas City, 1955.

Despard, G. P., HOPE DEFERRED, NOT LOST, London, 1854.

Drysdale, J. M., A HUNDRED YEARS IN BUENOS AIRES, Buenos Aires, 1929.

Edwards, F. C., THE ROLE OF THE FAITH MISSION: A Brazilian Case Study, South Pasadena, 1969.

Elliot, Elizabeth, THROUGH GATES OF SPLENDOR, New York, 1957.

Ellis, J. B., THE DIOCESE OF JAMAICA, London, 1913.

Enns, Arno, MAN, MILIEU AND MISSION IN ARGENTINA, Grand Rapids, 1971.

Enyart, P. C., FRIENDS IN CENTRAL AMERICA, South Pasadena, 1970.

Every, E. F., TWENTY-FIVE YEARS IN SOUTH AMERICA, London, 1929.

Fanstone, A. B., MISSIONARY ADVENTURE IN BRAZIL, Worthing, Sussex, 1972.

Ferreira, J. A., HISTORIA DA IGREJA PRESBITERIANA DO BRASIL, São Paulo, 1960.

Findlay, G. G. & W. W. Holdsworth, HISTORY OF THE WESLEYAN METHODIST MISSIONARY SOCIETY, London, 1921-1924.

Frodsham, S. H., WITH SIGNS FOLLOWING, Springfield, 1946.

Gee, Donald, THE PENTECOSTAL MOVEMENT, London, 1949.

Ginsburg, Solomon, A MISSIONARY ADVENTURE, Nashville, 1921.

Glover, R. H., THE PROGRESS OF WORLD-WIDE MISSIONS, New York, 1960 (edition enlarged by J. Herbert Kane)

Goddard, B. L., ENCYCLOPEDIA OF MODERN CHRISTIAN MISSIONS, Toronto, 1967.

Gonzales, J. L., THE DEVELOPMENT OF CHRISTIANITY IN THE LATIN CARIBBEAN, Grand Rapids, 1969.

Good, Thelma, MORAVIAN MISSIONS IN BLUEFIELDS, 1974.

Grose, H. B., ADVANCE IN THE ANTILLES, New York, 1911.

Grubb, K. G., THE NORTHERN REPUBLICS OF SOUTH AMERICA, London, 1931.

Grubb, K. G., RELIGION IN CENTRAL AMERICA, London, 1937.

Grubb, W. Barbrooke, A CHURCH IN THE WILDS, London, 1941.

Guerra, J. G., SARMIENTO, SU VIDA Y SUS OBRAS, Santiago, 1901.

Hamilton, J. T., A HISTORY OF THE CHURCH KNOWN AS THE MORAVIAN CHURCH, Bethlehem, Pennsylvania, 1900.

Harrell, David E., ALL THINGS ARE POSSIBLE; the Healing and Charismatic Revivals in Modern America, Indiana, 1975.

Harris, John, A CENTURY OF EMANCIPATION, London, 1933.

Hasse, E. R., THE MORAVIANS, London, 1911.

Henderson, G. E., GOODNESS AND MERCY, Kingston, 1931.

Herr, Richard, THE EIGHTEENTH CENTURY REVOLUTION IN SPAIN, Princeton, 1958.

Hicks, Tommy, MILLIONS FOUND CHRIST: HISTORY'S GREATEST RECORDED REVIVAL, Los Angeles, 1956.

Hinton, J. H., A MEMOIR OF WILLIAM KNIBB, London, 1847.

Hogg, W. R., ECUMENICAL FOUNDATIONS, New York, 1952.

Holleran, M. P., CHURCH AND STATE IN GUATEMALA, New York, 1949.

Hoover, W. C., HISTORIA DEL AVIVAMIENTO PENTECOSTAL EN CHILE, Santiago, 1931.

Hopkins, C. H., HISTORY OF THE Y.M.C.A. IN NORTH AMERICA, New York, 1951.
Horner, N.A., PROTESTANT CROSS-CURRENTS IN MISSIONS, New York, 1968.
Horton, A. G., AN OUTLINE OF LATIN AMERICAN HISTORY, Dubuque, 1966.
Howard, David, HAMMERED AS GOLD, New York, 1969.
Hudspith, Margarita, RIPENING FRUIT, Harrington Park, N.J., 1958.
Hutton, J. E., A HISTORY OF MORAVIAN MISSIONS, London, 1923.
Jordan, W. F., ECUADOR: MISSION ACHIEVEMENT, New York, 1926.
Kahn, M. C., DJUKA: THE BUSH NEGROES OF DUTCH GUIANA, New York, 1931.
Kessler, J.B.A., PROTESTANT MISSIONS AND CHURCHES IN PERU AND CHILE, Goes, Netherlands, 1967.
Kinsolving, A. B., BIOGRAFIA DE L. L. KINSOLVING, New York.
Kramer, Beckman & Fehlauer, EVANGELISCHE LUTERISCHE KIRCHE IN ARGENTINA, Buenos Aires, 1955.
LaFetra, I. H., CHILE MISSION OF THE METHODIST EPISCOPAL CHURCH, Santiago, 1894.
Landes, P. S., ASHBEL GREEN SIMONTON, Fort Worth, 1956.
Latin American Mission, EVANGELISM IN DEPTH, Chicago, 1961.
Latourette, Kenneth Scott, A HISTORY OF THE EXPANSION OF CHRISTIANITY, Volumes III, IV & V, New York, 1938-1945.
Latourette, Kenneth Scott, CHRISTIANITY IN A REVOLUTIONARY AGE, Volume V, New York, 1962.
Lea, H. C., THE INQUISITION IN SPANISH DEPENDENCIES, New York, 1908.
Leonard, E. G., O PROTESTANTISMO BRASILEIRO, São Paulo, 1963.
Lessa, V. Themudo, PADRE JOSE MANOEL DA CONCEICAO, São Paulo, 1938.
Loetscher, L. A. TWENTIETH CENTURY ENCYCLOPEDIA OF RELIGIOUS KNOWLEDGE, Grand Rapids, 1955.
Lovett, Richard, THE HISTORY OF THE LONDON MISSIONARY SOCIETY, Volume II, London, 1899.
Luiggi, A. H., SIXTY-FIVE VALIANTS, Gainesville, 1965.
Luz, Fortunato, A IGREJA EVANGELICAL FLUMINENSE, Rio de Janeiro, 1932.
Lyra, J. B., ORIENTAÇÃO EVANGÉLICA, São Paulo, 1960.
MacDonald, F. C., BISHOP STIRLING OF THE FALKLANDS, London, 1929.
MacFarland, C. S., CHAOS IN MEXICO, New York, 1935.
McGavran, D. A., CHURCH GROWTH IN JAMAICA, Lucknow, 1962.
McGavran, D. A., et al, CHURCH GROWTH IN MEXICO, Grand Rapids, 1963.
McLean, J. H., HISTORIA DE LA IGLESIA PRESBITERIANA EN CHILE, Santiago, 1954.
McLoughlin, W. G., MODERN REVIVALISM, New York, 1959.
Mackay, J. A., THE OTHER SPANISH CHRIST, London, 1932.
Malcolm, C. W., TWELVE HOURS IN THE DAY, London, 1956.
Marotta, Orestes, Dr. SIDNEY McFARLAND SOWELL, Buenos Aires, no date.
Marty, M. E., THE NEW SHAPE OF AMERICAN RELIGION, New York, 1959.
Mecham, J.L., CHURCH AND STATE IN LATIN AMERICA, Chapel Hill, N. C., 1966.
Miller, E. R., THY GOD REIGNETH, Fontana, 1964.

Mitchell, D. R., 'The Evangelical Contribution of James Thomson to South American Life, 1818-1825,' Doctoral dissertation, 1972, Princeton Theological Seminary.

Montgomery, J. D., DISCIPLES OF CHRIST IN ARGENTINA, St. Louis, 1956.

Moody, W. R., THE LIFE OF DWIGHT L. MOODY, New York, 1900.

Murray, S. W., W. P. NICHOLSON: FLAME FOR GOD IN ULSTER, Belfast, 1973.

Neill, S. C., A HISTORY OF CHRISTIAN MISSIONS, London, 1964.

Nichol, J. T., PENTECOSTALISM, New York, 1966.

Odell, E. A., IT CAME TO PASS (Puerto Rico), New York, 1952.

Orr, J. Edwin, ALWAYS ABOUNDING (Oswald Smith), London, 1950.

Orr, J. Edwin, EVANGELICAL AWAKENINGS IN EASTERN ASIA,

Orr, J. Edwin, EVANGELICAL AWAKENINGS IN SOUTHERN ASIA,

Orr, J. Edwin, EVANGELICAL AWAKENINGS IN AFRICA, 1975.

Orr, J. Edwin, EVANGELICAL AWAKENINGS IN THE SOUTH SEAS, Minneapolis, 1976.

Orr, J. Edwin, EVANGELICAL AWAKENINGS IN LATIN AMERICA, Minneapolis, 1977.

Orr, J. Edwin, THE EAGER FEET, Chicago, 1975.

Orr, J. Edwin, THE FERVENT PRAYER, Chicago, 1974.

Orr, J. Edwin, THE FLAMING TONGUE, Chicago, 1973.

Orr, J. Edwin, FULL SURRENDER, London, 1950.

Orr, J. Edwin, GOOD NEWS IN BAD TIMES, Grand Rapids, 1953.

Oyarzun, Artura, LA OBRA EVANGELICA EN CHILE, Valdivia, 1921.

Pannier & Mondain, L'EXPANSION FRANCAISE OUTRE-MER ET PROTESTANE, Paris, 1931.

Pattee, Richard, EL CATOLICISMO CONTEMPORANEO EN HISPANO AMERICA, Buenos Aires, 1951.

Pattee, Richard, THE CATHOLIC REVIVAL IN MEXICO, Washington, D. C., 1944.

Payne, E. A., FREEDOM IN JAMAICA, London, 1933.

Payne, William, PIONEERING IN BOLIVIA, London, no date.

Penzotti, Francisco, SPIRITUAL VICTORIES IN SOUTH AMERICA, New York, 1916.

Peters, G. W., INDONESIA REVIVAL, Grand Rapids, 1973.

Pierson, P. E., A YOUNGER CHURCH IN SEARCH OF MATURITY, San Antonio, 1973.

Pollock, J. C., A CAMBRIDGE MOVEMENT, London, 1950.

Pollock, J. C., BILLY GRAHAM, New York, 1966.

Raine, Philip, PARAGUAY, New Brunswick, N.J., 1956.

Ranaghan, Kevin, THE CATHOLIC PENTECOSTALS, Toronto, 1969.

Rankin, Melinda, TWENTY YEARS AMONG THE MEXICANS, Cincinnati, 1875.

Read, Monterroso & Johnson, LATIN AMERICAN CHURCH GROWTH, Grand Rapids, 1969.

Read, W. R., NEW PATTERNS OF CHURCH GROWTH IN BRAZIL, Grand Rapids, 1965.

Ridout, G. W., SHOWERS OF BLESSING, Lexington, 1933.

Rippy, J. A., LATIN AMERICA: A MODERN HISTORY, Ann Arbor, 1958.

Ritchie, John, INDIGENOUS CHURCH PRINCIPLES, New York, 1956.

Ritchie, John, THE INDIGENOUS CHURCH IN PERU, London, 1932.

Rivera, R. P., INSTITUCIONES PROTESTANTES EN MEXICO, Mexico City, 1962.

Roberts, W. D., REVOLUTION IN EVANGELISM, Chicago, 1967.
Salmon, David, LANCASTER AND BELL, Cambridge, 1932.
Samuel, Peter, WESLEYAN METHODIST MISSIONS IN JAMAICA
AND HONDURAS, London, n. d.
Scharpff, Paulus, GESCHICHTE DER EVANGELISATION, Giessen,
1964.
Schlatter, Wilhelm, GESCHICHTE DER BASLER MISSION, 1815-1915,
Volume I, Basel, 1916.
Shedd, C. P., TWO CENTURIES OF STUDENT CHRISTIAN MOVE-
MENTS, New York, 1934.
Smith, George, HISTORY OF WESLEYAN METHODISM, London,
1862 (Three Volumes)
Smith, O. J., WORLD-WIDE EVANGELISM, Toronto, 1972 (1964)
Smith, T. L., REVIVALISM AND SOCIAL REFORM, Nashville, 1947.
Speer, R. E., MISSIONS IN SOUTH AMERICA, New York, 1909.
Stillwell, H. E., PIONEERING IN BOLIVIA, Toronto, 1924.
Stokes, Louie, THE PENTECOSTAL MOVEMENT IN ARGENTINA,
Buenos Aires, 1968.
Stowell, J. S., BETWEEN THE AMERICAS, New York, 1930.
Stuart-Watt, Eva, DYNAMITE IN EUROPE, London, 1939.
Sumrall, L. F., THROUGH BLOOD AND FIRE IN LATIN AMERICA,
Grand Rapids, n. d.
Sweet, W. W., THE STORY OF RELIGION IN AMERICA, New York,
1950.
Taylor, Clyde & Wade Coggins, PROTESTANT MISSIONS IN LATIN
AMERICA, Washington, 1961.
Taylor, William, OUR SOUTH AMERICAN COUSINS, New York, 1879.
Thomson, James, LETTERS ON THE MORAL AND RELIGIOUS
STATE OF SOUTH AMERICA, London, 1830.
Tognini, Eneas, O PREÇO DA GRANDE BENÇÃO, São Paulo, 1970.
Tron & Ganz, HISTORIA DE LAS COLONIAS VALDENSES SUD-
AMERICANAS, 1858-1959, Montevideo, 1958.
Tucker, H. C., THE BIBLE IN BRAZIL, New York, 1902.
Tucker, Leonard, "GLORIOUS LIBERTY," London, 1914.
Vergara, Ignacio, EL PROTESTANTISMO EN CHILE, Santiago, 1962.
Wagner, C. P., LOOK OUT! THE PENTECOSTALS ARE COMING,
Carol Stream, Illinois, 1973.
Wagner, C. P., THE PROTESTANT MOVEMENT IN BOLIVIA, South
Pasadena, 1970.
Watson, Tom, T. J. BACH: A VOICE FOR MISSIONS, Chicago, 1965.
Weld, Wayne, AN ECUADOREAN IMPASSE, Chicago, 1965.
Wheeler, W. R., MODERN MISSIONS IN CHILE AND BRAZIL,
Philadelphia, 1926.
Winans, R. G., GOSPEL OVER THE ANDES, Kansas City, 1955.
Winter, R. D., THEOLOGICAL EDUCATION BY EXTENSION, South
Pasadena, 1969.
Winter, R. D., THE TWENTY-FIVE UNBELIEVABLE YEARS, South
Pasadena, 1970.
WORLD CHRISTIAN HANDBOOK, London, 1952, 1957, 1962, 1967.
Young, Robert, FROM CAPE HORN TO PANAMA, London, 1905.
Zubiar, J. B., SINOPSIS DE LA EDUCACION EN LA REPUBLICA
ARGENTINA, Buenos Aires, 1901.

INDEX OF PERSONS